THE
COMPACT HISTORY
of the
AMERICAN NEWSPAPER

THE COMPACT HISTORY

of the AMERICAN NEWSPAPER

John Tebbel

HAWTHORN BOOKS, INC.   PUBLISHERS
NEW YORK

First Edition, November, 1963.

H-1242

Contents

THE
COMPACT HISTORY
of the
AMERICAN NEWSPAPER

THE NEWSPAPER
as
PROPAGANDA

The Colonial Press:
License and Freedom

"THIS IS PUBLISHED TO PREVENT FALSE REPORTS." So runs the subhead on the news broadside titled "The Present State of the New-English Affairs," published in Boston in 1689, the first attempt to print a domestic news report in America.

In that declaration, and the phrase "published by authority," is the essence of newspaper history in the United States during its first fifty years. In that period the broad outlines of a great struggle were clearly laid down, one which continues to the present day. For the history of the American newspaper is a record of the Establishment's effort to control the news and of private individuals to disclose it without restriction.

There is much more subtlety in the story, however, than such a simple definition would indicate. It is not, as some historians and modern commentators would have us believe, a well-defined plot in which government is always cast as the villain and publishers are the voice of the people. That is the black-and-white language of contemporary sophistry. If one follows the line of historical theory which sets men above events, the inevitable conclusion is that the motives have been mixed on both sides. The results of license or freedom cannot be easily filed away under "bad" and "good."

It is still widely believed by Americans brought up under the cliché method of teaching our history that the Massachusetts Bay colonizers, fleeing from English oppression, immediately established a free society on these shores. In fact, they did nothing of the kind. They set up a system of politico-religious control of thought and daily life fully as oppressive as the one they had left. A key element in this system, common to all authoritarian governments past and present, was control of the press. There was, of course, no press as such in earliest New England, but there were men with printing presses and the colonizers had personal experience with the power of that combination.

Two of them, William Brewster and Edward Winslow, had fled to Holland before they sailed on the *Mayflower*, and there in Leyden they had published news sheets, actually no more than pamphlets, which were designed to stir up revolt against civil and ecclesiastical rule in England. These sheets were smuggled across the North Sea and sold secretly.

Once established in America, men like Brewster and Winslow were not inclined to give any dissenters in the colony the same opportunity. The powerful and zealous Mather family, the real rulers of the colony, were intellectuals who well understood the power of the printed word and "published by authority" was their watchword from the beginning. None of the early news broadsides, of which "The Present State" was one, could be printed without license. Those who dared to do otherwise would be "accounted enemies to Their Majesties' present government and be proceeded against as such with uttermost severity," a proclamation of 1689 asserted.

Nevertheless, someone attempted it and became the first publisher of a newspaper in America. His name was Benjamin Harris, and it is safe to say no major American institution has been launched by so unworthy a pioneer. He was a bigot and an opportunist who had been the proprietor of a London paper called *Domestick Intelligence*, in which he had "exposed" that imaginary conspiracy known as the Popish Plot, an invention of the Whigs designed to convince the citizens that the Roman Catholics meant to kill the Protestants in London and burn the city. Harris had prepared for his career of Pope-baiting by publishing and selling from his Bell Alley bookshop various scurrilous pamphlets attacking Catholics and Quakers.

Harris had faulty news judgment. He could not distinguish between what was safe bigotry, approved by the authorities, and implicit criticism of the Crown. For the latter offense, his newspaper was suppressed and the infamous Chief Justice Scroggs, as corrupt as any prisoner who ever faced him, sentenced him to King's Bench Prison in default of his fine.

Free again in nine months as the result of a forged discharge, Harris resumed his career in a new guise as the proprietor of a coffee shop where he sold books, patent medicines and playing cards with anti-Catholic propaganda printed on the backs. But he could not stay away from pamphleteering, and he was soon in imminent danger of arrest again, whereupon he fled to Boston.

Harris was certain he would find a welcome in Boston, and he was right. The Calvinist authorities there were as anti-Popish as he was, consequently more than willing to have him set up as publisher and bookseller. It was not surprising to see the Mathers on his list of authors, nor to find them among the patrons of the London Coffee House which he opened in August 1690.

Success spoiled Ben Harris. Displaying his deplorable lack of judgment once more, he did not bother applying for a license to publish his *Publick Occurrences Both Foreign and Domestick*, which appeared only a month after the coffee shop opened. Apparently he felt himself so secure in the favor of the authorities that he could print whatever he pleased. He promised to publish once a month, or oftener if the "glut of occurrences" warranted.

This first American newspaper was unpretentious. It was printed on three sides of a folded sheet 6 by 9½ inches, set double column, with the fourth page blank so that readers could add their own news in longhand before they forwarded it to friends who lived elsewhere. Those who meant to do so had to move rapidly, because as soon as the Mathers saw the publication they suppressed it. Not only had it been published without a license, which was reason enough, but it contained two stories particularly offensive to the authorities. The nature of this offensiveness has a peculiarly contemporary ring.

One story dealt with the mistreatment of prisoners taken captive by the Mohawk Indians during the sanguinary border warfare between the colonies and Canada. No one doubted the story. It was common knowledge that the Indians showed little mercy to captives, but the recital of atrocities concerned Indians presumably friendly to the colony, who would certainly be displeased when they heard about this unfavorable publicity and saw themselves referred to as "miserable Salvages." Of course there had been some provocation. Harris reported the tale of two English captives who related that a Captain Mason had "cut the faces, and ript the bellies of two Indians, and threw a third Over board in the sight of the French," whose Indian allies had retaliated at once by butchering forty of their own prisoners.

While this item was embarrassing, the other was doubly so because it impugned the morals of His Christian Majesty, the King of France. "France is in much trouble (and fear)," Harris reported, "not only with us but also with his Son, who has revolted against him lately, and has great reason if reports be true, that the Father used to lie with the Sons Wife."

Thus the counts against Ben Harris and his paper were serious. Everyone knew that whatever was published in the colony was licensed, and people reading *Publick Occurrences* in England, France, or elsewhere would have reason to believe that the authorities had countenanced the insulting of valuable Indian allies and the French monarch in a single issue. No wonder it was suppressed, and existing issues called in and destroyed.

Harris lingered awhile, not entirely out of favor. He continued to run his coffee shop, to sell Cotton Mather's "Wonderful Works of God Commemorated," and occasionally to do some official job printing. By 1694, however, he was back in London, publishing a paper he called the *Post*. Its character, and his own, are aptly summarized in the opinion of a former friend, John Dunton: "He is so far from having any dealings with Truth and Honesty, that his solemn word, which he calls as good as his bond, is a studied falsehood, and he scandalizes Truth and Honesty in pretending to write for it. His 'London Post', or weighing of Truth and Honesty, resembles the Bird of Athens; for it seems to be made up of face and feathers . . ."

To those observing the fate of Ben Harris and his paper, it was obvious that the publication of news had to have official sanction to exist. As the colony grew, there was an equally obvious necessity to disseminate information, but nobody appeared anxious to publish an approved gazette. It had taken nearly seventy years of colonizing to produce Harris's first abortive attempt, and it took fourteen more before someone dared try again.

It was entirely logical that Boston's sour-faced Scottish postmaster, John Campbell, should make the second attempt. He was, in the first place, at the news center of the colony. As postmaster he could and did read everything that wasn't sealed, and the post office itself was a community gathering place where news and gossip were traded as freely as they are in a Washington cloakroom today. He was also at the center of distribution. The post-boys who carried the mail could also carry a newspaper. Finally, as a man who owed his valuable position to the authorities, he was unlikely to print anything that would offend them.

These facts guaranteed that the resultant product would be the dissemination of dull, approved news, which was exactly the case with Campbell's Boston *News-Letter* when it appeared on April 24, 1704. It hardly needed the large type under the title which proclaimed that it was "Published by Authority." In the box at the left of the title, now called an "ear," there was a sailing ship, signifying that most of the news came from abroad, four months old by the time it reached Boston. In the right ear was the figure of a galloping post-boy, who was soon a familiar symbol on the front pages of colonial newspapers. The post-boys, it may be added, idled along between communities, amusing themselves, and when they approached a village, blew a warning blast on their bugles and came thundering into town, giving the impression that they had been riding posthaste for hours.

As Campbell prospered in his business affairs, he lost interest in his newspaper and by 1722 it had passed into other hands. It had never been a profitable operation, with few subscribers and fewer advertisers. Word of mouth was still a faster way to spread the news, and consumers had comparatively few choices as to stores.

There were also other factors at work. By this time the colonists had lost much of their earlier interest in English and European affairs, and a lull of sorts had occurred in the intermittent fighting with the Canadians and their Indian allies, before the bush skirmish of a Virginia colonel of militia named George Washington touched a flame to the Seven Years' War. Momentarily there was little news at home, and eager mouths spread it faster than Campbell could print it.

It was significant that Campbell's successor as publisher was his printer, Bartholomew Green, whose shop on Newbury Street was considered the best in the country. With this succession a pattern was established in the print media which would persist for decades, and would be repeated across the nation as printing presses moved by oxcart and flatboat over the mountains and along broad rivers to carry the printed word from Atlantic to Pacific. The pattern was the printer as publisher. Out of his shop came books, a newspaper, pamphlets, broadsides, job printing of every description, and in time, magazines. In the front of the shop most of these products were on sale, particularly the books and newspapers, along with candy, violin strings and the sundries of a general store. The printer was becoming at once publisher, editor, and bookseller—in brief, the central figure in American publishing.

Since no man could wear all these hats with equal grace, the early products of the printshop, like the *News-Letter*, displayed a natural division of talents. The newspapers were often admirable typographically, and printed on excellent paper, although others were less well done, reflecting the competence of the individual printer. Editorially, however, they were abominable, innocent of grammar and syntax and badly written.

In the early Boston papers, the combination of unlettered printers and dull postmasters produced an uninspiring series of newspapers before a change in the pattern occurred, a change which would also spread until it became dominant in the East. Wherever the printer traveled in the westward migration, the same change occurred, with varying speed and results. This change was the domination of the paper by an editor who might or might not be a printer himself. More and more, as time went on, he was not. He was, rather, a young intellectual with a talent for writing who gathered around him men like himself. As young men, they were quite naturally in revolt against the Establishment. First they defied the local civic and religious authorities, and later the Crown itself.

The pioneer was James Franklin, Benjamin's older brother, who became the first real newspaper editor in America, and whose *New-England Courant* was the first American newspaper worthy of the name.

The *Courant* was born out of anger and prospered in it. When John Campbell lost the postmastership in 1718, he refused to pass along the *News-Letter* with his job to William Brooker, his successor; Bartholomew Green inherited it, as noted before. Brooker was so angry he started his own paper, the *Boston Gazette*, equally dull and official. Casting about for a printer, Brooker gave the job to a young Bostonian named James Franklin. But in less than a year Brooker had lost his position to Philip Musgrave, who inherited the *Gazette* and transferred the printing contract to a friend. Franklin thereupon became an angry young man too, and founded a third paper, the *Courant*. There was now competition in Boston.

Some of Franklin's friends tried to talk him out of the venture, his brother Ben recalled later. They termed it an undertaking "not likely to succeed." James persevered nonetheless, Ben went on, "and after having worked in composing the types and printing off the sheets, I was employed to carry the papers through the streets to the customers."

The newspaper was, in fact, a godsend to Franklin's business. He was one of several printers in a town of no more than twelve thousand people, and there was not enough job printing to go around. He and Ben, who had been apprenticed to him in 1718 at the age of twelve, were compelled to turn out all kinds of odd jobs—Ben's ballads, pamphlets, even printed linens, calicos and silks.

In starting the *Courant*, James could not have become a publisher at a better time, nor one more calculated to demonstrate the newspaper's future usefulness as a propaganda medium. It had already demonstrated its value as a government-controlled press, designed to serve the purposes of authority. Now it became a vehicle for the growing body of dissent in the colony.

At the bottom of the new dissent was resentment against the

Mathers and the powerful Congregationalism which had dominated the colony for so long. Enough Episcopalians and deists had arrived to form a core of resistance to the Mathers and the magistrates. Two of them who came to James Franklin's aid and helped him launch the *Courant* were John Checkley, a bookseller and apothecary who had already been in trouble with the authorities; and William Douglass, a Scottish doctor, whose medical degree (earned in Edinburgh, Leyden and Paris) had been the only one in America when he arrived in Boston.

The ground on which these three chose to defy authority in the first issue of the *Courant* was, ironically, one of the few issues on which the Mathers happened to be right. The paper appeared in August of a steaming summer during which smallpox had been rampant, and the authorities had been trying to fight it by means of the new inoculation. Cotton Mather had heard of this development from one of his slaves, who had known it in Africa, and he had read in a London newspaper that it was being practiced in Constantinople. Mather persuaded a Boston doctor, Zabdiel Boylston, to inoculate two of his sons and a slave. The results were so successful that Boylston set up a clinic and became the hero of the hour.

Douglass, despite his learned medical degree, declared in the *Courant's* first issue that inoculation derived from "the Greek old women," and the paper came out hotly against this "doubtful and dangerous practice." In subsequent issues the *Courant* led a pack of doctors, selectmen, other newspapers and citizens who howled for Boylston's blood, and even threatened his life and Mather's. The young Boston intellectuals were delighted with the *Courant* and its first campaign; they came around willingly to write for it.

James Franklin's rôle in the new paper was apparently far more professional than intellectual. When the Mathers struck back through the pen of Increase's grandson, Thomas Walter, it was James who printed Walter's broadside, called *The Little-Compton Scourge; or, The Anti-Courant*. The language of this duel set the tone for the next hundred years or more of American journalism. Walter asserted the *Courant* appealed only to "men of passion and resentment." Checkley, in the *Courant's* third issue, called Walter an "obscene and fuddling Merry-Andrew," a drunkard and a debauchée.

Cotton Mather found the *Courant* intolerable. He termed its writers the Hell-Fire Club and asserted that "the practice of supporting and publishing every week a libel on purpose to lessen and blacken and burlesque the virtuous and principal ministers of religion in a country, and render the services of their ministry despicable, even detestable, to the people, is a wickedness that was never known before in any country, Christian, Turkish, or Pagan, on the face of the earth."

As the epidemic waned, so did the *Courant's* interest in the inoculation battle. More and more it turned to lighter matters. It was only a single sheet, printed on both sides, and the real news in it was scant, consisting mostly of shipping reports and snippets of information from neighboring towns, or letters from Europe. The meat of it was contained in the letters to the editor from the Boston wits, poking Addisonian fun at the city's morals and manners, but being careful of what they said about authority.

The letters were signed with the quaint conceits of the day— Timothy Turnstone, Tom Penshallow, Ichabod Henroost, Abigail Afterwit. One, appearing on April 2, 1722, was the first authentic prose of Benjamin Franklin, who signed himself "Silence Dogood," and promised to provide the paper's readers once every fortnight "with a short Epistle, which I presume will add somewhat to their entertainment." Ben suspected correctly that his brother "would object to printing anything of mine in his paper if he knew it to be mine," and so his contributions were slid under the shop door anonymously.

In spite of the *Courant's* milder tone, the Mathers regarded it as a troublesome threat to authority and they waited for an opportunity to suppress it. The fact that they waited at all was a measure of how much freedom the press had already gained. Twenty years earlier the *Courant* would have been suppressed arbitrarily; now it had popular support and the magistrates had to be wary.

As it was, the excuse they ultimately used was trivial enough—a sarcastic, fictitious letter from Newport, reporting pirates off the coast and adding that the Massachusetts government was fitting out a ship to go after them, "to be commanded by Captain Peter Papillon, and 'tis thought he will sail some time this month, wind and weather permitting." The Council thought, with reason, that this was contempt. They had James Franklin arrested and thrown into jail. In a week James had apologized, and in a month he was free again, on the certification of Dr. Boylston that his health had been impaired in prison.

Meanwhile, Ben operated the shop, and the Dogood papers he continued to write attracted more and more attention by their wit and wisdom. But James returned to his post, and early in 1723 resumed his attacks on the magistrates. "There are many persons who seem to be more than ordinary religious," the *Courant* gibed, in its January 14 issue, "but yet are on several accounts worse, by far, than those who pretend to no religion at all."

The Council had no doubt who was meant by "many persons." At once it issued a sweeping decree against James, forbidding him not only to publish the *Courant* but "any other pamphlet or paper of the like nature, except it first be supervised by the Secretary of this Province." The press was not yet free, by any means.

But the *Courant's* influential friends were determined their paper should continue, and they devised an ingenious, if flimsy, method of doing it. Ben was made publisher in place of his brother, obtaining from James a release from his indenture, duly executed, to be shown to the authorities if they should charge that the apprentice was merely acting for the printer. Privately, however, Ben was to sign new indentures.

The *Courant* also pretended to take a new direction. "The present undertaking . . . is designed purely for the diversion and merriment of the reader," the new publisher assured his readers blandly, and the paper was indeed more discreet. Ben knew how to prod without inviting trouble. At seventeen he was, as Carl Van Doren has said, "the best mind in Boston and . . . the best apprentice in the world." His identity as "Silence Dogood" was now known to the other contributors, who were extravagant in their praise of his papers.

It was too much for a jealous older brother. There were quarrels, the situation became intolerable for both, and as Ben put it, "I took upon me to assert my freedom." Indenture or no, he was determined to leave, which he did, secretly by night aboard a sloop bound for New York.

Both Franklins continued to be newspapermen for a time. James deserted the *Courant* three years later and took his press to Rhode Island, the first one that colony had seen. There, in the pleasant precincts of Newport, surrounded by dissenters like himself, he became public printer and publisher of the *Rhode Island Gazette.*

As for Ben, after a few well-known vicissitudes in New York, he went on to Philadelphia and there, on October 2, 1729, he began to publish the *Pennsylvania Gazette,* at once the best newspaper in the colonies because it was almost entirely written and edited by a man of undoubted genius.

Franklin understood what a newspaper ought to do, and what kind of man should edit it. "To publish a good newspaper is not so easy an undertaking as many people imagine it to be," he wrote in the first issue of the *Gazette*. An editor, he went on, should

be qualified with an extensive acquaintance with languages, a great easiness and command of writing and relating things clearly and intelligibly, and in few words; he should be able to speak of war both by land and sea; be well acquainted with geography, with the history of the time, with the several interests of princes and states, the secrets of courts, and the manners and customs of all nations. Men thus accomplished are very rare in this remote part of the world.

They were. The only man, in fact, qualified to be an editor on those terms was Franklin himself. As long as he was satisfied to confine his surging, diverse talents to the *Gazette*, it remained a sophisticated, superbly edited journal, far ahead of its time and foreshadowing the newspaper of the future. In policy it was conservative in its attitude toward the authorities, yet never subservient. "If all printers were determined not to print anything till they were sure it would offend nobody, there would be very little printed," its proprietor remarked.

The issues raised by James and the *Courant* in defying the Mathers and the Boston Council were soon to be tested anew in another place, with far greater celebrity. It was inevitable that this would happen. Revolt against authority ran in underground ripples through the colonies, lapping at the seats of the mighty. It had not yet become a voice of protest against the King and his ministers, but the basic principle involved was the same. The colonists were restless under the authoritarian rule of church and state, whether separate or linked. They resented the absolute power of governors, often used ruthlessly. Most of all, perhaps, they hated the silencing of protest, whether the suppression came from the governor, other royal appointees, or their own councils and assemblies.

Dissidents had learned something from the *Courant's* experience. They had seen how a printer with courage could become the means of attacking authority, if enough determined and able men supported him. The printer might be jailed, but his friends, who were the real life of the paper, could continue it under other auspices. If these friends preserved a discreet anonymity, they were not likely to be jailed; the printer was the man who took the risk. That meant he had to have the courage of his convictions, or be inspired by some other motive.

In New York City, where the population suffered the rule of a corrupt and oppressive governor, William Cosby, a printer appeared who satisfied the needs of those who sought relief. John Peter Zenger has long been celebrated as the man who struck the first blow for press freedom in America, but as a folk hero, this immigrant from the German Palatinate has acquired an immortality not entirely merited, nor is his famous trial for libel quite the landmark in jurisprudence it has been made out to be.

Zenger was not qualified by intelligence or ability to be a leader in the battle. An indifferent printer and an untalented writer, he had come up to New York with William Bradford, a Philadelphia printer under whom he had served his apprenticeship. Bradford, a man of ability, immediately established himself as the official printer and ran a successful shop, in which Zenger joined him as partner. In less than a year, the partnership ended and Zenger set up his own place on Broad Street, where he struggled along with what work he could get that was left over from Bradford's enterprise.

He had arrived in the city at a time when public anger over Governor Cosby's behavior was approaching a climax. Of all the royal governors, Cosby had proved himself to be the worst. He was a lazy, lecherous, dissolute man who ruled by whim through a clique of sycophants. Cosby had alienated nearly everyone except these favored cronies. He had antagonized the middle-class merchants by levying excessive taxes, and the common people were constantly irritated by the public display the governor made of his debauchery, which the people were painfully aware they were financing.

These irritations would have made enough trouble for him, but Cosby committed a high-handed error which precipitated open conflict. He deposed one of the colony's best-loved elder statesmen, Chief Justice Lewis Morris, and appointed in his place James DeLancey, the enterprising young son of a rich merchant who was one of Cosby's friends. The younger DeLancey had only recently returned from his training at Temple Bar in London. His appointment as Chief Justice was a brutal affront to every lawyer in the community, as well as a shabby substitute for Lewis Morris' experience and wisdom.

Morris and several of his most influential friends sought redress. Since there was no legal avenue open to them, they turned to the printed word. They knew it would be useless to approach William Bradford; he was the government's official printer and not likely to risk his profitable business. Zenger was the alternative.

He was not lacking in courage. Talent or education were not among his attributes, but as a refugee from authoritarian rule he understood and sympathized with Morris. Moreover, he was prepared to risk his little business to fight Cosby.

It was no inconsiderable risk. To a far greater extent than James Franklin had been, Zenger was the tool of other men. Where Franklin had been an editor as well as a printer, using his friends to poke dangerous fun at the rulers of Massachusetts, Zenger was only a stalking horse for determined men who meant to make a frontal assault on no less a personage than a royal governor. Franklin might face jail and suppression, but at least the clergy and magistrates of Boston were not monsters. No one could predict what a savage tyrant like Cosby might do.

One can believe the governor was more than annoyed when he saw the *New York Weekly Journal*, which Zenger and Morris's supporters began to publish on November 5, 1773. In this small, unpretentious four-page sheet, printed with Zenger's usual lack of craftsmanship, Cosby no doubt saw that threat to power which has always disturbed governments in similar circumstances. Perhaps he recognized the educated hand of the *Journal's* real editor, James Alexander, an accomplished young lawyer.

Other readers of the *Journal* were so delighted to see it that Zenger was kept busy reprinting editions. Morris had recently been elected an assemblyman in Westchester, in spite of the machinations of the High Sheriff, a comic-opera figure who had tried to rig the election in favor of one of Cosby's appointees, and the *Journal* satirized the sheriff in a mock advertisement.

A Monkey of the larger Sort, about 4 Foot high, has lately broke his chain and run into the country," the ad read. ". . . Having got a Warr Saddle, Pistols and Sword, this whimsical Creature fancied himself a general; and taking a Paper in his Paw he muttered over it, what the far greatest Part of the Company understood not . . .

The governor replied in kind through the columns of his own newspaper, Bradford's *New York Gazette,* in which Zenger's erstwhile partner directed a stream of vituperation at him in the unbridled style of the era.

In the ensuing battle between the two papers through the pens of their studiously anonymous supporters, the Morris faction had a clear margin. Its writers were better, and through their prose like a bright thread ran the appeal to freedom from tyranny, the plea for representative government. They drew heavily on Cato's *Letters* and Swift's *Tale of A Tub,* as well as Addison, whose essays appeared to serve the other side equally well.

Cosby was impatient with this literary tilting. He directed his new Chief Justice to get a grand jury indictment against what he considered unmistakable libel, but two terms of the jury refused to hand up an indictment—naturally, because the jurors were ordinary citizens, who uniformly hated Cosby. The governor then instructed

his hand-picked Council to dispose of Zenger, and the Council, having tried and failed in several legal maneuvers, abandoned circumspec-
tion, issued a warrant on its own behalf, and had Zenger clapped in
jail.

Thus the New York printer followed his Boston counterpart, but
there the similarity ended. Zenger was charged with criminal libel,
a more serious charge than the usual civil variety, since it involved
imprisonment as well as a fine, following conviction. It has been
invoked only twice in New York City since Zenger's day, the second
time as recently as 1963.

By an ironic coincidence, William Bradford, Zenger's *Gazette* opponent and erstwhile partner, had already tested the libel law in
Philadelphia. There he had printed some indiscreet speculations about
the honesty of the Quaker authorities, which cost him his official printing contract, his type and paper, and his freedom. In court he had
argued his own case, setting forth two principles: his right to challenge
obviously biased jurors peremptorily in such an action, and acceptance
of the burden of proof by his prosecutors.

Under English common law, by which the case was being tried,
Bradford had nothing to support his contentions at the time, but
he was so eloquent in his address to the jury, citizens like himself,
that these gentlemen, no friends of authority, confessed themselves
unable to agree after forty-eight hours of deliberation, and Bradford
was freed. His career was over in Philadelphia, however; he had lost
the tools of his trade through seizure. That was why he had come up to
New York, bringing his apprentice Zenger with him. It was why he
supported Cosby's government, to whom he owed his re-establishment
in business and his success as official printer.

It must have seemed strange to Bradford, as a veteran fighter for
freedom of the press, to find himself now labeled as its enemy, and
Zenger, the man he had started in business, hailed as the hero of
the people. Presumably he watched the proceedings which now un-
folded in court with more than ordinary interest.

As had been the case in Philadelphia, the law, as law, did not support Zenger. Cosby and DeLancey, moreover, did whatever they
could to abet the statutes. They refused reasonable bail to Zenger as

a guarantee of his appearance, and when his lawyers attacked the
Chief Justice's commission in a desperate effort to prevent his sitting
on the case, DeLancey simply disbarred them and appointed one
of his own friends to defend the printer. This lawyer, however, apparently had a conscience. He did what any good attorney would have
done and asked for a month's delay so he could prepare his case. It
was granted. DeLancey and his fellow justice, Frederick Philipse,
who were hearing the case, could hardly have done otherwise since
this was standard procedure.

The interval gave the Morris forces an opportunity to plot their
course, and it served to stir the population to a pitch of excitement,
not only in New York but in all the colonies. The Sons of Liberty,
who would soon be patriots in another cause, kept the issue alive
everywhere through their cells up and down the coast. Zenger's disbarred lawyers looked about for another counsel, and down in Philadelphia, Ben Franklin took an interest in the case. It may have been
Franklin who persuaded his friend Andrew Hamilton, the great liberal
lawyer who was then in his eighties, to consider taking up one more
battle for liberty.

Whether it was Franklin or the issue itself which was persuasive,
Hamilton rode to New York in the deep summer heat and sat in the
back of the courtroom on August 4, 1735, as the trial got under way
at last. He watched the jury being impaneled, and in these good men
and true he may have seen Bradford's hung jury reincarnated, and
plotted his campaign accordingly.

He sat quietly while Zenger's DeLancey-appointed attorney, John
Chambers, entered a plea of "not guilty" to the charges as read; then
he rose and came to the bar, a striking figure with his white hair fall-
ing to his shoulders, his ancient body erect and eyes keen. The justices
greeted him with respect and accepted his request to appear for the
defense.

"I cannot think it proper," he began in his resonant actor's voice,
notable in so many courtroom dramas, "to deny the publication of a
complaint which I think is the right of every free born subject to
make." He turned so that he was addressing the jury as much as the

judges. "Therefore I'll save Mr. Attorney the trouble of examining his witnesses to that point; and I do confess (for my client) that he both printed and published the two papers set forth in the information. I do hope in so doing he has committed no crime."

Those in the courtroom who were familiar with law were astounded. Under the statutes, the jury had only to decide whether the publications had actually been made by the defendant, yet Hamilton had opened his case by admitting it.

The attorney-general was puzzled but grateful. "Then, if your honors please," he interposed, rising quickly, "since Mr. Hamilton has confessed the fact, I think our witnesses may be discharged; we have no further occasion for them." With publication admitted, he went on, there was nothing further for the jury to do but bring in a verdict of guilty.

"Not so, neither, Mr. Attorney," Hamilton answered coolly. "There are two sides to that bargain. I hope it is not our bare printing or publishing a paper that will make it a libel. You will have something more to do before you make my client a libeler. For the words themselves must be libelous—that is, false, malicious, and seditious —or else we are not guilty."

On this point of law, Attorney-General Bradley and Hamilton stood before the bench and argued. The old lawyer cited the Magna Carta and the abolition of the Star Chamber. Bradley simply said that the law was the law. He was right, but Hamilton's superb courtroom manner had even the partisan justices momentarily hypnotized. It was only when Hamilton asserted that "the falsehood makes the scandal, and both the libel," and added he would "prove these very papers that are called libel to be true," that DeLancey interposed. Young and unqualified he might be for his post, but he had been to Temple Bar and he knew something about English law.

"You cannot be admitted, Mr. Hamilton, to give the truth of a libel in evidence," he admonished. "The court is of the opinion you ought not to be permitted to prove the facts in the papers." He was correct, and he cited a long list of precedents to prove it. Hamilton listened patiently. He knew the citations by heart.

"These are Star Chamber cases," he said, when DeLancey had finished, "and I was in hopes that practice had been dead with that court."

DeLancey was both confused and angered by this unexpected reply, and he responded as a young man would. "The Court have delivered their opinion, and we expect you will use us with good manners. You are not permitted to argue against this Court."

It was the moment Hamilton had been waiting for. He knew he had no case in law, but he had provoked DeLancey into acting in the arbitrary way every man on the jury would recognize as Cosby's. Accomplished actor that he was, Hamilton then gave the magnificent, historic performance which has been so often quoted.

Bowing to the Chief Justice with a courtly, "I thank you," he turned his back on both judges and addressed the jury, his resonant voice ringing clearly in the courtroom. "Then it is to you, gentlemen," he began, "that we must now appeal for witnesses to the truth of the facts we have offered, and are denied the liberty to prove . . . I beg leave to lay it down as a standing rule in such cases that the suppressing of evidence ought always to be taken for the strongest evidence, and I hope it will have that weight with you."

DeLancey interrupted. Doggedly, he pointed out that the jury had no right under the law to do any more than decide whether Zenger had published the papers. It was the prerogative of the judges to decide whether they were libelous.

"The jury *may* do so," Hamilton swept on grandly, scarcely glancing at the bench, "but I do likewise know that they may do otherwise. I know they have the right, beyond all dispute, to determine both the law and the facts; and where they do not doubt of the law, they ought to do so.

"A proper confidence in a court is commendable, but as the verdict (whatever it is) will be yours, you ought to refer no part of your duty to the discretion of other persons. If you should be of opinion that there is no falsehood in Mr. Zenger's papers, you will, nay (pardon me for the expression), you ought to say so; because you do not know whether others (I mean the court) may be of that opinion. It is your right to do so, and there is much depending upon your resolution, as well as upon your integrity."

The justices and every lawyer in the courtroom could see what Hamilton was doing. He was telling the jurymen to be freemen, to follow their consciences and assert the liberties guaranteed them by English law. Winding up in a peroration that had these jury members fascinated with their own position, he declared:

"Old and weak as I am, I should think it my duty, if required, to go to the utmost part of the land where my service could be of any use in assisting to quench the flame of prosecutions upon informations, set on foot by the government to deprive a people of the right of remonstrating (and complaining too) of the arbitrary attempts of men in power. Men who injure and oppress the people under their administration provoke them to cry out and complain, and then make that very complaint the foundation for new oppressions and prosecutions.

". . . The question before the court and you, gentlemen of the jury, is not of small nor private concern. It is not the cause of the poor printer, nor of New York alone, which you are now trying. No! It may in its consequences affect every freeman that lives under a British government on the main of America. It is the best cause. It is the cause of liberty, and I make no doubt but your upright conduct this day will not only entitle you to the love and esteem of your fellow citizens, but every man who prefers freedom to a life of slavery will bless and honor you as men who have baffled the attempt of tyranny, and by an impartial and uncorrupt verdict have laid a noble foundation for securing to ourselves, our posterity and our neighbors that to which nature and the laws of our country have given us a right—the liberty—both of exposing and opposing arbitrary power (in these parts of the world, at least) by speaking and writing—truth."

DeLancey must have known, after this stirring appeal to the passions and prejudices of the jury, that he was defeated, but he clung to what he knew. He gave what amounted to a directed verdict, insisting again that the jury could not go beyond deciding the fact of publication, which had already been admitted, leaving the question of libel to the justices. But the jury was transformed. They saw themselves in the afterglow of Hamilton's words as freemen upholding the ancient rights of Magna Carta, and they brought in a unanimous verdict of not guilty.

It must be said for the Chief Justice that he did not do what it was in his power to do. He could have set aside the verdict as being in direct contradiction to the evidence, as it was. He could even have cited Hamilton for contempt. That he did none of these things was one of the first indications British government in America was inclined to move cautiously. It was plain to DeLancey that the verdict was not simply the result of Hamilton's histrionics, but an expression of deep and intense popular feeling. It was in the faces of the inspired jurymen, and in the electric atmosphere of the courtroom, which erupted in riotous cheering after the verdict.

Hamilton, of course, was on impeccable moral grounds and his victory was a moral one. But the fact remains that the principle he argued, the jury's right to determine both law and fact, was not recognized either in England or America until more than a half-century later, and the verdict of this jury, as DeLancey correctly maintained, was contrary to law. In those days, the recognized principle was "the greater the truth, the greater the libel."

Nor did the verdict have any immediate effect on the law. Truth as a defense was not recognized generally in America until 1804, when another famous libel action, the Croswell case, was argued as brilliantly by another Hamilton, Alexander, a byproduct of which was the quarrel which led to that great man's death on the heights of Weehawken.

Zenger might well have been rearrested after his trial, but Cosby too was cautious now: Morris had gone to England to argue his case against the governor personally with the Crown. While Cosby was awaiting the results, he fell ill that winter and died the following March. Zenger published a verbatim account of the trial which made him momentarily famous in the colonies, and got him appointments as public printer in both New Jersey and New York. But in spite of the apologists who have made his name a landmark in American journalistic history, the truth is that Zenger was not an outstanding figure in his own right. He was not competent enough to take advantage of his opportunities after the trial, and died poor in 1746. Yet Zenger achieved lasting historical recognition, while Andrew Hamilton, the true hero of the case, is known today only to scholars and American history buffs.

If the trial established no legal precedents, it had a powerful effect on other juries, which now felt emboldened to uphold critics of government, no matter what the law might be. It also encouraged citizens to believe that these laws, as laid down by the governors, were not immutable and could be changed by popular demand. In short, the seeds of revolution had been planted, and the newspaper was recognized as the vehicle of popular revolt.

two

Newspapers in the Revolution

WHILE THE NEWSPAPERS WERE STRUGGLING for their freedom, they were also proliferating. There were five of them in Boston by 1741, including the *New England Weekly Journal,* first newspaper to have a system of correspondents in neighboring towns.

The urge to make newspapers spread as the need for information increased, and as more politicians came to understand how valuable newspapers could be in disseminating ideas. The transition from ownership by printer-proprietors to editors continued, and there were some who combined both skills. One of the best of these was William Parks, who had learned his trade from the finest printers in England. He supplemented his art with a good education and excellent literary taste. Parks made Maryland the fourth colony to have a newspaper when he established the *Maryland Gazette* at Annapolis in 1727. In 1736 he added Virginia to the list with the *Virginia Gazette,* published in Williamsburg, where his shop is now part of the Rockefeller restoration of the village and facsimile copies of the *Gazette* are tourist trinkets.

These papers of Parks' were among the best to appear in colonial America. They were typographically superior to most of the others, and much better written. The editor's cultivated tastes gave them a literary flavor well suited to the educated English gentry who were settling in the tidewater South, and who were their principal readers. George Washington and his friends were constant readers of the *Virginia Gazette,* in their splendid plantations along the James and the Potomac.

Published now without license in substantial numbers—there were fourteen weeklies in the six colonies with the highest population by 1750—the press was becoming an essential part of daily life. Business was beginning to depend upon it as the transmission belt between producer and consumer, as it does today. The rise of business in pre-Revolutionary America had been so spectacular that any number of early Calvin Coolidges, particularly in Philadelphia, were already prepared to assert that the business of America was business. The colonies themselves were no longer struggling, isolated settlements, clinging to the edge of a savage continent. They were populous provinces, growing every day, and linked by a thousand mutual interests which were served by the newspapers' unmatched ability to communicate information.

By mid-century circulations were substantial enough, aided by advertising revenue, to make a few publishers rich. These were the men who had known best how to take advantage of climbing population figures, better means of communication, and the mounting political temperature in the colonies. Such publishers were producing better newspapers with more news in them. After 1750 the papers also began to appear more frequently, some as often as three times a week.

The news was largely political, whether foreign or domestic. Everything the monarchy did was news, and Americans followed the succession of the three Georges with absorbed interest. The War of the Austrian Succession and the Seven Years' War were major stories, particularly the latter, which profoundly affected Americans because the North American phase of it involved all the colonies in bloody conflict with the French and Indians on their borders.

Aside from wars and rumors of them, the news columns were filled with the continuing struggle between royal governors and popular assemblies. Some publishers believed freedom of the press meant newspapers should publish any submitted comment on a public issue, particularly if the writer paid for it. Franklin announced himself opposed to this idea. He was not operating a stagecoach with seats for everybody, he said. Such controversy ought to be carried on through pamphlets, he added, and these he was prepared to print for anyone.

Pamphleteering was, in fact, the chief method of carrying on controversy for some time, and the newspapers treated this activity as a profitable source of job work. In their own columns, they were usually careful to avoid trouble, perhaps bearing in mind the tribulations of James Franklin and Zenger. Since those days an uneasy truce had existed between newspapers and government, the press pretending it was free but acutely aware that there was nothing to prevent the Crown from closing any shop. Sometimes one newspaper was more outspoken than the others, and then the authorities, whether governor or assembly, would make threatening noises. It was usually enough. The press was no longer licensed, but it was censored through intimidation, or the possibility of it.

As the complicated issues between colonies and Crown moved closer toward an open break, however, one act of government, the Stamp Act of 1765, did more than anything else to precipitate outright opposition and unite the colonial newspapers as they had not been united before.

This Act pleased no one, but it hurt publishers and lawyers more than any other segment of the population because it fell heaviest on newsprint and legal documents. Thus the British ministers antagonized the two elements in America capable of doing them the most harm. It did no good to argue that tax money was absolutely essential to put Britain, bankrupted by the long war with France, on its feet again, nor to point out to Americans that British armies had saved a Protestant population from being ruled by the Pope. Nor was business consoled by the knowledge that the British fleet had made normal commerce possible again. There was simply the normal, perennial reaction to taxation. Everyone hated it, and none more than the elements in the population on whom the greatest burden was imposed.

Publishers resisted the tax according to their temperaments. Some declared the levy insupportable and suspended their papers. That produced a sharp reaction in the business community, whose interests were immediately affected, and among the general public, who were deprived of their chief source of information. The patriotic opposition consequently gained a good deal of ground.

Other publishers, probably the majority, fought the law by evading it. If a newspaper were published without title or masthead, it was technically no longer a newspaper and therefore not taxable. Some papers appeared without the tax stamp, which the law said must be pasted on each issue, and explained editorially that they could not find any stamps to buy, which was credible in those cities where the mob had stopped the sale.

The papers were nearly unanimous in treating the tax as a direct assault on what freedom they possessed. Several pretended solemnly that the press was dead. In Philadelphia, the *Pennsylvania Journal and Weekly Advertiser* appeared with its column rules turned over, as in public mourning, but in the shape of a tombstone. Both the *Boston Gazette* and the *Maryland Gazette* carried a skull-and-cross-bones on their front pages.

From the day in November 1765 that the Stamp Act took effect until the end of the Revolution, American newspapers were pre-occupied with politics. The news was subordinated to the uses of propaganda. At one level it was the classic propaganda of the class struggle—the have-not mobs of Boston and New York, for example, against the privilege and position which the Crown and its rich friends represented. On another level, it was the revolt of men who felt them-selves unjustly deprived of basic freedoms—the kind of deprivation which inspired the cry of "taxation without representation."

That slogan, however, did not represent Sam Adams and the demo-cratic mob, but rather the capitalist, or Whig, viewpoint of men like John Dickinson, who believed in the sanctity of property rights and free enterprise, and considered the arbitrary action of governments, whether the King's or a provincial assembly's, to be a direct threat to both institutions.

These political ideas—Tory, Whig and democratic—were the sub-stance of the propaganda which dominated newspapers for nearly twenty years and reduced their news function largely to highly colored, partisan accounts of the tremendous events which swept the land. Wars of ideas attract brilliant men, and the editors of the Revolution were splendid intellects and superior craftsmen for the most part. Most of them were young. Collectively they gave a distinction to the writing and editing of the American newspaper which transcended whatever it lost as a propaganda medium. They swore that they were telling the truth, and they believed it. Each side was convinced the others were a pack of liars, and there was some truth in that too.

What the patriot newspapers did for the cause before the climactic events at Lexington and Concord can hardly be underestimated. They were confronted with a country dangerously divided, from the standpoint of those who believed war was the only way out. It was difficult enough to oppose the Tories, who were in league with the Establishment, but there was also the wavering stance of the Dickinsonian capitalists, the incipient Whigs, who would not believe in the failure of conciliation and compromise until the blood flowed. Worst of all was the division among the patriots themselves, not all of whom were as entirely dedicated to freedom as the hotbloods of the big Eastern ports, where the conflict was most abrasive.

The editors of newspapers in these port cities were conscious that the settlers who had begun moving toward the west were not as ardent in the cause. The daily lives of these farmers were demanding, and they were far away from such clear and present irritations as the British troops and Crown tax collectors who inhabited the port cities, the centers of revolt. Consequently the editors in these cities made particular efforts to reach those in the hinterlands and arouse them to the coming struggle. They were not finicky about how they did it. The British were depicted as so hungry for tax money that they would stop at nothing. It was solemnly declared in one paper that kissing would be taxed. The difficulties of collection were ignored.

By these and other exhortations, the will of the colonies to resist was crystallized and the common spirit, so far as it was common at all, was communicated by dozens of newspapers circulating everywhere men lived, even as far as the Ohio Valley, where the settlers were more concerned with the Indians than they were with the British.

The newspapers were conscious of what they were doing, of their collective strength. "The press hath never done greater service since its first invention," the *New Hampshire Gazette* proclaimed.

What the papers did was not always admirable, but it seldom failed to be exciting. It was a matter of courage as well, because censorship by government, which drew nearer to a close every day, was being replaced by the blind censorship of the mob, which was likely to descend on an offending paper, break its type and presses, and the proprietor in the bargain if he were unwise enough to linger.

It was the fire-eaters among the patriots who incited these passions, and no better example could be offered of their handiwork than the Boston *Gazette*, known to the Tories of that city as the "Weekly Dung Barge." It was the product of two "men of bold and fearless hearts," as they were aptly described, whose names were Benjamin Edes and John Gill. They had been brought up in Charlestown, Massachusetts, and had become friends there. In 1775, when they were only twenty-three, they set up a print shop at the corner of Court Street and Franklin Avenue and began to publish the *Gazette* from it. Like so many other patriot papers—and it declared itself at once —the *Gazette* became a gathering place for like minds. There was publishing in the front room and sedition in the back, according to current journalistic practice.

One of the seditious acts discussed in the *Gazette's* back room must have been the plot to dump the tea into Boston harbor, since Edes was one of the chief conspirators. The plan was perfected at the Green Dragon, a notorious patriot public house, and the plotters put on their disguises either there or in Edes' house.

The *Gazette* caused the British so much pain in the years before hostilities began that when Boston was about to be occupied, General Gage's officers issued orders placing the newspaper high on the list of places to be captured and destroyed when the recalcitrant farmers were pushed back. The troops were to pay special attention to "those trumpeters of sedition, Edes and Gill."

In the hours of crisis before the city was occupied, the partners held a hasty conference and dissolved their business on the spot. In the dead of night Edes loaded press and type on a wagon and escaped to nearby Watertown, just far enough away to be safe. Publication was resumed there, and in Boston again after the British left it. The *Gazette* remained a gadfly to the British as long as the war lasted. But when it ended, the real reason for the *Gazette's* existence ended too. Edes was an able propagandist for the cause he believed in so ardently, but he was unable to sustain a newspaper without a cause in the post-Revolution years. The *Gazette* suspended in 1798, and Edes died five years later, a poor man.

Gill, left alone in Boston to face the advancing British, did not choose to flee, for some reason. Consequently he was arrested at once and was fortunate enough to endure nothing worse than prison until General Washington's triumphant army liberated him. Starting in business again, Gill quickly disclosed where the strength of the partnership had been. His new paper was a colorless affair which not even the events of the Revolution itself could sustain, and Gill himself did not long survive the end of the war. He died in 1785, as poor as his former partner.

The *Gazette,* in retrospect, was a true child of the times, a propaganda organ, pure and simple, flamboyant and rabble-rousing in its style, valuable and powerful in its own context but contributing little to the development of the press.

By contrast the newspaper of a young contemporary was a work of art, and its publisher a man to be remembered far beyond his time. Isaiah Thomas rises above the journalists of the eighteenth century like those giants who followed him a few decades later.

He was a man whose life was dedicated to the printer's craft. Apprenticed when he was only six years old, so that he could help support a widowed mother, he never had a chance for schooling but he emerged from a lifetime of study as one of the finest scholars in America, the possessor of one of its best private libraries, a historian of note, and a founder and first president of the Antiquarian Society. Thomas got his education from setting type and reading galley proofs, and from living with books all his life.

He was only twenty-one, in 1770, when he began to publish the *Massachusetts Spy* in Boston, in partnership with Zechariah Fowle, to whom he had once been apprenticed. It was a brief merger. Fowle was a lazy, commonplace printer and Thomas approached genius; the apprentice soon bought out the master.

Following the Whig line, Thomas carried a slogan under the *Spy's* name, asserting that it was "A Weekly Political and Commercial Paper—Open to All Parties, but *influenced* by None." As war approached, however, Thomas lost his faith in the Whig policy of conciliation and the tone of his paper began to take on the radical coloration of Edes' *Gazette*. It was far better written than the *Gazette* or any other paper except one, James Rivington's *New York Gazetteer*, which was to become the leading Tory voice after the war began.

Until actual hostilities were under way, both Thomas and Rivington tried to approach the issues of the coming Revolution objectively, but objectivity was not a quality desired by most newspaper readers. Rivington was denounced by both sides, especially the Sons of Liberty and their friends. Thomas was not attacked because his differences with the radicals at the beginning were only one of method, not of principle, and as the open break came nearer, he was hand-in-glove with them, not only in the pages of the *Spy*, but in the revolutionary underground conspiracy itself. It was Thomas who sat in the belfry of the Old North Church that April night, along with other Minutemen, and flashed the signals which sent Paul Revere on his ride.

At Lexington next day, Isaiah Thomas became the first American war correspondent. His eyewitness report of the skirmish was not intended to be an objective account—objectivity fled that day from what few remaining papers were committed to it—but it is an excellent story for the times. This is how Thomas reported the affair:

> About ten o'clock on the night of the eighteenth of April, the troops in Boston were disclosed to be on the move in a very secret manner, and it was found they were embarking on boats (which they privately brought to the place in the evening) at the bottom of the Common; expresses set off immediately to alarm the country, that they might be on their guard. When the expresses got about a mile beyond Lexingon, they were stopped by about fourteen officers on horseback, who came out of Boston in the afternoon of that day, and were seen lurking in by-places in the country till after dark. One of the expresses immediately fled, and was pursued two miles by an officer, who, when he had got up with him presented a pistol, and told him he was a dead man if he did not stop, but he rode on till he came up to a house, when stopping of a sudden his horse threw him off, having the presence of mind to halloo to the people in the house,
>
> "Turn out. Turn out. I have got one of them."
>
> The officer immediately retreated and fled as fast as he had pursued. The other express [Paul Revere] after passing through a strict examination, by some means got clear.

The body of troops in the meantime, under the command of Lieutenant Colonel Smith, had crossed the river and landed at Phipp's Farm. They immediately, to the number of 1,000, proceeded to Lexington, about six miles below Concord, with great silence. A company of militia, of about eighty men, mustered near the meeting house; the troops came in sight of them just before sunrise. The militia, upon seeing the troops, began to disperse. The troops then set out upon the run, hallooing and hussaing, and coming within a few rods of them, the commanding officer accosted the militia, in words to this effect,

"Disperse, you damn'd rebels—Damn you, disperse."

Upon which the troops again hussaed and immediately one or two officers discharged their pistols, which were instantaneously followed by the firing of four or five of the soldiers; and then there seemed to be a general discharge from the whole body. Eight of our men were killed and nine wounded.

That story was printed in Worcester, where Isaiah had moved his type and presses two nights before, under cover of darkness, about the time Edes was embarking across the Charles River to the safety of Watertown.

In Worcester, Thomas was more successful than he had ever been in Boston. The war years were difficult, as they were for every printer, but when the conflict was over, Thomas expanded his activities until he was the leading publisher in the colonies. He not only continued to put out the *Spy* with distinction, but he published three magazines, an almanac and a distinguished list of more than 400 books, including Blackstone's *Commentaries,* Bunyan's *Pilgrim's Progress,* Defoe's *Robinson Crusoe* and more than a hundred children's books. After he retired rich in 1802, he devoted himself to scholarship, producing his *History of Printing in America,* still a valuable source work.

Thomas's Worcester shop was the marvel of the printing industry in post-Revolutionary America, with its 150 employees and seven presses. It was supplied by its own paper mill and bindery, and the apprentices Isaiah trained opened branches in eight other cities, with his money and advice to help them. The books he turned out at Worcester were not only first publications, as in the case of the first folio Bible and the first dictionary, among others, but they were typographically superb. Franklin called him "the Baskerville of America."

The *Spy* itself continued to be a distinguished newspaper. Thomas had established it so solidly that it persisted until 1904.

No other publisher of his day approached Thomas. Even among the partisan newspapers of the Revolution, his *Spy* was a model of reporting. It served the propaganda uses of the patriots, but it did so with distinction. Compare, for example, Thomas's Lexington reporting with the *Boston Gazette's* coverage of a Boston incident four months earlier, probably written by Edes. The story ran:

A little after ten o'clock this evening, two young men passing down Milk Street, near the entrance into Long Lane, they were accosted by an officer, not in the English, but as they supposed in another language, which they did not understand; they asked him what he meant; he replied he meant to tell them to go about their business. They had not gone far before the officer called to them to stop. They stopped till he came up to them, and angry words ensued. The young men, however, parted from him the second time, and went on their way towards their homes. The officer followed and overtook them near the head of the lane, and stopped them again, telling them he supposed they were stiff Americans; to which one of them said he gloried in the character. Here again words ensued, and the officer drew his sword, flourished it and struck one of the young men on the arm, who immediately seized him. At this junction, three or four of the town watch, who were upon the patrol, came up and separated them, advising them to go home. The two young men did so, but the officer refused, saying he was prisoner of the watch and would go with them; they told him he was not their prisoner, but might go where he pleased, and if he desired it, they would see him safe home: but he insisted upon it that he was their prisoner. The watchmen went down the lane towards their head-quarters in King Street, where they had been going before, and the officer accompanied them. In the way they met with several persons, whom they took to be servants of officers, who, supposing the officer to be in custody of the watch, attempted to rescue him, but he insisted upon being a prisoner, and said the watchmen were his friends, and he *would* go with them. They then went forward, and in Quaker Lane, which leads into King Street, they were met and assaulted by more than twenty officers of the army, who took several of their watch poles from them, and wounded some of them.

By way of further contrast, here is the story of the same incident, as reported by Rivington in the *New York Gazetteer*:

You have read in that fund of lies and sedition, Edes and Gill, of a "high-handed riot." There have been five field officers on a court of inquiry, to inspect into the conduct of the officers concerned on that occasion. It commenced by Lieutenant Myers, 38th Regiment, being, without the smallest cause, insulted by two townspeople, who not only called him a Tory, rascal, scoundrel, &c., but damned the king, governor, army, and every friend to government; the former he put up with, the latter resented, by knocking the person down. He was immediately surrounded by the watch; and though he immediately surrendered, and gave his sword to a Mr. Winslow, who came up at the time (a private gentleman), and informed them, and this gentleman, of the cause of the quarrel, they treated him with every indignity possible; not only allowed the two men to knock him down in the midst of them, but they themselves kicked and beat him all the way to the watch-house, a little short of a quarter of a mile. The noise about the watch-house brought together a few officers, whom Mr. Myers requested not to interfere, concealed from them the cruel treatment he had met with, and insisted on remaining in custody. The insolence of the watch to those gentlemen occasioned a fresh riot, when the interposition of a party from the main guard prevented any bad consequences. Immediately after, Myers was released, by order from the governor. Complaints were immediately lodged against the officers, and bail is to be given to-morrow for their appearance. I cannot quit this subject without observing that the high-flyers are much disappointed in the event of this riot; not only at the little mischief done, but at the ready submission of every officer concerned, to the laws of the country.

The spirit of the people here seems to subside a little; and we have every reason to believe, that, in order to keep it up, the vagabonds of the town are employed to insult the troops, which they do daily, in hopes of bringing about another massacre.

"Jemmy" Rivington, who wrote these words, was by all odds the most exciting newspaper publisher of his time, as Isaiah Thomas was the most distinguished. He was a Tory by instinct, since his father had been a prominent London bookman whose chief business was to be the Church of England's official publisher, as the Rivington family had been for generations. Jemmy grew up in this "official" atmosphere of a united authoritarian church and state. It not only explains his Tory viewpoint, but may also throw some light on his early life in London, where his success in his father's business—he cleared ten

thousand pounds alone by publishing Smollett's History of England—
was accompanied by the profligate life he led after hours, and sometimes during them.

Rivington, a handsome man like Thomas but built along much
more generous lines, was excessively fond of horses and women. He
lost much of his money at Newmarket, squandered more of it on
expensive mistresses, and came to America in 1762 to recoup his
fortunes. Incidentally, he meant to advance the Tory cause.

He set himself up in Philadelphia as a bookseller, advertising as
"the only London book-seller in America." Rivington imported books
from Britain and distributed the works of Tory sympathizers in
America. Since the people who read books were mostly in the upper
class, and many of them were likely to be Tories, Rivington prospered,
so well that he opened branches in Boston and New York, thus becoming the first chain bookstore operator in America.

His income from bookselling was so encouraging that Rivington
decided in 1773 to begin a newspaper in New York. The name he
selected reflected his expansive character: *Rivington's New York
Gazetteer, or the Connecticut, New Jersey, Hudson's River and
Quebec Weekly Advertiser.* Jemmy may have had circulation in all
these places, but most of the 3,600 copies he was circulating after his
first year in business were read in New York City. It was like Rivington, however, to proclaim that his paper was circulated "thro' every
colony of North-America, most of the English, French, Spanish, Dutch,
and Danish West India islands, the principal cities and towns of Great
Britain, France, Ireland, and the Mediterranean."

The editorial policy of the *Gazetteer* was also enunciated in Jemmy's
grandiloquent prose as one calculated "Never to admit any Performance, calculated to injure Virtue, Religion, or other public Happiness, to wound a Neighbor's Reputation, or to raise a blush in the
face of Virgin Innocence." He added that he intended to print both
sides of public questions, and in that at least he was entirely scrupulous
at the beginning.

Behind all this flamboyance was an ability which more impartial
critics could admire. Isaiah Thomas, who had little reason to love
his rival, wrote of him that "few men, perhaps, were better qualified

. . . to publish a newspaper." The *Gazetteer* itself, Thomas added, was admirable: "No newspaper in the colonies was better printed, or was more copiously furnished with foreign intelligence."

Rivington pursued a reasonably objective line before 1775, just as Thomas was doing in Boston, but the time came when both men had to choose, and they chose opposite sides. Jemmy could have made no other choice; he was a Tory in his bones, with a contempt for popular rule, which he termed hypocritical. The patriots, he asserted, were not willing to wait for the processes of English law and government to redress their grievances; their only answer to injustice was violence.

As though to confirm this accusation, a party of the Sons of Liberty from Connecticut swept down on Rivington's shop in November 1775 and destroyed it. He was bitter, and with reason. The *Gazetteer* had been printing both sides of public issues, as the proprietor had promised. It had carried patriot versions of events even when Rivington knew them to be untrue. He had done his best to be impartial, according to his conception of what an editor and a newspaper should be, but the patriots disdained impartiality. For them there was only one truth, and that was their own. Thus fanaticism won a short-term victory, as it so often does, and Jemmy was destroyed. He went home to England.

By the time he returned, two years later, the British were in control of New York and he resumed publication of the *Gazetteer* under their protection. Now it was an entirely different paper, and there were those who had reason to regret their callous treatment of it in its first phase. For Jemmy turned the full force of his clever, vitriolic pen against the patriots and all their works, with telling effect. The patriot papers were as one-sided in their propaganda as Rivington, but their editors for the most part lacked his diabolical ingenuity and savage wit.

Rivington's *Gazetteer*, in its wartime incarnation, was as superbly written and edited as ever, but it was also conducted on the most unprincipled lines. Jemmy had no compunction about printing scurrilous forgeries, spreading any kind of rumor which seemed likely to discomfit the Continentals, and repeating gossip, whether real or imaginary, about the leading figures in the other camp, from General

Washington on down. The General, a serious man with little of humor in his nature and even less to cheer him during most of the war, was constantly annoyed by Rivington's jibes, and horrified by his scandalous forgeries. No doubt it was this experience that helped to form in Washington's mind a distaste for newspapers which became a passionate hatred when he was President, as will be seen.

A man who was even more angered by the *Gazetteer* than the Commander-in-Chief was the hero of Vermont, General Ethan Allen, whom Rivington pursued with ridicule through the war years, depicting him as a country bumpkin in uniform. Allen was so irate he swore he would "lick Rivington the very first opportunity" when the war was over.

Rivington's description of how the General came down to New York to carry out this vow is at once an excellent sample of his style and a revealing glimpse of his charming personality. He wrote:

I was sitting after a good dinner, alone, with my bottle of Madeira before me, when I heard an unusual noise in the street, and a huzza from the boys. I was in the second story, and stepping to the window, saw a tall figure in tarnished regimentals, with a large cocked hat and an enormous long sword, followed by a crowd of boys, who occasionally cheered him with huzzas, of which he seemed insensible. He came up to my door and stopped. I could see no more. My heart told me it was Ethan Allen. I shut down my window and retired behind my table and bottle. I was certain the hour of reckoning had come. There was no retreat.

Mr. Staples, my clerk, came in paler than ever, and clasping his hands, said, "Master, he is come . . . He entered the store, and asked if James Rivington lived there. I answered, 'Yes, sir.' 'Is he at home?' 'I will go and see, sir,' I said; and now, master, what is to be done? There he is in the store, and the boys peeping at him from the street."

I had made up my mind. I looked at the bottle of Madeira—possibly took a glass. "Show him up," said I; "and if such Madeira can not mollify him, he must be harder than adamant."

There was a fearful moment of suspense. I heard him on the stairs, his long sword clanking at every step. In he stalked.

"Is your name James Rivington?"

"It is, sir, and no man could be more happy than I am to see Colonel Ethan Allen." [Rivington's use of "colonel" remains unexplained.]

"Sir, I have come—"

"Not another word, my dear colonel, until you have taken a seat and a glass of old Madeira."

"But, sir, I don't think it proper—"

"Not another word, Colonel. Taste this wine; I have had it in glass for ten years. Old wine, you know, unless it is originally sound, never improves by age."

He took the glass, swallowed the wine, smacked his lips, and shook his head approvingly.

"Sir, I have come—"

"Not another word until you have taken another glass, and then, my dear Colonel, we will talk of old affairs, and I have some droll events to detail."

In short, we finished two bottles of Madeira, and parted as good friends as if we never had cause to be otherwise.

The other enmities Rivington had fostered were not so easily disposed of, unfortunately for him. After the British evacuated the city, he thought it expedient to apologize for his acts, which he did, but the expediency was too apparent for a good many citizens. It was said in his defense that he had given secret help to the spy ring Washington had maintained in New York, but that has never been proved to this day and is doubted by most historians who have examined it. There was also the fact that he had become a familiar New York character. His portly figure, carefully dressed in the claret coats he fancied, with scarlet waistcoat trimmed in gold lace and buckskin breeches, was seen in the best places and with the best people.

Nevertheless they could not forget the cutting, false things he had said in his paper, and the fact that they had been written with wit and style did not mitigate them. Once he was set upon in the street and beaten by a citizen who remembered too well. Even his generosity earned him a cell in debtor's prison when those whose bills he had guaranteed failed to pay. People no longer patronized his newspaper, and in truth, without the politics it was not as sharp and readable as it had been during the war—a fate which overtook many another gazette. There could be only one ending to Rivington's story. He went bankrupt and died poor—on Independence Day, 1802, leaving behind him a growing store of legends and a street named after him on the lower East Side.

Rivington was far from being the only wartime editor who failed to survive the strong feelings the papers had stirred up by virtue of their excesses. Another New York publisher, Hugh Gaine, was the victim of his own opportunism. Gaine was an Irishman who had anticipated the great migration by coming to New York from Belfast in 1753 and founding the *New York Mercury*. He was a hardworking, frugal young man who was apparently without any real convictions except the desire to make money. Almost at once he involved himself in the quarrel between Episcopalians and Presbyterians over which church should control the newly established King's College, later Columbia University. Gaine contrived to work both sides to his own profit.

By the time the Revolution was on his doorstep, Gaine's *Mercury*, now the *Gazette and Weekly Mercury*, was a prosperous newspaper, but its proprietor appeared on the streets in the same worn clothes of his lean years. He was still the frugal worker, prepared to serve any man. Naturally, he announced himself as nonpartisan in the quarrel with Britain, but he could no more take this stance successfully than the other publishers. Poor Gaine! His nonpartisanship was founded on the notion of obtaining revenue from both sides, as he had done before, but the Sons of Liberty hinted at his total destruction if he did not advocate their cause.

For a time, in a frantic effort to avoid losing advertising and circulation, he tried being mildly partisan for the cause, with a good many qualifications and fence-sitting observations. Then the British, driven out of Boston, occupied New York after ousting General Washington from it, and Gaine prudently removed himself to Newark, taking one of his presses and some type with him, and waited to see which way the military cat was going to jump. Meanwhile he continued to publish the *Mercury* in Newark as an exceedingly mild patriot paper, in which references to "the enemy" and reports of the Continental Army's progress, or lack of it, were nicely balanced with stories of what was going on in New York, written with a dispassionate, even a sympathetic flavor.

Gaine was not happy in Newark. It was difficult to get supplies, his business had fallen off badly, and he missed the good friends and good drink he had left behind him in New York. Surveying the military situation with the assurance of one who knew nothing about it, he concluded that the war would soon be over and the British would win it. Consequently he decided it was best to be on the winning side, and returning to New York, made his personal peace with the British. They were glad to welcome him. They had taken the equipment he had left and were continuing to publish their own version of the *Mercury* from his shop. Now they appeared happy to give it back to him, as long as he published a paper in their interest.

That it did not take him long to embrace it is apparent in one of the first issues he published after his return. In the issue of December 16, 1776, those who had known Gaine in his patriot guise, lukewarm as it was, were somewhat surprised to find him declaring: "The shattered Remains of the Rebel Army, 'tis said, are got over into the Jersies. Humanity cannot but pity a Set of poor misguided Men who are thus led on to Destruction, by despicable and desperate Leaders, against every idea of Reason and Duty, and without the least Prospect of Success."

As a convert, Gaine was more Tory than the Tories. His versions of the war's news were so wildly partisan that it was even difficult for the British to believe some of them. The *Pennsylvania Journal*, printing a sarcastic "New Catechism," asked, "Who is the greatest liar upon earth?" and answered itself without hesitation, "Hugh Gaine, of New York, printer." The British had no particular love for him either, and suffered him only until Rivington came back from his flight to England. General Howe, the British commander, felt himself much more akin to a man who loved drink and women, like Jemmy, than to the penurious Gaine who spent all his time working. As a result, Rivington got most of the Tory business and Gaine's switch of allegiances profited him not at all. By the time the war had ended, he was too discouraged to continue his paper.

While the most colorful editors of the Revolution were in Boston and New York, it must not be supposed that Philadelphia, the colonies' third important city, was not represented. It could boast three excellent newspapers, and one of them was a newspaper of considerable distinction—the *Pennsylvania Journal,* conducted by William Bradford III. There was no Whig equivocating about Bradford, no lofty purpose to print both sides of controversy. He was an unabashed patriot editor from the beginning, although he was never as fiery as Edes and Gill. He fought the Stamp Act, was among the first to come out flatly for independence, and published the first of Thomas Paine's "Crisis" papers. Bradford, who came from the old Philadelphia printing family whose founder had given Zenger his first job, was a man of parts. As a businessman, he operated a coffee house and conducted a marine insurance business. As a publisher, his shop turned out a splendid line of books as well as the *Journal*. As an active patriot, he had fought in the French and Indian War, and when the Revolution began, this vigorous 57-year-old man enlisted in the cause and ended the war as a colonel.

That effort, however, was too much even for Bradford. The British occupation of Philadelphia, which had forced suspension of the *Journal*, virtually ruined his business affairs, and the privations of field duty so impaired his health that he could never get properly started again. The *Journal* was carried on for a decade longer after the war by his son Thomas.

Philadelphia also had its Hugh Gaine, who was far more accomplished in opportunism than the unfortunate Irishman. Benjamin Towne, who published the *Pennsylvania Evening Post,* one of three Tory newspapers, began his career as a patriot who used his patriotism to get advertising away from his chief Tory rival. Towne's paper was the first in Philadelphia to print the Declaration of Independence, but when the British occupied the city not long afterward, Towne cynically switched his politics and stayed after the other patriot editors had fled. Now he competed with his old Tory rivals, who had returned to the city, and did so with astonishing success. When the British evacuated Philadelphia, the Tory editors fled once more—all but Towne, who succeeded in pacifying the returning American authorities enough to let him keep on publishing.

Like Gaine, the Philadelphia turncoat discovered that while he might be able to placate governments he could not win back people who remembered what he had written. Advertisers did not return in any substantial number, and subscribers were now in short supply. The contributors who had once given the *Journal* what quality it possessed as a patriot paper now refused their pens to Towne, in spite of his protestations of reform. The story is often told of how John Witherspoon, president of Princeton, author of stirring Revolutionary pamphlets and once a contributor to the *Journal*, encountered Towne one day after the war in a bookstore. The editor had the temerity to ask him to write again for the *Journal*.

"I will do it," Witherspoon said, "if you will publish in the *Journal* a confession, recantation and apology, which I shall write for you."

Towne agreed, with an easy pliability confirming Witherspoon's opinion of him, but when the publisher read what the doctor had written, he found something which gagged him at last in the prose of his learned ghostwriter, who caused him to say that, "instead of being suffered to print, I ought to be hanged as a traitor to my country." The apology never appeared in the *Journal*, but Withersooon passed it on to other papers. They, of course, were delighted with it.

More and more, in the heat of the Revolution, censorship of newspapers passed from governmental authority to public opinion, and some editors found it harsher than the old order. Governments could be conciliated, bargained with, and dealt with by various political means, but there was no way to argue with an angry mob of patriots who insisted that a paper print only the propaganda of the cause. In at least one instance, a provincial government found itself upholding freedom of the press against the mob rule of its own people.

The case, historic but forgotten now by everyone except historians, was that of William Goddard, a zealous printer-editor who had published papers in Providence, New Haven, New York and Philadelphia before he came down to Baltimore in 1773 and established the *Maryland Gazette*, which he operated with the help of his sister Mary, who was a printer and editor in her own right, as well as a bookseller and the town's postmistress for a time.

Goddard was another man of principle. He was neither Tory nor Whig, but one who believed that a newspaper ought not to close its columns to unpopular ideas. He was not a neutralist who intended to print both sides of public questions impartially; he simply desired, as editor, to make the decisions about what went into his newspaper.

When the British offered peace terms to the Americans in 1777,

Goddard wrote a piece in ironic style suggesting that the terms be accepted. The Whig Club in Baltimore failed to grasp the irony, and peremptorily ordered Goddard to close his paper and get out of town within forty-eight hours. The editor turned to the Maryland government and demanded protection from such intimidation, which he said must be granted if freedom of the press meant anything at all. The Maryland legislature agreed. He was granted protection by the House of Representatives, which rebuked the Whig Club at the same time.

Goddard was in trouble again before two years had gone by. This time it was an article by Charles Lee, that eccentric, moody, uncouth general who had been a perplexity and a problem to Washington from the day he first appeared in Cambridge at the siege of Boston. Now their long quarrel had come to a climax with Lee's insubordination at the Battle of Monmouth, for which Washington had had him dismissed from the army. Lee's article in the *Maryland Journal* was an angry defense of his conduct, and a slashing attack in his peculiarly vituperative manner on Washington, who in spite of all his difficulties, was a national idol.

The patriots were outraged. A mob descended on his office, and under pistol point Goddard was forced to write and publish a repudiation of Lee's article. Some of these zealots, whose conduct would have dismayed Washington if he had known of it, would have hanged Goddard if they had not been restrained. Once more the editor appealed to the state, and once more the legislature responded with protection for his person and property. As soon as it was provided, he hastened to repudiate his recantation, and to assert again the principles in which he believed. When the war was over, he was one of the few such editors who escaped the lingering wrath of the populace, perhaps because he had been so firm, courageous and highminded in defense of his ideas.

For one reason or another—disaffection among the readers, or wartime difficulties with print and paper—the Revolution caused some attrition among newspapers. Thirty-seven of them had been in existence on the day the muskets sounded at Lexington; only twenty of these survived Yorktown, which does not count the eighteen new ones begun and discontinued during the war years. Other wartime arrivals were luckier, so that the total at the time hostilities ended was thirty-five, a net loss of two. The political balance of power in the press was heavily tilted in favor of the patriots; only fifteen papers were Tory, either constantly or for a time, like those of Gaines and Towne.

Physically, newspapers looked much the same as they had before the Revolution, except that many used smaller type. Because supplies were cut off from England, press makers and type founders had begun to spring up. Goddard, for example, had a handsome mahogany press made for him by a Hartford watchmaker. These new industries in presses and type appeared, for some reason, to be centered in Connecticut.

What was new in newspapers as a result of the Revolution was the great improvement in quality brought about through the brilliant young editors attracted to print by the great issues of the time. The variation from paper to paper was marked, and it was not always the best ones which survived. The differences extended through the whole range of the news. The *New London Gazette,* for example, noting a local death, would say, "Last Monday there died here Mr. Edward Ashby, a very inoffensive man, in the hundred and ninth year of his Age." But Rivington, covering the same kind of minor story, wrote: "On Monday afternoon, the Spirit of that facetious, good tempered, inoffensive Convivialist Mr. John Levine, ascended to the Skies."

The real significance of the American newspaper during the Revolution was astutely observed by Ambrose Serle, in charge of New York's Royalist press in 1776, who wrote home to Lord Dartmouth about the papers: "One is astonished to see with what avidity they are sought after, and how implicitly they are believed, by the great Bulk of the People . . . Government may find it expedient, in the Sum of things, to employ this popular Engine."

The engine, indeed, had become truly popular for the first time. As an instrument of propaganda it had already exceeded the pamphlet and the sermon in usefulness, and people were beginning to depend on it, in a way they had not in the early Boston days.

Wars have always stimulated the art of communication, and the Revolution was no exception. The newspapers held the colonies together during the struggle, in a sense, keeping up spirits which had ample reason to be depressed, and gathering the news of a conflict which was scattered over most of the eastern half of the country. As a news gatherer, morale upholder and propaganda medium the newspaper was unexcelled during the war. What it did for the unity of the colonies can hardly be underestimated.

No one knew what direction the press would take after the war. There was a brief hiatus as the new nation caught its breath, so to speak, and turned to the high purpose of establishing itself in the world community. In that interval the popular engine found, unhappily, the powerful use Ambrose Serle had suggested.

three

Weapons in the Great Debate

FROM THE VANTAGE POINT of the twentieth century, journalism historians look back on the period between 1789 and 1808 as the "dark ages" of the American newspaper. Like the dark ages of medieval history, however, these early years of the Republic are not quite as black as they have been assumed to be, on closer examination.

The partisan divisions of the Revolution were simply carried over into another arena—the great debate over the balance of power in the new Republic. That debate is far from being settled today. Stated briefly in its simplest form, it was (and is) the debate between those who favor a strong, central government and those who want states' rights and as much freedom for the individual as possible. The terms of the dialogue are different in our time than they were in the first troubled decades of the nation, but the essence of the argument is the same.

As in the debate between Tories and patriots over the relationship between colonies and King, the argument between Federalists and Republicans was one involving men of principle, and they used the press in exactly the same way. The difference was that the newspapers themselves were more sophisticated by this time, and the men who manipulated them as propaganda weapons were among the finest intellects our country has produced. The result was that these weapons were transformed from blunderbusses into deadly artillery. Worse, the use of newspapers as propaganda organs at the highest level of government encouraged the same usage everywhere, with the result that in a country which was rapidly filling up with people in its Eastern half, the abrasion was severe among disputing groups, all of whom now had access to some kind of newspaper.

Yet the great debate was conducted at times on a very high plane, as only men like Thomas Jefferson and Alexander Hamilton could conduct it. The extreme vilification and lies were the work of lesser men, of fierce partisans who would stop at nothing. The element absent from the press was responsibility. It was as free now as it would ever be, restrained only by the libel laws, which were not yet backed up by a body of precedent sufficient to impose more than a mild restraint on what was printed.

The propaganda attacks of these partisan newspapers perhaps seem more extreme to us now because they were directed at men like Washington, John Adams, Jefferson and Hamilton. But they were no worse than those suffered by Jackson and Lincoln, and were different only in degree from those endured by Grover Cleveland, Wilson, and Franklin D. Roosevelt. The restraint that has been progressively imposed over the years, mitigating the excesses of freedom, is the concept of responsibility, which was as slow of development in the Fourth Estate as it was in the business community.

Americans got a taste of what was to come as soon as Washington took office, and it must have been shocking to some who believed that a man who was already a national saint would be spared the indignities of public office. Certainly no man ever entered the Presidency under circumstances of such universal veneration. Nor was there ever a President whose standards, personal and public, were as high as Washington's.

This honest, humorless, yet intensely sincere man, whose real nature was little better understood by his contemporaries than it is today, had deep reservations about the nature and function of the press. As Commander-in-Chief, in the dark days of 1777, he had expressed some of these doubts to the President of Congress in words which have a startling present-day ring. "It is much to be wished that our Printers were more discreet in many of their Publications," he wrote. "We see almost in every Paper, Proclamations or accounts transmitted by the Enemy, of an injurious nature. If some hint or caution could be given them on the Subject, it might be of material Service." Nearly two hundred years later, the President and his Secretary of Defense were still wrestling with that problem.

Like other Americans, Washington depended on newspaper advertising. Shortly before he came to New York to assume the Presidency, he wrote to his Secretary of War, who was already there: "Having learnt from an Advertisement in the New York Daily Advertiser, that there were superfine American Broad Cloths to be sold at No. 44 Water Street; I have ventured to trouble you with the Commission of purchasing enough to make me a suit of cloaths. As to the colour, I shall leave it altogether to your taste . . ."

Still, the doubts remained. In the interval between the end of the Revolution and the Presidency, he wrote to Clement Biddle: "I have such a number of Gazettes crouded upon me, (many without orders) that they are not only Expensive, but really useless; as my other avocations, will not allow me time to Read them oftentimes, and when I do attempt it, find them more troublesome, than Profitable . . ." In general, he found newspapers inaccurate, meddlesome, or both, although he frequently found occasion to defend them if he observed any restrictions on their circulation, which he considered essential to the public's information.

When he came at last to New York, as the nation's first President, he had one of his gloomy premonitions that the day would not be long in coming before "the extravagant (and I may say undue) praises which they are heaping upon me at this moment" would be turned into "equally extravagant (that I will fondly hope unmerited) censures."

This prophecy came to pass almost at once. As soon as Washington was in office, partisan politics entered the national scene and with it the press began to reflect immediately the deep divisions among the American people over the fundamental nature of government, issues which divide us today. Even before his inauguration the journalistic knife throwers were at work, repeating the whispering campaign that he had misappropriated Virginia property belonging to his old friend and patron, Lord Fairfax.

Stirred to the anger he constantly strove to control, Washington issued a public challenge in the newspapers to the slanderer, inviting him to prove his charge. Not long afterward he wrote to a friend: "It is to be lamented that the Editors of the different Gazettes in the Union, do not more generally, and more correctly (instead of stuffing their papers with scurrility and nonsensical declamation . . .) publish the debates in Congress on all great national questions, and this with no uncommon pains, every one of them might do."

Still, there was no open quarrel between the President and the newspapers until Washington was drawn unwillingly into the public battle between his two Cabinet members, Hamilton and Jefferson. The outlines of that epic struggle are too well known to be rehearsed here, but the part the newspapers played in it is less familiar, except to specialists.

At the beginning, the Federalists had matters their own way. They were in power, with Washington at their head, and in Hamilton they had a leader of surpassing intelligence who fought cleverly and well to establish the nation solidly and soundly on Federal principles. As an artilleryman in the Revolution, Hamilton had gotten about the colonies and read the colonial gazettes from Boston to Virginia. He knew that there was no better means of persuasion available to a government than a newspaper dedicated to its interests. Hamilton understood, too, that the best way to be certain of a newspaper's dedication was to hand-pick its editor and control it yourself, and that is why in 1789 he established what was in reality the official organ of the Federalist administration, the *Gazette of the United States*.

Hamilton was the *Gazette's* mainspring. He and his influential friends in the party had put up the money to start it, they were always in the wings to provide it with more when it faltered, and Hamilton was the paper's chief contributor. He had picked the editor himself, and in that selection had committed his only error. John Fenno was not the best man for the job. True, any editor would have been overshadowed by Hamilton's personality, but Fenno was only a mediocre writer, and little better as an editor. A Bostonian, his education had been no more elevated than attendance at Samuel Holbrook's Writing School. In the Revolution he had kept General Artemas Ward's orderly book, and after the war had gone into trade, unsuccessfully. Following that disaster he had drifted down to New York and begun a new career as a printer.

The *Gazette* he printed was unpretentious in size, three columns wide on a page 17 by 21 inches, and undistinguished except for what Hamilton and other Federalist leaders wrote for it. It was given regular transfusions of government printing, on contracts engineered by Hamilton, and it published nothing except what the government approved of publishing. If Washington said almost nothing about the paper in his correspondence, it was because the *Gazette* never said anything to irritate him.

It may come as a shock to those who presently debate the matter, but George Washington was a firm believer in "managed news," in exactly the context of the argument carried on between the press and President John F. Kennedy's administration. He believed in the broad principle that the press should keep the public informed, and he was against direct censorship by the government except in time of war, nor was he for indirect censorship by post office regulations or taxation. Nevertheless he believed there were some matters which were the business of government, and others which should not be published if it hurt the image of the United States abroad.

Thus he advised the Secretary of War: "Orders or advertisements, which are intended to be put into the public Gazettes, ought to be well weighed and digested before they are inserted, as they will not only appear in all parts of Europe, but may be handed to the enemy. To publish beyond the limits of the army, or the vicinity of it, the dastardly behavior of one's own Troops, is not a very pleasant thing."

It was inevitable, in the nature of partisan politics, that the opposition to the Federalists should have its own newspaper voice. That did not occur, however, until the government moved to Philadelphia, taking the *Gazette of the United States* with it. There Thomas Jefferson undertook to redress the balance of power by establishing his own newspaper, although he denied that he had ever done it.

In choosing an editor, Jefferson was careful to pick one who would be Fenno's superior—not a difficult task. The editor he found was a better man in every respect than any other editor of his time. He was Philip Freneau, who is best known today as a poet.

Freneau was a complicated personality, a fierce idealist with a deep love of the sea, a fine writer of excellent literary taste, utterly devoted to Jefferson and the cause of Republicanism. He came of a

cultured Huguenot family in New York, who had given him private
tutors for his beginning education and then sent him at fifteen to the
College of New Jersey, later Princeton, where he entered as a sophomore and found a congenial roommate in an ambitious boy named
James Madison. During the war he had written the burning patriotic
poetry which later caused him to be known as the Poet of the Revolution, but his best verse was composed in the Caribbean, where he was
briefly secretary to a Santa Cruz planter. These shimmering lyrics are
full of sea moods and island colors.

In the war itself, Freneau was less fortunate. On one of his trips to
and from the Indies, his brig was captured by the British, who in-
terned him for long, miserable months on a prison ship anchored in
New York harbor. When the war was over and he was released, he
went to work in the Philadelphia post office, but Freneau could not
stay on land for long periods of time. He was off again, as the master
of a brig bound for Jamaica, and for the next few years he sailed
the Atlantic and the Caribbean, writing more of his haunting lyrics.

Marriage brought him to land once more, and to the relative
stability of a job as editor of the New York *Daily Advertiser*, with
which he was occupied when Jefferson invited him to come to Philadelphia and fight Federalism as editor of the *National Gazette*. Freneau
found both Jefferson and his former Princeton roommate, Madison,
backing the *Gazette*, although for political reasons the backing had to
be discreet.

There is, in fact, considerable dispute about Jefferson's rôle in the
newspaper. Freneau once signed an affidavit denying that the Secretary of State had ever had anything to do with the *Gazette,* but near
the end of his life he swore to the opposite, charging Jefferson with
authorship of some of the paper's most violent pieces, and producing
a marked file to prove it. In a famous 4,000-word letter to Washington defending himself against Hamilton's charges, Jefferson denied
any connection with the *Gazette,* and went to some lengths in explain-
ing why it was that Freneau was also working in the State Department as a translator, at $250 a year. It was because Freneau was a
"man of genius," he said, and he had been glad to help him as he
had aided other such men.

In the savage quarrel between the two Secretaries, which the President was now pleading for them to end, Hamilton had made a direct charge to Washington about Jefferson: "I cannot doubt from the evidence I possess, that the *National Gazette* was instituted by him for political purposes, and that one leading object of it has been to render me, and all the measures connected with my department, as odious as possible."

Defending himself to Washington, Jefferson said of the *Gazette:* "As to the merits or demerits of his [Freneau's] paper, they certainly concern me not. He & Fenno are rivals for the public favor. The one courts them by flattery, the other by censure, & I believe it will be admitted that the one has been as servile, as the other severe . . ."

Jefferson went on to tell the President what he thought the rôle of newspapers should be in a democracy. "No government ought to be without censors," he wrote, "& where the press is free, no one ever will. If virtuous, it need not fear the fair operation of attack & defence. Nature has given to man no other means of sifting out the truth either in religion, law, or politics. I think it as honorable to the government neither to know, nor notice, it's [sic] sycophants or censors, as it would be undignified & criminal to pamper the former & persecute the latter."

These noble words which Jefferson truly believed, as he demonstrated later, nevertheless could not conceal the facts in the *Gazette* case, and it is not to Jefferson's credit that the great man stooped to a course of equivocation and evasion in an inexplicable attempt to escape his responsibility for the paper. The evidence is clear that Jefferson and Madison negotiated with Freneau when he was still in New York to come to Philadelphia and start a national paper in the Republican cause, after Jefferson had failed to persuade Benjamin Franklin Bache, proprietor of the Philadelphia *Advertiser,* to make a national organ out of his paper. Freneau, having agreed, was subsidized by Jefferson with a job in the State Department, where he also had access to all the information and government advertising which the Secretary could throw his way. Jefferson's feigned indifference to the paper's merits or demerits—"they concern me not"—is belied by his many expressions of satisfaction with the paper, and by his earnest efforts to get subscriptions for it, even after he left office.

It is difficult to see why Jefferson was so anxious to disavow what was, in reality, "his" paper. Hamilton was almost openly operating a newspaper, through his hand-picked editor, attacking him and everything in which he believed, and was diverting Treasury advertising to it. In the context of the times, there was certainly nothing wrong with replying in kind, in defense of what Jefferson believed.

As for Washington, he wanted this undignified quarrel to stop. He deplored the violent language and wild charges in both papers as calculated to divide the new nation irrevocably, which was his greatest fear as President. More than once Freneau's slashing pen drove Washington into one of his fits of temper which he found so hard to control as he got older, as they had been when he was young. Jefferson recorded one of these outbursts in May 1793:

> He adverted to a piece in Freneau's paper of yesterday, he said he despised all their attacks on him personally, but that there has never been an act of the government . . . which that paper had not abused . . . He was evidently sore & warm, and I took his intention to be that I should interpose in some way with Freneau, perhaps withdraw his appointment of translating clerk in my office. But I will not do it. His paper has saved our constitution which was galloping fast into monarchy, & has been checked by no means so powerfully as by that paper.

On another day, Washington was even more disturbed by a particularly vicious thrust of Freneau's, and according to Jefferson's report of the incident,

> The President was much inflamed, got into one of those passions when he cannot command himself, ran on much on the personal abuse which had been bestowed on him, defied any man on earth to produce one single act of his since he had been in the govmt which was not done on the purest motives, that he had never repented but once the having slipped the moment of resigning his office, & that was every moment since, that *by god* he had rather be in his grave than in his present situation. That he had rather be on his farm than to be

made *emperor of the world* and yet they were charging him with wanting to be king. That that *rascal Freneau* sent him 3 of his papers every day, as if he thought he would become the distributor of his papers, that he could see in this nothing but an impudent design to insult him. He ended in this high tone . . .

The President was not even satisfied with his own paper, deploring Fenno's intention to defend him on one occasion by attacking Benjamin Franklin. No wonder Washington wrote to his friend Edmund Pendleton: "We have some infamous Papers calculated for disturbing if not absolutely intended to disturb, the peace of the community."

In the two-year struggle between the papers, Freneau was the clear victor, although his *Gazette* did little to shake the foundations of Federalism. But he was so far superior to Fenno as writer and editor that he was a constant irritant to the whole Federal camp, which was delighted when the yellow fever epidemic of 1793 forced the *Gazette* to suspend. Jefferson's retirement from the cabinet led at once to Freneau's departure.

Peace was not restored, however. The Administration was under constant attack from other papers, and one of them, Benjamin Franklin Bache's *General Advertiser,* which Jefferson had wooed before Freneau consented, proved to be far worse in its campaign of vilification than the *Gazette* had ever been.

Bache was only twenty-one when he started his paper in 1790. Because of his youth and his immediate ancestry, he was known familiarly if not always affectionately in Philadelphia as "Lightning Rod Junior." The name of his paper had a popular usage, too, after 1794, when the proprietor's habit of centering the name of a popular London paper, the *Aurora,* above the *Advertiser's* title, led people to use the shorter version.

The *Aurora* was not entirely a bad paper. It did give a full account of the proceedings in Congress, at a painstaking length which the other papers did not emulate. Aside from that, however, its news columns were devoted to a virulent campaign against Washington, the Federalists and all their works, in much the same way some

newspapers devoted themselves to similar attacks on Presidents like
Lincoln, Wilson and Franklin Roosevelt.

Among other things, the *Aurora* accused Washington of over-
drawing his salary, and professed to regard most of his acts as
unconstitutional. The President called such stories "outrages on common decency." Bache answered by reprinting forged and long since
discredited letters of Washington, which the British had used in Jemmy
Rivington's paper in 1776.

The worst of the *Aurora's* sins was an incident which again has
contemporary overtones. In 1795, John Jay had come back from
London with the treaty he had negotiated with Great Britain, and
while it was reasonably satisfactory to the Federalists, Washington
well knew it would not satisfy the hotheads in Congress or Republicans in general. In his view, the treaty ought to remain secret until
it could be discussed in the Senate with as much discretion as possible,
before submitting it for ratification. But Bache somehow learned of
the treaty's contents, at least in a general way, and published them,
although the account was full of inaccuracies. Seeking at least to
correct these errors, now that the secret was out, a Virginia Senator
gave an exact copy of the treaty to Bache, who printed it and attacked
it again, not only in the *Aurora* but in a pamphlet which he published.

With that a storm of criticism burst upon Washington and the
Administration, zealously fed by the Republican newspapers. "I have
brought on myself a torrent of abuse in the factious papers in this
country," Washington remarked gloomily to Gouverneur Morris,
"and from the enmity of the discontented of all descriptions therein
. . . I have nothing to ask, and discharging my duty, I have nothing
to fear from invective."

He may not have feared it, but he hated it, particularly when he
read in the *Aurora* that he "had violated the Constitution and made
a treaty with a nation abhorred by our people; that he had answered
the respectful remonstrances of Boston and New York as if he were
the omnipotent director of a seraglio, and had thundered contempt
upon the people with as much confidence as if he had sat upon the
throne of Industan."

That was the mildest of the abuse he had to endure. His old friend,

Tom Paine, who had been such a mainstay in the darkest days of the Revolution, published an open, bitter letter to him, concluding, "And as to you, sir, *treacherous in private friendship* . . . and a *hypocrite* in public life, the world will be puzzled to decide, whether you are an *apostate* or an *impostor,* whether you have abandoned *good principles;* or whether *you ever had any?*"

The man who had entered office a national hero found himself now referred to in the *Aurora* and other papers as one whose character was composed of "little passions," "ingratitude," "want of merit" and "insignificance," and whose fame was spurious. His trips North and South as President were, according to Bache, a "stately journeying through the American continent in search of personal incense." He was "a frail mortal, whose passions and weaknesses are like those of other men, a spoiled child, a despot, an anemic imitation of the English kings."

In the face of this kind of invective, Washington can easily be forgiven for managing the news when he decided to leave the Presidency. He prepared his Farewell Address carefully, in consultation with Hamilton, and determined to have it published initially under the best possible auspices, rather than give it to all the papers simultaneously without favor. The paper he chose was, naturally, a Federalist organ, the *Pennsylvania Packet and Daily Advertiser,* published by John Dunlap and David Claypoole, which later became the first morning daily in America, and in fact the nation's first successful daily of any description. Claypoole, who was summoned by the President, has left us an account of their meeting:

> I received a Message from the President by his Private Secretary signifying his desire to see me. I waited on him at the appointed time, and found him sitting alone in the Drawing room. He received me kindly, and after paying my respects to him, desired me to take a seat near him; then, addressing himself to me, said, that he had for some time past contemplated retiring from Public Life, and had at length concluded to do so at the end of the (then) present Term;—that he had some Thoughts and Reflections on the Occasion, which he deemed proper to communicate to the People of the United States, in the form of an address, and which he wished to appear in the Daily Advertiser,—of which I was Editor.—He paused, and I took the op-

portunity of thanking him for having preferred that Paper as the
channel of his Communication with the People . . . He silently as-
sented and asked when the Publication could be made.—I answered
that the time should be made perfectly convenient to himself,—
and following Monday was fixed on;—he then told me that his Secretary would bring me the copy on the next (Friday) morning, and I
withdrew.

In his first draft of the speech, Washington had written that "some
of the Gazettes" had "teemed with all the Invective that disappointment, ignorance of facts, and malicious falsehood could invent, to
misrepresent my politics and affections; to wound my reputation and
feelings; and to weaken, if not entirely destroy the confidence you had
been pleased to repose in me; it might be expected at the parting
scene of my public life that I should take some notice of such virulent
abuse. But, as heretofore, I shall pass them over in utter silence never
having myself, nor by any other with my participation or knowledge,
written or published a Scrap in answer to any of them."

But he changed his mind and omitted this paragraph, as part of a
rewriting in which he characteristically reduced references to himself
to an absolute minimum. The change did not save him. When he
delivered that historic address, Bache greeted it next day in the
Aurora with these words:

> If ever a nation was debauched by a man, the American nation
> has been debauched by Washington. If ever a nation has suffered
> from the improper influence of a man, the American nation has suf-
> fered from the influence of Washington. If ever a nation was de-
> ceived by a man, the American nation has been deceived by
> Washington. Let his conduct then be an example to future ages. Let it
> serve to be a warning that no man may be an idol.

Bache's final shot as Washington left Philadelphia in March 1797
was an exultant editorial which declared: "If ever there was a period
for rejoicing, this is the moment—every heart in unison with the
freedom and happiness of the people, ought to beat high with exulta-
tion that the name of Washington from this day ceases to give a
currency to political iniquity, and to legalized corruption."

The attacks on Washington are worth considering at length, not only because they provide an insight into the excessive partisanship of the day, but for the pattern they set in relations between the President and the American press. Every President since Washington has been attacked by some proportion of the press, the percentage varying with the stature of the Chief Executive. Mild, ineffectual Presidents have incurred the least criticism. Nor has the language changed a great deal. That is why the language of the *Aurora* can hardly be considered as typical only of the "dark ages" of journalism, when it is reproduced substantially in some excessively partisan newspapers of our own time.

Washington's attitude toward this criticism is also revealing in a special way. Back home in the safety of Mount Vernon, he wrote to Secretary of State Timothy Pickering just before his death: "The crisis [meaning the Alien and Sedition Acts], in my opinion, calls loudly for plain dealing, that the Citizens at large may well informed, and decide, with respect to public measures, upon a thorough knowledge of facts. *Concealment* is a species of mis-information; and misrepresentation and false alarms found the ground work of opposition."

There is no doubt Washington honestly believed what he wrote, but he was not then President. In office, he concealed and managed the news as every President has done with varying skill, and from what he considered the highest motive, that is, the best interests of the country. There has always been this difference between belief and practice. Unfortunately, people remember the belief but not the practice, and the press casts doubt on both.

The departure of Washington and the accession of John Adams brought no change whatever in the character of the press, nor could it, because it still had no prime reason for existence except to be the tool of political parties. Its news function, even a substantial part of its advertising, was subverted to that purpose.

Adams found himself attacked by the *Aurora* and defended by the mob, in a manner reminiscent of early Revolutionary days. A gang of Federalist hoodlums wrecked Bache's shop, and on another occasion a sympathizer of Adams whom Bache had slandered came into the editor's office and beat him severely. Bache was arrested for libeling the President, but he was quickly released. Encountering his rival editor, Fenno, on the street, words and blows were exchanged but no serious damage was done. Both men were dead little more than a year later, victims of the yellow fever which made Philadelphia a ghost city for a time.

The Federalist press did not mourn Bache's passing. *Russell's Gazette,* a Boston paper, observed: "The Jacobins are all whining at the exit of the vile Benjamin Franklin Bache. So they would do if one of their gang was hung for stealing. The memory of this scoundrel cannot be too highly execrated."

A convenient marriage, however, assured the *Aurora's* continuance along the same lines Bache had conducted it. His Danish-born widow, Margaret, who took up the paper's management, married its associate editor, William Duane, a fanatic Irishman better able in some respects to carry on the crusade. He had the same caustic style, with ornamentations of his own, and a courage which could only be described as reckless. He made the *Aurora's* columns "an uninterrupted stream of slander of the American Government," as Pickering observed to Adams.

Duane was not always on the wrong side. He discredited the war with France which threatened the new nation, and indeed helped to avert it by his marshaling of public opinion. He fought hard against the Alien and Sedition Laws, a piece of bad legislation, and was a factor in their repeal. In the campaign of 1800, he led the journalistic crusade to get Jefferson elected. In return for the latter service, he expected to be rewarded by the new administration, but Jefferson as President was not Jefferson the Secretary of State. Adams had remained completely aloof from the press, and the man from Monticello followed his example for the most part. When he moved the seat of government from Philadelphia to Washington, he did not invite Duane and the *Aurora* to follow him.

Bache's heir had survived two indictments against him for libel, brought by the Federalists, and he had also lived through a time when his life was in constant danger, but he could not survive indifference. He did not even get the government contract for printing and stationery. Although he remained a Jeffersonian in spite of the rebuff, something of the conviction went out of the *Aurora* and it died a lingering death, expiring at last in 1822.

Through all the abuse at the hands of Freneau, Bache and Duane, the Federalists did not have to depend on the relatively weaker voice of Johnny Fenno for defense. They had two strong supporters in *Porcupine's Gazette* and *The American Minerva,* representing the radical and conservative wings of Federalism.

William Cobbett, an English political refugee, was Peter Porcupine, the prickly radical. He had come to America in 1792, fleeing the disturbance aroused by his exposure of a graft ring among British Army officers. Cobbett was known all his life as "The Contentious Man," and with reason, since he appeared to love argument and controversy for their own sake, rather than out of any profound convictions. The *Aurora* had another name for him. It called him "the celebrated manufacturer of lies, and retailer of filth." He called himself Peter Porcupine, for obvious reasons.

There was no hypocrisy about Cobbett, whatever virtues he might lack. In the first issue of *Porcupine's Gazette,* he declared honestly, "Professions of impartiality I shall make none." A master of cutting, sardonic prose, he returned Bache's vituperation with interest, attacking not only the *Aurora's* young proprietor but his honored grandfather as well, whom he described as a "crafty and lecherous old hypocrite . . . whose very statue seems to gloat on the wenches as they walk the State House yard."

No doubt of it, Cobbett was a bold and unabashed rascal who invited trouble. Even before he started the *Gazette* he had been threatened with the mob's tar and feathers by unashamedly opening a bookshop whose windows displayed portraits of George III, Lord Howe, and other prominent Royalists. In the columns of the *Gazette,* Cobbett came out strongly for an alliance with England, beat the drums for war against France, and in the process consigned the whole Republican movement to perdition.

Like Duane, Cobbett lived a dangerous life in which he survived threats of deportation by the government, libel actions, and personal threats. In the end he defeated himself by attacking a man with more power than the government, the redoubtable Dr. Benjamin Rush.

Ironically, it was one of the occasions when Cobbett was telling the truth. He had excoriated Rush, a patriot leader and one of the most influential Philadelphia citizens, for his yellow fever treatment, which consisted of plentiful bleeding and the mercurial purge. Rush sued for libel, and after two years of legal sparring, the case came to trial before a judge and jury consisting of Rush's friends, who returned a verdict for the doctor of $5,000 damages and $3,000 costs.

Cobbett had no intention of paying any such fine. Before the verdict was in, he was on his way to New York, where he delivered a parting fusillade at Rush with the publication of one *Gazette* and five editions of a libelous paper he called the *Rush-Light,* after which he took ship for England and did not return.

A paper of an entirely different character was Noah Webster's *American Minerva.* It was bound to be different because Webster himself was not a political adventurer like Cobbett, nor was he a born propagandist, like Duane and Bache. When the Federalists persuaded him to start the *Minerva* in 1793, it was only an episode in the life of a man of genius. For a time he made himself a political writer, in which he excelled as he did in everything else. He declared in his first issue that he was in the newspaper business for the purpose of "vindicating and supporting the policy of President Washington," and for the next five years he devoted himself to that idea.

Webster's contributions, written under the pseudonym of "Curtius," in the manner of the times, were by far the best things in the paper. His defense of Jay's treaty was a masterpiece of argument and political writing, free of the invective which marked other discussions of it. Hamilton also wrote frequently for the *Minerva,* but these articles were not among his best.

While he was at it, Webster made some contributions to the newspaper business itself. By running his editorial in the same prominent place every day, he started the first editorial page in an American newspaper. His semi-weekly edition, the *Herald,* "for country readers," was the first bulldog edition.

Webster's ideals were too high for the political arena. Disillusioned in 1798 by what he considered Hamilton's betrayal of Adams, he moved to New Haven and gradually eased his way out of journalism, selling the *Minerva* at last in 1803.

There were hopes, with the election of Jefferson in 1800, that the excesses of the past would be forgotten and an enlightened era would dawn. Instead, the press descended to lower depths. It was in fact worse because the new papers were edited by lesser men. Jefferson, whose ardent belief in freedom of the press was a foundation stone in his character, found himself the victim of greater vilification than either Washington or Adams had endured. The corruption and irresponsibility of the press was at its lowest point at a moment when its best defender was its principal target.

Again the antagonists were Jefferson and Hamilton, with different papers supporting them, but this time it was Hamilton who had by far the best editor. That was undoubtedly because Jefferson, as noted before, was much more the moderate as President, and his paper, the tri-weekly *National Intelligencer and Washington Advertiser,* reflected his moderation. Its editor was Samuel Harrison Smith, who had been an inconsequential publisher in Philadelphia and had been invited by Jefferson to follow him to Washington in preference to the unfortunate Duane, a fighter too brutal for the President's taste.

Smith's character, which he imparted to his newspaper, can best be estimated by the name the opposition gave to the *Intelligencer:* "Mr. Silky-Milky Smith's National Smoothing Plane." His wife Margaret was the Perle Mesta of her day, and gave splendid Washington parties at the Smith country place, Sidney, where Catholic University now stands. These parties were the forerunners of the soirées given in the 1940's by Evelyn Walsh MacLean at Friendship, where the eminences in attendance might find themselves cheek by jowl with enemies from the opposite party, soothed for the moment by good food and wine.

Samuel Smith was a connoisseur of both. The moderate tone of the *Intelligencer* may have reflected high living as well as the fact that its editor was scarcely a fighter by nature. He was not, however, an unintelligent man. There was a certain well-bred distinction about the *Intelligencer,* and its coverage of domestic and foreign news was the best available in Washington. In a time of controversy, it appeared bland beside the other gazettes, but its solid qualities were of a kind to make it last longer than its rivals. Changed to a daily in 1813, it remained as one of the best papers in America until its eventual demise after the Civil War.

Hamilton's paper, the *New York Evening Post,* was of far different character, as one might expect. Again, he and his friends were the undoubted founders of the paper, but Hamilton had now grown more cautious and, like Jefferson, he made efforts to disassociate himself from the *Post,* at least as far as the public was concerned. Privately, he wrote for it as he had for his *Gazette,* carrying on his old feud with Jefferson, now on a somewhat more philosophical level, and discussing public questions of the day.

The *Post* was begun on November 16, 1801, and it is still in existence, the longest-lived daily in the United States, having passed through several different incarnations since its founding. By the devious route of politics, it has arrived about where it was at the beginning —that is, a supporter of strong Federal government, which was Hamilton's argument, although it adheres to the Democratic party of which Jefferson was the spiritual founder, notwithstanding its initial cognomen, Republican.

The *Post's* beginnings were humble enough. Hamilton had not been able to raise much cash to start it, and its first issues had to be printed on an old hand press, like the one Ben Franklin had used. Its quarter-size sheets were well circulated in a city which by this time had grown to 60,000.

This time Hamilton had done well in selecting an editor. He was William Coleman, who would have been perfectly cast as the Hollywood kind of big-city editor—a large, handsome man with a hearty voice who loved women, alcohol, food, argument and politics, not always in the same order. He had been a lawyer in Massachusetts in his early days, and there he had been the rare combination of scholar and athlete, the kind of man who would read Greek in the morning and skate the twenty miles from Greenfield to Northampton in the evening.

Coleman began his tenure as editor on a high note of principle.

In the *Post's* first issue he declared that he abhorred "personal virulence, low sarcasm, and verbal contentions with printers and editors." He would not be swerved, he said, from "the line of temperate discussion."

In reality, he had no such intention. It was all window dressing, of a kind that was to become increasingly common as the century wore on. Paper after paper appeared with high-minded declarations from the publisher on the front page of the first issue, which were promptly forgotten as soon as the publisher got into politics, as he inevitably did.

It was not long before Coleman was swinging the meat-ax with as much good will as the others, but one of his articles, by a rather devious route, resulted in a blow for freedom of the press more effective than any since the Zenger trial.

By this time the long-continued violence of the partisan press had produced the inevitable reaction, and there was public debate about finding a means to control it. The Federalists had attempted to throttle it wholesale through the Sedition Act, an ill-considered and fortunately short-lived piece of legislation. Following the Republican philosophy, Jefferson thought this was a job which might better be done by the states, and he advocated bringing a few libel cases under state laws as an example to the worst offenders.

The first opportunity came in New York State, with a story which originated in the *Evening Post*. This piece, written by Coleman, was a roundabout assault on Jefferson. It had been said, the editor reported without denying it, that "the burden of the Federalist song" was the party's charge that "Jefferson paid Callender [James Callender, editor of the Richmond *Examiner*] for calling Washington a traitor, a robber, a perjurer; for calling Adams a hoary-headed incendiary and for most grossly slandering the private characters of men he knew well were virtuous. These charges not a democratic Editor has yet dared or ever will dare to meet in an open and manly discussion."

This charge, in spite of the devious way it was presented, was a serious one and the clumsy subterfuge was no protection whatever against its libelous content. It was picked up on "exchange" and republished by Harry Croswell, editor of a paper in Hudson, New York, called *The Wasp,* a publication so vicious that the more respectable Federalists would have nothing to do with it.

It was exactly the kind of case Jefferson had been talking about. Here was one of the worst offenders, who could now be prosecuted under New York State law. Croswell was indicted on a charge of libeling the President and duly tried. Found guilty, he took the case on appeal to the State Supreme Court.

As had been the case with Zenger, Croswell found a distinguished advocate waiting to defend him when he rose in court. It was no less than Alexander Hamilton himself, and like that earlier Hamilton, he made one of the most eloquent pleas for freedom of the press that had ever been heard in a courtroom. His argument was that the press had "the right to publish with impunity truth, with good motives, for justifiable ends, though reflecting on Government, Magistracy, or individuals." Once more it was being argued that truth, by itself, was the only defense needed in a libel action, if it could be proved.

There was no doubt in Hamilton's mind that Coleman had printed the truth. Callender was an utterly unprincipled man who had been badly treated by the Federalists when they were in power. Convicted and jailed under the Sedition Act, he had been released and pardoned by Jefferson, who was then petitioned by this opportunist for a postmaster's appointment in Richmond as reward for the great sacrifice he had made for the cause. Refused, he had turned against his former benefactor and offered to the Federalists, for a price, everything he knew about the interior workings of the Republican party.

This did not prove, of course, that what Coleman and Croswell had printed was true. It was, in fact, most unlikely that Jefferson had ever paid Callender directly to defame such men as Washington and Adams, although it was true that he had helped Callender financially on a fairly regular basis, as a man whose paper was valuable to the party. Hamilton knew that if truth were admitted as a defense in libel, the links between Jefferson and Callender were strong enough possibly to confuse a jury and quite certainly to plant suspicions in the public mind which might be enough to disgrace Jefferson, whether the actual charge was true or not.

Whatever Hamilton's motives, and they were not of the best, the argument he presented was the keystone in building a truly free press. He lost the case in court—the four justices were evenly divided—but his defense had been so impressive that the New York Assembly soon passed a law admitting truth as evidence in a libel case, and providing further that the jury must judge the law as well as the facts, both points that old Andrew Hamilton had argued more than a half-century before.

The sad by-product of the Croswell case was an idle but derogatory remark Hamilton made about Aaron Burr in a tavern, while he was in Albany to argue the appeal. The remark was picked up by someone, possibly a reporter, and appeared in an Albany newspaper, where it was read by Burr, who challenged Hamilton to the duel which ended in his death.

This episode was one of the last in the sorry history of the post-Revolution press. It was a time of unparalleled scurrility, when the press was entirely in the hands of politicians, but it had not been such a "dark age" as the vituperation suggested. Some of the politicians had been great men, and a few of the editors had been formidable in their own right. There was excellent writing, stirring writing, along with the gutter words and phrases. Mechanically, there had been some progress too, with improved presses, and the number of newspapers, both daily and weekly, was increasing at an astonishing rate. The rise of the dailies accounted for much of the growth. By 1828, there were more newspapers and newspaper readers in America than anywhere else in the world.

It must be said that Jefferson emerges, in spite of seeming equivocations on the subject, as the real champion of the press in this, one of its darker periods. Even at the most abysmally low point in the campaign against him, Jefferson continued to defend press freedom, although he was as exasperated on occasion as Washington and Adams had been. At such times he could write, "The newspapers of our country by their abandoned spirit of falsehood, have more effectually destroyed the utility of the press than all the shackles devised by Bonaparte."

That was true, but it did not represent Jefferson's views on press freedom. He might deplore the "abandoned spirit of falsehood," but he was in favor of permitting the newspapers to keep on telling lies rather than restraining them by any other law except libel, and even that must be invoked on a state level. He wrote in one of his most quoted statements on the subject,

> I am persuaded that the good sense of the people will always be found to be the best army. They may be led astray for a moment, but will soon correct themselves. The people are the only censors of their governors; and even their errors will tend to keep these to the true principles of their institution. To punish these errors too severely would be to suppress the only safeguard of the public liberty. The way to prevent these irregular interpositions of the people, is to give them full information of their affairs through the channel of the public papers, and to contrive that those papers should penetrate to the whole mass of the people. The basis of our government being the opinion of the people, the very first object should be to keep that right; and were it left to me to decide whether we should have a government without newspapers, or newspapers without a government, I should not hesitate a moment to prefer the latter. But I should mean that every man should receive those papers, and be capable of reading them.

The last sentence is usually omitted from the quotation today.

Perhaps the best illustration of how much freedom the press had attained in Jefferson's administration, however badly the papers used it, is the story of how the Prussian minister, calling on the President one day, picked up a copy of a Federalist paper from the table, scanned its headlines, and burst out, "Mr. President, why do you permit such libels?"

"Put that paper in your pocket, Baron," Jefferson answered, "and should you ever hear the reality of our liberty, the freedom of our press questioned, show them this paper—and tell them where you found it."

With Jefferson's departure from the arena at the end of his second administration, an era began drawing to a close. The chief actors were disappearing. Washington was dead, and so was Hamilton. Freneau, the man who had navigated the oceans with impunity, had retired to his New Jersey farm, making occasional new voyages, but he would soon die incongruously halfway between his house and barn in a December blizzard. Fenno, his rival, and Bache, his compatriot, were already dead of the fever.

There was still unbridled passion on the lower echelons of journalism, even though the big guns had ceased to roar. The *Washington Monitor* lamented on August 23, 1808: "It is full time that some effort should be made to purify the presses of the United States, from their froth, their spume, and their coarse vulgarisms. Newspapers of all descriptions teem with bombastic invective, with ridiculous jargon, and empty declamation. The popular taste becomes vitiated, and is prepared to receive the pestilential banquet of every noxious creature that wields a pen or controls a press."

Dr. Samuel Miller had put his finger on the source of the trouble five years before, in his *Brief Retrospect of the Eighteenth Century,* when he wrote: "Too many of our Gazettes are in the hands of persons, destitute at once of the urbanity of gentlemen, the information of scholars, and the principles of virtue. To this source, rather than to any peculiar depravity of national character, we may ascribe the faults of American newspapers, which have been pronounced by travelers, the most profligate and scurrilous public prints in the civilized world. These considerations, it is conceived, are abundantly sufficient to account for the disagreeable character of American newspapers. In every country the selfish principle prompts men to defame their personal and political enemies; and where the supposed provocations to this are numerous, and no restraints are imposed on the indulgence of the disposition, an inundation of filth and calumny must be expected.

"In the United States the frequency of Elections leads to a corresponding frequency of struggle between political parties; these struggles naturally engender mischievous passions, and every species of coarse invective; and, unhappily, too many of the conductors of our public prints have neither the discernment, the firmness, nor the virtue to reject from their pages the foul ebullitions of prejudice and malice. Had they more diligence, or greater talents, they might render their Gazettes interesting, by filling them with materials of a more instructive and dignified kind; but, wanting these qualifications, they must give such materials, accompanied with such a seasoning, as circumstances furnish. Of what kind these are no one is ignorant."

With the expiration of the Alien and Sedition Acts, hundreds of libel cases were brought in the first decade of the nineteenth century. Few editors went to jail, however, and most were let off with fines, although these might range from a few dollars to $8,000. The best-known editors accumulated the most suits. Duane, for example, had had sixty actions brought against him by 1806. Every editor ran the danger of a challenge to a duel, or of being horsewhipped or otherwise attacked by irate readers. These dangers persisted well into the second half of the century.

Yet the wisest men realized the indispensability of the press, whatever its faults. Jefferson had upheld its freedom. Adams had not answered it in kind. Washington, whose personal sufferings were the most severe because of his character, had canceled most of his newspaper subscriptions when he left the Presidency, but he renewed many of them in the quiet of Mount Vernon. On the night before he died, he sat up until nine o'clock reading the newspapers, and his last utterance on any public matter that last evening was to argue "with some degree of asperity" about something he had read in the paper.

four

Party and Press:
The Alliance Ends

AS THE TIDE OF SETTLEMENT MOVED WESTWARD, the printing press and the newspaper went with it. Presses and type were loaded into wagons, lashed onto barges, carried by hand when it was necessary. Everywhere they went the colonial pattern was repeated—the printer-proprietor turning out newspapers, pamphlets, local laws, commercial announcements, bills, legal forms and an occasional book from the same shop. Often the equipment was inadequate for the work—the first novel printed in Alabama, "The Lost Virgin of The South," was set in two different type sizes—but if the press was successful, it did better work and soon began to specialize, either in newspapers or else book and magazine work.

The migration had begun as early as 1786, when the first paper west of the Alleghenies, the Pittsburgh *Gazette,* began publishing in that city, then a struggling settlement of only three hundred people. In that same year, a Philadelphia printer, John Bradford, loaded his press on a wagon and with the further aid of flatboat and packhorse made his way as far as Lexington, Kentucky, where he began publishing the *Kentucky Gazette* in August 1787.

While Jefferson was retiring from the Presidency, Joseph Charles was crossing the Mississippi and setting up the *Missouri Gazette* in St. Louis. In Texas a Baltimore printer, Sam Bangs, was busy turning out propaganda in both pamphlet and newspaper form on behalf of the Mexican revolutionary movement against Spain.

In 1834, the first press in California was set up by a man from Florida, Agustin Zamorano, who had come by way of Mexico City, and with that event printing spanned the continent. It was a dozen years later before there were presses in Monterey and San Francisco, but no later than 1839 when a Honolulu missionary brought a press all the way from the islands, at the behest of Christian women there, to convert the Nez Perces in the Pacific Northwest.

There were 512 newspapers being published in the United States by 1820, twenty-four of which were dailies, sixty-six semi- or tri-weeklies and 422 weeklies. These were read largely by the upper economic and social classes—the people who could read and had the money to pay. That meant the circulations were never large, not often above 1,500, except for the largest big-city papers. Beyond the cities, the spread of newspapers was even greater, increasing sixfold in the first two decades of the century. Advertising was not quite keeping pace with these advances; retailing, which was to be the biggest source of newspaper income, was only beginning its spectacular rise.

In the East, where the politics were still hottest, the dying embers of controversy were fanned into life again by the onset of the War of 1812, and in Baltimore occurred one of the ugliest incidents in the entire era of the propaganda press.

The Federalists were out of power, but as the prospect of war began to develop, they had an issue once more, and President Madison was attacked with something of the old vigor. The most outspoken of the "out" party's newspapers was the *Federal Republican,* whose publishers were Jacob Wagner and Alexander Hanson. Their assault on the President raised again the troublesome question which had plagued Washington and is still with us today: How far should press criticism go when the country's security is threatened by an enemy? What Wagner and Hanson were saying in the columns of the *Federal Republican* was clearly dangerous, but Madison hesitated to impose the censorship that was clearly called for. He could not help remembering that it was his party which had fought for freedom of the press ever since it had been threatened by the Sedition Act. To restrict a newspaper now would be widely regarded as a violation of party principle.

To the dismay and shock of more responsible citizens, the mob took charge of this situation, as it had been doing since before the Revolution. The President's supporters, although certainly never authorized by him, destroyed the *Republican's* buildings and presses. The editors saved their lives only because of a timely warning by their friend John Howard Payne, who was then far away from his "Home, Sweet Home" in Easthampton, Long Island.

Wagner and Hanson were possessed of courage, if not of good judgment or reasonable restraint. Equipped with another press, they resumed publication in a second building, and thoughtfully provided themselves with food and water behind stout barricades, in case they were besieged.

The first issue they put out from this fortress was calculated to infuriate the mob all over again. What they called the President was exceeded only by what the Baltimore fanatics called them when they read it. The common word of the Republican mob was "traitor," which seemed ungrateful to at least two members of the *Republican's* staff, James Lingan and "Light Horse Harry" Lee, who had been generals and heroes only a generation before in the Revolution.

When the mob came again, there was a short, furious siege battle which threatened to end in a blood bath when the besiegers brought up a cannon. Those in the mob who could still think prevailed at this critical point and a truce was arranged, by which the paper's entire staff was given safe conduct to a jail. It was not enough to satisfy the mob. They destroyed building and press once more, and then assaulted the jail. This time there were no restraints. A few staff members escaped, but nine others were savagely beaten by the mob. Lingan was killed; Lee was maimed for life. It was hard to place the blame accurately for this sorry affair, whether on the vicious stupidity of the mob, or the intransigent foolhardiness of the editors who had provoked it.

Such intransigence was characteristic of the Federalist press, which carried its fight against the Madison administration right into the war years. Reading their papers, it could scarcely be told whether the President or the British were the enemy. If this seems one of those remote excesses, happily in the past, it may be recalled that the same unsavory history was repeated by a few American newspapers during the second World War, and again in the Korean War.

The seat of dissension in the War of 1812 was in New England, which was in greatest danger of losing life and liberty. There a firebrand named Major Benjamin Russell was publisher of the Boston *Columbian Centennial,* a rabid Federalist organ which went so far as to back a secession movement among the more myopic New Englanders during the darkest days of the war. Madison correctly termed this action treason, and the fact that the *Centennial* and some other regional papers supported it was a severe test of his tolerance. Still, he restrained himself and the end of the war, and of his administration soon after, prevented the issue from becoming a national one.

With this transition in Washington there began the period which Major Russell named "the era of good feelings," a durable label but no more accurate than a good many of the major's other political analyses, since it was in reality a time when the old disputes were merely being supplanted by others. The Federalist-Republican quarrel was nearly dead. Far more serious antagonisms were stirring beneath the surface, however, in the grassroots democratic revolt which would shortly send General Andrew Jackson to the White House, and in the slowly developing controversy between North and South.

For the time being, there was little of the old factionalism. James Monroe, an inveterate newspaper reader, was in the Presidency. He was an admirer of the Washington *National Intelligencer,* which was as safe and sane as his administration. "Mr. Silky-Milky Smith" had retired from the paper in 1810, and it was now in the hands of two partners, Joseph Gales, Jr., and William W. Seaton, who worked as Congressional reporters, dividing Senate and House between them and taking down the proceedings in the new labor-saving device, shorthand. They had converted the *Intelligencer* from a tri-weekly to a daily, and it was making money. In a partisan era, it was a quiet, steady, conscientious voice, as the *New York Times* would shortly be in the turbulent years of the Civil War, and for a century after that.

Newspapers were somewhat overshadowed in the first decades of the century by magazines, which had been the last of the printed media to establish themselves but were suddenly in the ascendancy.

They had been held back by circulation problems, and because Americans had been slow, for various reasons, to acquire the magazine reading habit. In the period before the Civil War, however, the magazine business entered its golden age and the newspapers, undergoing a slow transition, could not always keep up with them in the competition for public interest.

There was an occasional echo of former days. Duane, who was still editor of the *Aurora,* appeared again as a petitioner to President Monroe for a special favor. During the War of 1812, he had been a quartermaster in the army and found himself short in his accounts at the conclusion of the conflict. Seeking a new start, he had used his Senatorial friends to try to get him an appointment as an American agent to Venezuela. But Monroe had a good memory, and he had no sympathy whatever for Duane, whom he described as an Irish adventurer, the editor for twenty-five years of "the most slanderous newspaper in the United States," as John Quincy Adams quoted him indirectly in his diary. "He is now poor, and growing old, and his present proposal is substantially to sell his silence," Monroe concluded.

There was close liaison between the *Intelligencer* and the White House, but it was never the administration's paper, body and soul, as newspapers had been owned by political parties before. Nevertheless, the press was still almost entirely political, as a cynical but substantially accurate analysis by Adams in his diary would indicate. Writing of how the press was pushing the candidacy of William H. Crawford for the Democratic nomination in 1824, Adams noted caustically:

> Among the most powerful of his agents have been the editors of the leading newspapers. The National Intelligencer is secured to him by the belief of the editors that he will be the successful candidate, and by their dependence upon the printing of Congress; the Richmond Enquirer, because he is a Virginian and a slave-holder; the National Advocate of New York, through Van Buren; the Boston Statesman and Portland Argus, through William King; the Democratic Press, of Philadelphia, because I transferred the printing of the laws from that paper to the Franklin Gazette; and several other presses in various parts of the Union upon principles alike selfish and sordid.

Of the subsequent newspaper war between Crawford and Calhoun, Adams wrote:

> This day the City Gazette has three columns of brevier type of the foulest abuse upon McKenney, and upon Mr. Calhoun personally . . . The Republican replies this evening with firmness and moderation to the National Advocate and Boston Statesman, and reviews its own progress hitherto. If this press is not soon put down, Mr. Crawford has an ordeal to pass through before he reaches the Presidency which will test his merit and pretensions as well as the character of the nation.

In spite of Adams' worries about the nation's character, and the briefly virulent character of the newspapers' campaign in the summer of 1824, the crisis passed (if it was a crisis) and Adams himself was in the White House, as a kind of intermission president between Monroe and Jackson. Like Monroe, Adams had used the *National Intelligencer* when he was Secretary of State as a willing mouthpiece when he thought it necessary to defend himself, but the paper's support of Crawford widened a rift that already existed. When he was safely installed as President, Adams turned to a new Washington paper, the *National Journal,* as his chief support. Its editor and publisher, Peter Force, who also was mayor of Washington during his career, was the President's friend, but Adams' relationship with the *Journal* was never particularly close. John Quincy, indeed, could not seem to come particularly close to any individual or institution.

The long, comparative peace in the partisan press came abruptly to an end with the campaign of 1828. The papers supporting Adams and Jackson appeared to be in a competition to see who could make the most scandalous charges. Jackson's papers declared that Adams, when he was minister to Russia, "attempted to make use of a beautiful girl to seduce the passions of the Emperor Alexander and sway him to political purposes." Adams' editors replied with the charge that Jackson's mother was a mulatto. The opposition answered by asserting that Adams' wife was English, not American.

Jackson's chief newspaper support came from a Frankfort, Kentucky, newspaper with a grandiloquent name, the *Argus of Western*

America, edited at different times by two remarkable men, Amos Kendall and Francis P. Blair. Kendall was a Groton-educated lawyer who, as a rugged editor in a rough town, had carried a knife and pistol to defend himself against his and the paper's enemies. Blair was a native of Virginia, raised in Kentucky, who survived a delicate childhood to become a fiery pamphleteer in his adopted state and eventually succeed Kendall as editor of the *Argus.*

The *Argus* had been a sarcastic, cheeky paper from the beginning, and its conduct during the campaign was reminiscent of the worst days of propagandizing. Adams' papers replied in kind, and there rose a great deal of bitterness between the contending factions, culminating in Jackson's failure to pay the White House call which protocol demanded when he arrived in Washington as president-elect. Nor did Adams ride with his successor to the inauguration ceremonies.

Jackson did not underestimate the rôle newspapers, including the *Argus,* had played in electing him, as he made clear when he dispensed patronage after assuming office. Adams complained of it bitterly:

> The appointments, almost without exception, are conferred upon the vilest purveyors of slander during the late electioneering campaign, and an excessive disproportion of places is given to editors of the foulest presses. . . . The appointments are exclusively of violent partisans; and every editor of a scurrilous and slanderous newspaper is provided for.

Among those provided for were Amos Kendall and Francis Blair, whose appearance in Washington occasioned both amazement and amusement. Blair was described only half-facetiously by his partner, John C. Rives, as "about five feet ten inches high, and would be full six feet if his brain were on the top of his head, instead of being in a and weighed last spring, when dressed in thick winter clothing, one hundred and seven pounds, all told . . . flesh he has none. His face is narrow, and of the hatchet kind, according with his meat-ax disposition when writing about his enemies. His complexion is fair, his hair sandy, and his eyes blue—his countenance remarkably mild."

Kendall was an even stranger sight, "bent, nearsighted, badly *poll* behind it. He looks like a skeleton, lacks but little of being one,

dressed, with premature white hair, sallow complexion and a hacking
asthmatic cough." He appeared in his white broadcloth greatcoat,
buttoned to the throat, even on the hottest days, and because he was
subject to migraine headaches, he sometimes had a white handkerchief
tied around his head. This apparition was remarked on the floor of
the House, where a wondering Congressman remarked: "Poor wretch,
as he rode his Rosinante down Pennsylvania Avenue, he looked like
death on the pale horse."

In the new administration, Kendall was initially made fourth auditor
of the Treasury and later became Postmaster General, but his real
job was to be Jackson's confidential adviser and aide, in substantially
the same relationship as Colonel House to Wilson, Harry Hopkins to
Franklin Roosevelt, and Sherman Adams to Eisenhower. Blair was
summoned to Washington from the *Argus* to edit a new newspaper,
the *Washington Globe,* which was to be the administration's mouthpiece. To help him as business manager, another shaggy giant of a
Kentuckian, Rives, was imported. These three constituted what came
to be known as Jackson's "Kitchen Cabinet."

The *Globe* appeared first in December 1830, and was changed
from a semi-weekly to daily by means of a polite pressure campaign
which resulted in six hundred of the President's friends subscribing
to the paper in advance. Kendall later denied in his autobiography
that Jackson had started the paper, attributing its origin to these
helpful friends of Jackson's, but there seems little doubt that the
President and his Kitchen Cabinet intended it from the beginning to
be their creation and the administration's kept paper, which in fact
it was.

Blair was the ideal man for the editor's job. He had never met
Jackson before he came to Washington, but the two men liked and
admired each other at once, and soon Jackson's familiar command,
"Give it to Blair," was resulting in immediate translation of whatever
the President was thinking on any given subject into one of the
editor's slashing editorials, which he wrote at such speed that two
copyboys at a time were kept busy running his copy to the typesetters.

Kendall and Blair had the help of another newspaperman, Isaac
Hill, editor of the *New Hampshire Patriot,* who had been one of

Jackson's most effective supporters during the campaign. Hill was a militant phrase-maker who supplied a good deal of the *Globe's* ammunition, along with making his own paper one of the most influential in New England.

The *Globe* was assured of success because Jackson was able to maneuver Congressional and Departmental printing into its shop, and this alone was worth $50,000 per year. Further, it was considered a mark of loyalty to the party to be a subscriber and the faithful flocked to the lists. The *Telegraph,* the opposition paper which had lost the job printing, could not survive without it, and by 1837 the *Globe* had the field virtually to itself. According to one of Blair's biographers, "Compared with the Richmond *Enquirer* or the *National Intelligencer,* the *Globe* was a radical paper. It was dogmatic, bold and defiant. At times the editor hesitated when it was politic to do so. His gift for satire played to his advantage and to the great discomfiture of the enemy. Blair's sarcasm bit like vipers, and friends and foes alike came to dread his editorial attacks."

A striking evidence of the *Globe's* peculiar position was the attention paid to it abroad, where it was read carefully as an index to whatever Jackson, and therefore the United States, might be thinking and planning. In a remarkable forecast of things to come, the Russians complained about certain items in the *Globe,* and did not believe it when the American minister, James Buchanan, told them the paper was not under control of the government. This, of course, was a diplomatic fiction.

An indication, however, that the press was no longer happy over its intimate connections with political parties could be seen in the criticism that arose when Jackson, elected again, rewarded even more friendly editors with government positions. Nor was it a question of sour grapes. The Richmond *Enquirer,* which had worked hard for the President's re-election, complained:

> We wish the Executive would let the Press alone. We cannot any more approve of the appointment of so many of its conductors to office, although they may be required to give up their papers, than we approved of the great pains which were taken by Mr. Clay to turn obnoxious Editors out . . . and to put in his devoted Partizans.—We

know that General Jackson solemnly disclaims all intentions to *reward*
his supporters or to bribe the Press to support his measures. And we
believe him—we know also, the reasons by which he justifies these
appointments . . . But we are better satisfied with his *motives* than his
reasons—with the integrity than with the expediency of the appointment.

Jackson defended himself in what could only be called a specious
manner. To John Randolph he wrote in 1831:

> I was never sensible of the justness of the exceptions stated to the
> employment of Printers in the public service. The press is the
> Palladium of our liberties. Disfranchise those who conduct it: or what
> is the same thing make the calling of an editor a disqualification for
> the possession of those rewards which are calculated to enlarge the
> sphere of talent and merit, and which are accessible to other callings
> in life, and you necessarily degrade it . . . I refused to consider the
> editorial calling as unfit to offer a candidate for office; and accordingly
> appointed them on a few occasions when they were deemed honest
> and capable.

While Jackson was in office, certainly, the *Globe* was his voice and
its editor one of his closest friends. Blair, or Hill, coined the phrase,
"The world is governed too much," and under this comfortable slogan,
Blair attacked such targets as the United States Bank, which Jackson
was against as an assumption of Federal power, and Henry Clay's
"American System," a convenient term for the new Federalism. In
conducting these campaigns, the editor was always in consultation
with the President. He traveled with him, ate and drank with him
frequently, and often he appeared at the White House to be with
Jackson before the President had breakfast.

It could be argued that Jackson needed a newspaper voice he could
rely on. As the first President to be elected as the result of a ground-
swell in the grassroots, he was, as the late Claude Bowers noted,
opposed by "two-thirds of the newspapers, four-fifths of the preach-
ers, practically all the manufacturers, and seven-eights of the banking
capital."

As soon as Jackson was out of office, these enemies clustered like
vultures around the *Globe,* and it was soon in trouble. The new

Congress which came in with Van Buren deprived the paper of government printing contracts as one of its first acts. After several years of ups and downs, the *Globe* was rewarded by James K. Polk for its lukewarm support of him by being abandoned as the administration's paper. Thomas Ritchie, the Richmond editor, took it over and changed its name to the *Union*. Blair and Rives continued to publish their *Congressional Globe,* a record of proceedings in Congress, which had long been an extremely profitable sideline.

This action of Polk's hurt the dying Jackson more than it did Blair. He could not understand it, wrote to Blair that he thought the President had shown "less good common sense . . . than any act of his life," and prayed that Polk would not "let the Globe fall into the *hands of Bankrupts*. I am too sick to say more."

As James Pollard summarizes the unique association of Jackson and Blair: "Other Presidents, before and after him, had official organs but not to compare with the *Globe*. It was not the paper itself, however, but the rare combination of Blair and Jackson that made it so effective, so feared and so profitable for its proprietors. No Washington paper, before or since, has reached such heights and no President has leaned so strongly upon an official newspaper as Jackson upon the *Globe*. But while he contributed greatly to the political influence of the press it was one-sided and concentrated."

If the *Globe* was the ultimate in the use of the newspaper as a propaganda organ, it also represented the end of a long era which had begun with Benjamin Harris's effrontery, quickly suppressed. The press had in that era won its freedom from government license, and then sold itself utterly and voluntarily to its former masters. From its use as a revolutionary propaganda machine to its hardly concealed official position as the private organ of a President, it had encompassed the range of partisan expression at the expense of truth and responsibility. As a tool of party and politicians, it had not attained any particular distinction except in the excellence of writing which the best statesmen and editors brought to it.

At the close of the first Jackson administration, the American newspaper was not yet a *news*paper in the sense we know it today, but a new era was about to begin. The fact that it was inaugurated by the genius of a single man was indicative of the personal character the new era was to assume.

These first two eras of American newspaper history overlapped in a curious way. While the *Globe* was at the peak of its career, during Jackson's second term, and was the admiration of the whole newspaper business, a struggling young journalist tried to use what little influence he possessed to get a job on it as associate editor. "I should like such a position remarkably well," he wrote to Levi Woodbury, one of Jackson's friends, and remarked confidently that he thought he could "add a good deal of reputation and patronage to the *Globe.*"

The aspiring editor was ignored by the President and Blair. If he had been accepted, the future of the *Globe* might have been entirely different, although one doubts whether Blair could ever have lived comfortably in the same office with James Gordon Bennett, who would soon show newspapers how to collect and print news. With the establishment of his New York *Herald,* the era of personal journalism began.

THE NEWSPAPER
as
PERSONAL
INSTRUMENT

one

The Giants of New York

TWO HISTORIC DEVELOPMENTS PAVED THE ROAD James Gordon Bennett traveled. One was the technological breakthrough in typography which occurred in the first half of the nineteenth century. The other was a tide of immigration rolling in from Europe at the same time which provided a mass market for the kind of mass production the new presses were able to provide.

Printing technology has always moved slowly. Before Bennett's time there had not been a substantial advance since the last half of the fifteenth century, when the type mold and the chase were invented. Before George Clymer's development of the celebrated Columbian Iron Press, a flatbed affair first used in 1813, printers had used the wooden press employed by printers in England long before the settlement of America, which employed the principle of the screw to transmit the impress. Then, abruptly, there came a rush of discoveries, new principles in typecasting and setting, paper-making, and press building, and with these revolutionary changes printing emerged from art to industry, from the household into the factory.

Dan Treadwell's horsepower press of 1822, using a real horse, was the forerunner by a year of Jonas Booth's machine which replaced the horse with steam. But the development that made the mass newspaper possible was the invention of the cylinder press. From experiments begun in England as early as 1790, the idea of such a press grew until Robert Hoe and his associates took the prototypes of the French Napier cylinder presses in 1825 and improved on them until they had produced the press which dispensed with the flat bed entirely, carrying the type forms on the cylinders while other cylinders made the impression.

The first true cylinder press, developed by Robert Hoe's son Richard, did not appear in a newspaper office until 1847, when the Philadelphia *Public Ledger* installed a four-cylinder machine, into which four boys fed the paper. It printed 8,000 sheets an hour on one side, and it revolutionized the newspaper business.

Bennett did not have the advantages of such a machine when he established the New York *Herald* in May 1835, but then he was a man who had never enjoyed any advantages at all except those supplied him by his fertile, eccentric brain. The eccentricity may have been a reflection of his undoubted genius. Yet this same eccentricity runs like a crimson thread through the lives and characters of the men who produced in New York before the Civil War the newspapers which towered above their contemporaries and set the patterns for nearly everything we have in newspaper journalism today. They were restless, pushing men, for the most part, egocentric and combative, possessed of a certain cynicism and devoted to the making of newspapers, although some had political ambitions as well.

They were true products of the new era—editors, not printers; their own bosses, not the hired, subsidized voices of greater men in higher places. Truth and responsibility were not their hallmarks, although most of them loudly professed these qualities. They were as partisan as some of their predecessors, but in their own right, not as party minions. The newspapers they produced were often guilty of excesses reminiscent of the past, but at the same time the competition of these strongminded men for readers produced a constantly refined conception of news which made the papers entirely different from anything that had gone before. News—distorted, perhaps, but news— was the criterion by which they lived.

With the help of developments in printing, they were now speaking to mass audiences. From the end of the Revolution to the eve of the Civil War, immigration expanded the new nation from a settled strip of coastal plain all the way to the Mississippi. The inhabitants of this area increased from three million to more than thirty-one million in that time, and the center of population moved steadily westward from Maryland to Ohio. America was no longer an agricultural nation by mid-nineteenth century, but a country entering an industrial phase which would shortly make it the marvel of the modern world.

In overcrowded, rowdy, pushing New York City, where the Irish and German immigrant masses were manipulated cleverly by politicians, the new generation of personal journalist publishers were soon an important factor, but the newspapers they made were read far beyond the borders of the city or state. Horace Greeley's *Tribune* was read and heeded nearly everywhere in the country.

Bennett was the prototype of the new publisher, a born editor who brought to the making of newspapers a fresh concept. Scottish-born, he had emigrated to Halifax in 1819, lived through some desperate years of poverty there and in Boston, and worked at badly paid publishing jobs in New York and Charleston before he got his first newspaper job on the New York *Courier,* a Sunday paper. His series for that journal exposing various sharp practices in the New York business world marked him as a superb reporter, and sharpened his hatred for the money men.

When the associate editor of the New York *Enquirer* was killed in a duel, Bennett got the job if not the title and was soon the paper's correspondent in Washington, where he produced some penetrating articles about politicians which would now be called profiles. James Watson Webb, the editor of the *Courier,* bought the *Enquirer* and merged the papers, making Bennett the editor, but when the paper switched its allegiance to the Whigs, he resigned.

After a few other abortive attempts to establish himself either in New York or Philadelphia, Bennett found himself broke and out of work. That was the point at which he tried to get a job on Francis Blair's *Globe.* He had no better luck with Benjamin Day's new paper, the New York *Sun.*

The *Sun* represented another revolutionary idea in the newspaper business. Ben Day, its proprietor, was a New Englander who had learned the printing trade on the excellent paper in Springfield, Massachusetts, the *Republican,* operated by Samuel Bowles. He had come down to New York as a compositor, but in the depression of 1833, which was casting a long premonitory shadow toward the crash of three years later, he made a move of near desperation. He started a penny newspaper, the *Sun.*

There was shrewd reasoning along with the desperate gamble. The other New York papers were selling for six cents and showed no signs of distress, but Day reasoned that a penny would do much better while hard times prevailed, and he was convinced that there was a substantial untapped market in the new masses, who were too poor to pay six cents. He was aware that three penny papers had already appeared, one each in Boston, Philadelphia and New York, and they had all failed, but Day attributed that to poor timing.

Whether it was timing or the inferior nature of the product to blame for the previous failures, Day's *Sun* was an instantaneous success. He did all the work himself, except to hawk it in the streets —the first time a newspaper had ever been sold in that fashion, by newsboys. It was snapped up eagerly. The *Sun* had eight thousand circulation in little more than six months.

Watching this success convinced Bennett that Day had the right idea, and if the proprietor of the *Sun* would not give him a job, he was determined to start his own penny paper.

It was a gamble as desperate as Day's had been. Bennett had only $500 to his name, but it was enough to establish him in a Wall Street basement with an ailing press, scarcely more than enough type, and a desk made of a wide plank laid across two flour barrels. Out of this cellar emerged one May morning in 1835 a newspaper which was to be different from any the world had ever seen. The first issue was a modest four-page double sheet, ten-and-a-half inches wide and fourteen inches long, containing a typographical error in the first word of the first item: *"Ptb*lished daily by James Gordon Bennett & Co., office Number 20 Wall Street, basement story."

There was not much in that first issue to foreshadow the future. Bennett was not yet organized, and what news he had been able to gather was smothered by such sententious space fillers as the "Biographical Sketch of Matthias the Prophet," which occupied most of the first page. The second page carried a prospectus revealing some of the essential Bennett. He wrote:

> Our only guide shall be good sound practical common sense, applicable to the business and bosoms of men engaged in everyday life. We shall support no party, be the organ of no faction or coterie, and care nothing for any election or any candidate from President down to

constable. We shall endeavor to record facts, on every public and proper subject, stripped of verbiage and coloring, with comments suitable, just, independent, fearless and goodtempered . . .

There are in this city at least 150,000 persons who glance over one or more newspapers every day and only 42,000 daily sheets are issued to supply them. We have plenty of room, therefore, without jostling neighbors, rivals or friends, to pick up at least 20,000 or 30,000 for the Herald, and leave something for those who come after us."

It was one of the few times in his life that Bennett could be accused of modesty. In only fifteen months, the *Herald* boasted 40,000 circulation, and it was climbing every day. To separate it from the competition of the other penny dailies, which were now becoming numerous, he raised the price to two cents.

The immediate reason for his success was a simple one. Like Day, he had given the masses a paper they could afford, but he also knew how to give them the news they liked to read—local news, of an unvarnished kind. New York was a raw, wicked city, growing much too fast for its own good, full of every kind of sin and corruption, and Bennett reported what was going on in a blunt, accurate style, far different from the wordy, mock-elegant manner which had become standard, except in partisan political attacks.

Bennett was not only entertaining in the news columns, but his editorials were far from the pontifications which were the stock in trade of other editors. He slashed away in his half-mocking manner at churchmen, politicians, businessmen or anyone else who came to his notice. He spared no one, respected no one, which was exactly what delighted his readers, who had the only half-concealed contempt of the masses for constituted authority. In New York, the war between the haves and the have-nots had already begun, and Bennett showed himself as clearly the friend of the have-nots.

It was difficult to separate Bennett's overwhelming personality from the hard, brilliant work he did in the newsroom, but it was there he made his real contribution to newspaper development, overshadowed at the time by the incredible eccentricities which made him one of the most controversial figures of his day. What he did was to organize the business of news gathering and editing along the lines which remain standard today.

As soon as he could afford help, Bennett set up a city staff of reporters who went out on more or less regular beats, as well as handling spot news. The publisher himself covered Wall Street and the business news with a thoroughness which had never been seen, and frequently with a savage criticism of the money changers he thought might be cheating the public.

His enterprise in getting the news forced other publishers to emulate him, and for the first time getting and printing the news became the chief object of newspapers. Bennett set them a fast pace. In 1838 he went to Europe and there organized a six-man staff to cover the Continent for him; no one had thought of doing such a thing before. At home he extended the *Herald's* national coverage with correspondents in strategic cities, and sensing the impending crisis long before other editors, he made a particular effort to get the news from the South, utilizing Samuel Morse's new telegraph as soon as it was invented. In Washington he organized the first bureau to cover the capital, and got its members admitted to sessions of Congress.

Bennett spared nothing to get the news first. His fast packets cruised off Sandy Hook, intercepting ships bringing dispatches from Europe and getting them into his paper hours before the steamers could dock. Once he met a ship bearing important European news at Halifax and carried the dispatch cases himself by hired locomotives to Boston, Worcester and New London, then by ferry to Long Island where another locomotive waited to whisk him into New York. The opposition despaired of beating the *Herald*.

Balanced against this news enterprise, which was making him richer by the day, was the exhibitionism which distressed his friends and made him more enemies than any other man in town. One of his first feuds was with James Watson Webb, his former employer and associate on the *Courier and Enquirer*. They had parted enemies. Webb was an egocentric, self-aggrandizing man in his own right, too much like Bennett ever to get along with him. As a Whig and a defender of the monied interests, he was a natural target for the *Herald's* publisher.

After Webb had grandly requested, and Bennett had ignored the request, that his name never appear again in the columns of the *Herald,* the two men met one day on Wall Street and there was a brief scuffle. Four months later they met again in nearly the same spot. This is Bennett's description in the *Herald* of their second meeting:

> As I was leisurely pursuing my business yesterday, in Wall Street, collecting the information which is daily disseminated in the *Herald,* James Watson Webb came up to me, on the northern side of the street—said something which I could not hear distinctly, then pushed me down the stone steps, leading to one of the broker's offices, and commenced fighting with a species of brutal and demoniac desperation characteristic of a fury.
>
> My damage is a scratch, about three quarters of an inch in length on the third finger of my left hand, which I received from the iron railing I was forced against, and three buttons torn from my vest which any tailor will reinstate for a sixpence. His loss is a rent from top to bottom of a very beautiful black coat, which cost the ruffian $40, and a blow in the face, which may have knocked down his throat some of his infernal teeth for anything I know. Balance in my favor, $39.94.
>
> As to intimidating me or changing my course, the thing cannot be done. Neither Webb nor any other man shall, or can, intimidate me. I tell the honest truth in my paper, and leave the consequences to God. Could I leave them in better hands? I may be attacked, I may be assailed, I may be killed, I may be murdered, but I never will succumb. I never will abandon the cause of truth, morals, and virtue.

The *Herald* was full of such Bennettisms, and nearly every one was calculated to offend someone. "All we Catholics are devilish holy," Bennett would remark in one of his ambivalent statements about the Church in whose faith he had been reared. The death of a beloved brother under the rigors of one of the harsher priestly orders had left him with a bitterness toward the Church he could not always suppress.

He could demolish with a stroke. "Ground was broken for the Erie Railroad yesterday," he wrote prophetically; "we hope it breaks nothing else." Sometimes it was no more than a pithy filler: "Great excitement among the Presbyterians just now. The question in dispute is, whether or not a man can do anything towards saving his own soul." Often he boasted of his paper: "Nothing can prevent its success but God Almighty, and he happens to be entirely on my side." Always he fought the conventional morality of his day, ordering his reporters to write "leg" instead of "limb," except when he himself satirically referred to the "branches" of dancers. Similarly, the *Herald* used "shirts" for "linen" and "pantaloons" for what was usually termed "inexpressibles." Once he lashed out: "Petticoats—petticoats—petticoats—petticoats—there—you fastidious fools, vent your mawkishness on that!"

For the other publishers he had nothing but contempt, and often expressed it, as he did in this August 1836 editorial, in which he incidentally discloses his working habits:

> We published yesterday the principal items of the foreign news, received by the *Sheffield,* being eight days later than our previous arrivals. Neither the *Sun* nor the *Transcript* had a single item on the subject. The *Sun* did not even know of its existence. The large papers in Wall Street had also the news, but as the editors are lazy, ignorant, indolent, blustering blockheads, one and all, they did not pick out the cream and serve it as we did. The *Herald* alone knows how to dish up the foreign news, or indeed domestic events, in a readable style. Every reader, *numbering between thirty and forty thousand daily,* acknowledges this merit in the management of our paper. We do not, as the Wall Street lazy editors do, come down to our office about ten or twelve o'clock, pull out a Spanish cigar, take up a pair of scissors, puff and cut, cut and puff for a couple of hours, and then adjourn to Delmonico's to eat, drink, gormandize, and blow up our contemporaries. We rise in the morning at five o'clock, write our leading editorials, squibs, sketches, etc., before breakfast. From nine till one we read all our papers and original communications, the latter being more numerous than those of any other office in New York. From these we pick out facts, thoughts, hints, and incidents sufficient to make up a column of original spicy articles. We also give audiences to visitors, gentlemen on business, and some of the loveliest ladies in New York, who call to subscribe—Heaven bless them! At one we sally out among the gentlemen and *loafers* of Wall Street—find out the state of the money market, return, finish the next day's paper—close every piece of business requiring thought, sentiment, feeling, or philosophy, before four o'clock. We then dine moderately and temperately—read our proofs—take in cash and advertisements, which

are increasing like smoke—and close the day always by going to bed at
ten o'clock, seldom later. That's the way to conduct a paper with
spirit and success.

It was also, in combination with other such stories, the way to
irritate other publishers and the upper classes, who did not think the
Herald was amusing. This irritation, originating particularly with
Bennett's rivals and the clergy, resulted in what came to be called
"The Great Moral War" against the publisher and his paper. Reminiscent of propaganda days, Bennett's enemies replied in kind through
press and pulpit, with familiar invective: "Stigma on the city . . . vice
and vulgar licentiousness . . . hypocrisy, ignorance and bloated con-
ceit . . . double apostate and traitor in politics . . . half-crazy, un-
educated wretch . . . immoral and blasphemous monstrosity . . . pest
. . . villain . . . forger." So it went.

The climax came on June 1, 1840, when Bennett announced his
approaching marriage on the front page of the *Herald* in headlines
and story that seemed incredible even to contemporaries who lived
daily with the man's execrable taste. He had met a pretty Irish girl,
Henrietta Agnes Crean, at a party and pursued her with his characteristic arrogance which may well have frightened her into consent. He
would have been a hard man for any girl to resist—six feet tall, somewhat florid, with an intensity in his eyes and voice that nearly everyone
thought compelling. Henrietta was compelled and found herself celebrated with the following headlines and story:

**TO THE READERS OF THE HERALD—DECLARATION OF
LOVE—CAUGHT AT LAST—GOING TO BE MARRIED—NEW
MOVEMENT IN CIVILIZATION**

I am going to be married in a few days. The weather is so beautiful;
times are getting so good; the prospects of political and moral reform
so auspicious, that I cannot resist the divine instinct of honest nature
any longer; so I am going to be married to one of the most splendid
women in intellect, in heart, in soul, in property, in person, in manner,
that I have yet seen in the course of my interesting pilgrimage through
human life.

. . . I cannot stop in my career. I must fulfill that awful destiny which
the Almighty Father has written against my name, in the broad

letters of life, against the wall of heaven. I must give the world a pattern of happy wedded life, with all the charities that spring from a nuptial love. In a few days I shall be married according to the holy rites of the most holy Christian church, to one of the most remarkable, accomplished, and beautiful young women of the age. She possesses a fortune. I sought and found a fortune—a large fortune. She has no Stonington shares or Manhattan stock, but in purity and uprightness she is worth half a million of pure gold. Can any swindling bank show as much? In good sense and elegance another half a million; in soul, mind, and beauty, millions on millions, equal to the whole specie of all the rotten banks in the world. Happily the patronage of the public to the *Herald* is nearly twenty-five thousand dollars per annum, almost equal to a President's salary. But property in the world's goods was never my object. Fame, public good, usefulness in my day and generation: the religious associations of female excellence; the progress of true industry—these have been my dreams by night and my desires by day.

In the new and holy condition into which I am about to enter with the same reverential feelings as I would enter heaven itself, I anticipate some signal changes in my feelings, in my views, in my purposes, in my pursuits. What they may be I know not—time alone can tell. My ardent desire has been through life to reach the highest order of human intelligence, by the shortest possible cut. Association, night and day, in sickness and in health, in war and in peace, with a woman of the highest order of excellence, must produce some curious results in my heart and feelings, and these results the future will develop in due time in the columns of the *Herald*.

While his readers were still recovering from this proclamation, Bennett and his Henrietta were married and took an entirely conventional honeymoon trip to Niagara Falls, an excursion which the bridegroom improved by sending back daily dispatches on the state of the American countryside. On their return to New York, Bennett intended to install his bride in the Astor House until the house he was building for her was completed, but he discovered that his enemies had gone so far as to persuade the courtly proprietor of the Astor, Charles Stetson, to refuse him the hospitality of the hotel.

Bennett's reaction was entirely typical. "These blockheads are determined to make me the greatest man of the age," he wrote. "Newspaper abuse made Mr. Van Buren chief magistrate of this republic

—and newspaper abuse will make me the chief editor of this country. Well—be it so, I can't help it."

In spite of the *Herald's* success, however, it was never an influential paper. It was, in fact, the first large daily to demonstrate that even though a paper has an oversized circulation and is apparently beloved by its readers, it does not necessarily follow that these readers will follow it politically. The *Herald's* readers were highly entertained by Bennett, and no doubt many of them appreciated the range of news to be found in the paper, but they often voted contrary to Bennett's specific instructions.

There was only one newspaper in New York which could be said to have any significant influence in the city and nation. That was one of Bennett's earliest rivals, the *Tribune* of Horace Greeley. To most Americans today the name of Greeley is remembered, if at all, for a passing remark taken out of context: "Go west, young man." He was an eccentric, like Bennett, but it was a different kind of eccentricity. Where Bennett was intensely egocentric, Greeley was a liberal reformer whose dreams were for humanity—except for the one dream which wrecked his life, in the end.

Bennett's tall, spare figure was a familiar sight on New York streets, but Greeley was so widely known everywhere in the country that he became a popular legend in his own time, much as William Randolph Hearst was in ours. His restless, crusading spirit dominated the American journalistic scene from 1830 to 1870, and although other editors and literary figures viewed him with contempt (William Cullen Bryant would not even speak to him), his was the only journalistic voice heard from New York to California. There were a good many people in the country who refused to believe anything in the papers was so unless "Uncle Horace," as he was affectionately known, confirmed it in the *Tribune*.

A master showman, an amiable medicine man, he was known to everyone, as a present-day biographer describes him, by his "moon-faced stare, his flopping trousers, his squeaky slang, his sputtering profanities, his unpredictable oddities, and his general air of an owlish, rustic sage . . ." Vernon Parrington writes of his "round moon-face, eyes blinking through spectacles, and a fringe of whiskers that invited the pencil of the cartoonist." In his frock coat and white hat, he could be seen talking endlessly to people, in New York and elsewhere.

Those who thought Bennett might have more than a touch of paranoia were certain Greeley was out of his mind, but they could not be outraged, or hurt, or angry about him, as they were about the *Herald's* publisher. Instead, they told stories of Uncle Horace's eccentricities, adding steadily to the legend.

They recalled, for example, how Greeley, an ardent vegetarian, once absentmindedly ate a large steak under the impression it was graham bread. They repeated with delight the incident of the visitor who poured out a tirade in Greeley's office, and when the editor seemed to be paying no attention, exclaimed, "I've treated you like a gentleman, which obviously you're not." To which Uncle Horace responded mildly, "Who in hell ever said I was?" He was a strongminded man who kept a goat in the backyard behind his house on East Nineteenth Street, and when his fellow Union League Club members censured him for befriending Jefferson Davis after the Civil War, called them "narrow-minded blockheads" and dared them to throw him out of the club.

In the *Tribune,* Greeley created a newspaper as legendary as he was, a training ground for other editors, a forum for every liberal idea directed to the betterment of humanity, without regard for its real merits, since Greeley's agile mind leaped from idea to idea, like Eliza among the ice floes, and he was likely to go whooping off after another before his readers had fully absorbed one.

Greeley's early career followed the well-worn nineteenth-century trail which would one day be indelibly labeled the Horatio Alger road from rags to riches. He came out of the poverty of a New Hampshire farm, from which his father went to debtor's prison, and got his education from the Bible and from working as a printer's apprentice. When he came to New York in 1831, at twenty, he was the very prototype of the Alger hero, with everything he owned in the world slung over his shoulder in a bandanna, and his total wealth, ten dollars, in his pocket.

After a discouraging start on the first penny paper in New York, the *Morning Post,* which died within three weeks, Greeley started his own Whig weekly, the *New Yorker,* on the proverbial shoestring. Its editorial page spoke with so much vigor and obvious talent that Thurlow Weed, the political boss of New York State, was attracted and hired young Greeley to edit some campaign papers for him. Out of his savings from this successful venture, Greeley was able to launch the *Tribune* on April 10, 1841, when he was only thirty years old. He supplemented the $1,000 he had saved with another thousand borrowed. Half the total went for printing equipment.

Bennett had a six-year start, but Greeley's editorial genius, expressed in a different way, enabled him to achieve the same immediate success. The *Tribune* reached 11,000 circulation in just seven weeks. It never matched the *Herald* or the others in circulation. Often it was behind with the news, and sometimes it was unpopular politically. But no paper could equal its national influence. That was because the whole staff, from Greeley on down, believed that the "New Morning Journal of Politics, Literature and General Intelligence," as Greeley called it in its first issue, really meant it when the publisher promised it would "advance the interests of the people, and promote their Moral, Political and Social Well-being."

Greeley's staff was by all odds the ablest on any American newspaper. Charles Anderson Dana, later the *Sun's* noted editor, was made city editor of the *Tribune* in 1847, when its combined daily and weekly circulation had reached 26,000, and eventually became managing editor. Margaret Fuller, friend of Emerson and utopian reformer, was literary editor until George Ripley succeeded her. Bayard Taylor started writing travel sketches and editorials, and soon became a regular staff member. Solon Robinson, that remarkable observer of New York life, was also agricultural editor.

For a time Karl Marx was London correspondent of the *Tribune,* but when Greeley cut his original $10-a-week salary to $5, Marx revolted and quit. He had been using the money to help support him while he wrote "Das Kapital." Greeley may well have been suspicious of Marx's socialism, which was certainly nothing like his own.

Greeley and Dana had working for them, by 1854, no fewer than ten associate editors and fourteen reporters, with an outside staff of thirty-eight regular correspondents. The *Tribune's* weekly edition, which condensed what had been printed in the daily, went to the remotest corners of the United States, and was passed from family to family. As Taylor remarked, "The *Tribune* comes next to the Bible all through the West." It had, as the historian James Ford Rhodes was later to write, "a power never before or since known in this country."

James Parton, a contemporary biographer of Greeley, has given us a splendid picture of the *Tribune's* remarkable staff at work. The sub-editors, including Taylor, Dana, Robinson and the others, came to work at 11 A.M. In the hour before noon they made a leisurely preparation for the day's work, waiting for Greeley's arrival, which was usually between noon and one o'clock. The editor, with papers spilling out of his pockets and in his usual hurry, would rush in, stop for a few moments to talk with the others, and then plunge into the letters, clippings and newspapers piled high on his desk. By four o'clock he would be at the bottom of the heap, after which he went to dinner.

Returning, Greeley would find the splendid machine of which he was master tuning up in earnest for the night's work, which was not well under way until about nine o'clock, in the manner of morning newspapers from that day to this. Parton describes what followed:

> The editorial rooms . . . have become intense. Seven desks are occupied with silent writers, most of them in the Tribune uniform— shirt sleeves and moustache. The night-reader is looking over the papers last arrived, with scissors ready for any paragraph of news that catches his eye. An editor occasionally goes to the copy-box, places in it a page or two of the article he is writing, and rings the bell; the box slides up to the composing room, and the pages are in type and corrected before the article is finished. Such articles are those which are prompted by the event of the hour; others are more deliberately written; some are weeks in preparation; and of some the keel is laid months before they are launched upon the public mind. The Editor-in-Chief is at his desk writing in a singular attitude, the desk on a level with his nose, and the writer sitting bolt upright. He writes rapidly, with scarcely a pause for thought, and not once in a page makes an erasure. The foolscap leaves fly from under his pen at the rate of one in fifteen minutes. He does most of the *thinking* before he begins to write, and produces matter about as fast as a swift copyist can copy. Yet he leaves nothing for the compositor to guess

at, and if he makes an alteration in the proof, he is careful to do it in such a way that the printer loses no time in "overrunning"; that is, he inserts as many words as he erases. Not infrequently he bounds up into the composing room, and makes a correction or adds a sentence with his own hand. He is not patient under the infliction of an error; and he expects men to understand his wishes by intuition; and when they do *not,* but interpret his half-expressed orders in a way exactly contrary to his intention, a scene is likely to ensue . . .

Midnight. The strain is off. Mr. Greeley finished his work about eleven, chatted a while with Mr. Dana, and went home. Mr. Dana has received from the foreman the list of the articles in type, the articles now in hand, and the articles expected; he has designated those which *must* go in; those which it is highly desirable *should* go in; and those which will keep. He has also marked the order in which the articles are to appear; and, having performed this last duty, he returns the list to the compositor, puts on his coat, and departs.

When Greeley summed up his philosophy in 1850 under the title, "Hints Toward Reforms," it was easy to see why the *Tribune* was known far and wide as "The Great Moral Organ." He believed, said Uncle Horace, that "the avocations of Life, and the usages and structure of Society, the relations of Power to Humility, of Wealth to Poverty, of master to servant, must all be fused in the crucible of Human Brotherhood, and whatever abides not the test rejected."

The truth was that Greeley lived in an America which was in transition from an agricultural to an industrial society, a highly painful process full of dislocations, maladjustments, indignities, oppressions and injustices, along with the normal complement of evil and stupidity. To a man like Greeley with a highly developed but largely unfocused moral sense, many of these things were intolerable, to be fought with whatever weapon lay at hand. That was why he preached thrift although he never practiced it himself; it was good for humanity. He could ally himself with the conservative Whigs because they were fighting slavery, but he also horrified them because he thought of himself as a philosophical socialist.

Greeley fought hard for his beliefs, with a splendid disregard for consistency. When the Republican Party was founded, he was at home within its inner circle, but when it failed to live up to the standards he set for it, he did not hesitate to run against it with the help of the Democrats. He was for labor unions and free homesteads, but he was also for vegetarianism and spiritualism. One of his most ardent crusades was to lift the laboring class "out of ignorance, inefficiency, dependence and want," and for five years or so he preached an imported French brand of socialism known as Fourierism, which advocated cooperative ownership of lands and homes. In time he abandoned Charles Fourier, the French thinker who had originated the idea, but not before he had carried on an intense debate for six months in the columns of the *Tribune*. When he finally lost interest in the idea, he never mentioned it again.

Not all of his crusades were ineffective by any means. As a printer himself and an advocate of unionism, he organized the New York Printers' Union and became its first president. As a teetotaler, he used the influence of his paper to get state prohibition laws passed. As a humanitarian, he was against capital punishment and succeeded in getting several states to repeal their laws permitting death by hanging.

Occasionally he supported the right things for what some would have considered the wrong reasons. As a Whig, for example, he came out strongly in favor of protective tariffs, not because he wanted to protect the nation's industrialists but because he thought the high standards of labor would be protected by them. His fellow Whigs, during their uneasy alliance, were confused when they read editorials arguing for protectionism and socialism in the same issue of the *Tribune*. The Whigs had something to thank him for, however. Greeley sold the idea of high tariffs to the nation's farmers, where the *Tribune* had perhaps its greatest influence, almost single-handedly. He sold it so well that it is still an article of faith in most parts of the rural community.

Many of Greeley's crusades stemmed from his passion to make the country strong internally. His "Go West, young man, and grow up with the country," was part of the *Tribune's* westward expansion campaign, in which he constantly urged the Federal government to aid the young men who took his advice by passing a Federal homestead law, and helping to build railroads and telegraph lines—all propositions which horrified his Whig friends and their Republican successors.

Greeley took his own advice in the summer of 1859 and toured the country as far west as California, stopping in Salt Lake City on the way for a two-hour interview with Brigham Young, which made newspaper history because it was the first interview conducted in question-and-answer form. Uncle Horace found himself opposed to Young's views on polygamy, not for the usual moral reasons but because he considered the practice an infringement on the natural rights of women. Through the *Tribune* he brought so much pressure to bear on Congress from his aroused readers, who were concerned for more customary reasons, that polygamy was outlawed three years later.

Viewed in today's terms, Greeley is as much a contradiction as he was in his own time, and if he were alive, he would probably be just as unclassifiable. He was for what the Republicans would now call creeping socialism, but he would also be considered an isolationist and in sympathy with the party's right wing. He believed that laissez-faire was suicidal, leading to the "anarchy of individualism," yet he preached the rights of the individual. He put his ultimate trust in the fundamental goodness of humanity, a romantic view which accurately forecast his total failure in politics.

However wrong or muddled he might be on occasion, Greeley's high-minded advocacy of principles and his utter sincerity were what separated his paper from Bennett's *Herald*. James Parton placed his finger squarely on the reason for the *Herald's* failure to achieve Greeley's influence despite its larger circulation when he wrote, "Influence over opinion no paper can have which has itself no opinion, and cares for none."

In the contentious time just before the Civil War, when opinions were violent as they had not been since the turn of the century, one new editor dared to found a newspaper which took the middle ground. People who were tired of Bennett's sensationalism and cynical views, and who may have been equally tired of Greeley's liberal highmindedness, turned to it with relief.

The new editor was Henry Jarvis Raymond, and his newspaper was the *New York Times*. Raymond was an exception to the Alger pattern.

Born in upper New York State, the son of a comfortably well-to-do farmer, he was well educated, having graduated with the highest honors from Genesee Wesleyan Seminary and the University of Vermont, where he had studied so hard his health was impaired. He had found enough time, however, to contribute occasionally to Greeley's *New Yorker* during its brief career, and quite naturally he came to the city after his graduation to ask Uncle Horace for a job on the new paper.

Raymond was no raw recruit from the country. He had traveled in Europe, he knew some of the influential men of his time, and he was worldly by comparison with most of his contemporaries in the business. It is not surprising, therefore, that Greeley astutely made him his chief assistant—at $8 a week—when he founded the *Tribune,* although the two men could hardly have been more unlike. Raymond was a born nonpartisan, and it is one of the oddest mischances of newspaper history that he was also in love with politics.

As Greeley's assistant, Raymond applied the sound principles of newspaper management which seemed to come naturally to him and saved the *Tribune* from disaster during its first few struggling months. He had the help of a friend in the business office, a Vermonter named George Jones, and in their spare time these two men planned their own newspaper.

The venture had to be postponed for lack of capital. Jones went to work for a bank in Albany, and after two years with Greeley, Raymond quit and moved to the *Courier and Enquirer,* where he soon got himself so deeply involved in Whig politics that newspapering was almost a sideline. He was elected to the State Assembly in 1849, and after his re-election to a second term, became Speaker in 1851. His alliance with the Free Soilers cost him his job with James Watson Webb, and after a brief tour of duty as editor of *Harper's New Monthly Magazine,* he and Jones, with whom he had been corresponding, contrived to accumulate the astonishing capital sum of $100,000 and with it they established the *Times* in 1851. Only ten years before Greeley had started the *Tribune* with $2,000, and sixteen years previously Bennett had done it with $500. The newspaper business was changing rapidly.

In the usual inaugural edition declaration, Raymond set the tone for his paper in words which have been its guidelines for more than a century: "We do not mean to write as if we were in a passion—unless that shall really be the case; and we shall make it a point to get into a passion as rarely as possible."

Coming as they did at a time when passion was the order of the day, in the shadow of approaching civil war, these words were greeted with utter disbelief by old hands in politics and newspaper making, but Raymond meant them and he carried out his policy successfully. He made the *Times* the kind of newspaper it remains today—balanced, accurate, written and edited on the highest level. Its rational fairness, free of abuse and passion, was at once in striking contrast to nearly every other newspaper in the country.

In these tense years before the war, the newspaper business was again proliferating as the result of Bennett's revolution, the rise of the other giants, and the general expansion of the nation. Magazines were still the dominant factor among the printed media, but newspapers were doing well. A foreign-language press, particularly German papers, had risen in the Northeast and Middle West. Specialized organs like William Lloyd Garrison's abolitionist *Liberator* were attracting a national audience. The war correspondent had made his appearance with the conflict in Mexico, and the distinguished poet-editor of the *Evening Post,* William Cullen Bryant, was sending home excellent news letters from Europe. The advent of the telegraph in 1844 was lifting dailies everywhere from their parochial concerns and making them reflectors of the national scene.

On the eve of the Civil War, the giants of New York were already caught up in the struggle. In his new building at the corner of Fulton and Nassau streets, Bennett was discovering as he got richer that he had more in common with the business community than he had supposed. Since the impending conflict was highly unpopular with these business-men, Bennett found himself supporting Stephen A. Douglas. People remembered that he had once worked in Charleston, and the Abolition-ists began charging him with being pro-Southern.

Bennett, of course, had his own unique solution for the nation's family quarrel. Let the seceding states go, he said in the *Herald,* and then reorganize the Republic under the South's new constitution, leav-ing out the New England states. It is doubtful whether Bennett really believed in this harebrained idea, but the paper's readers took him seriously and a mob of several thousand gathered outside the *Herald's* new building with the intention of burning it down.

Saved from this disaster narrowly, Bennett thought better of his policies after Fort Sumter was fired on. Overnight he switched party lines, turned in his yacht to the Union, and offered his son as a sacrificial lamb, ordering him to enlist in the Navy. After completing these rituals, he supported Lincoln in a lukewarm way, except when it pleased him to do otherwise.

As for Greeley, he was a moving force in the Abolitionist cause, and consequently faced the New York mobs who were in sympathy with the other camp. The war was not popular in New York. It was opposed not only by businessmen, but by the Irish and German laboring masses, who were not interested in the ideology of the quarrel and could foresee only fighting and perhaps dying for a remote cause, or else enduring the rigors of wartime living and probably losing jobs to liberated Negroes drifting up from the South and flooding the labor market. Some of these unsympathetic citizens made a practice of hounding Abolitionist editors, and Uncle Horace once had to flee a pack of them, intent on destroying the *Tribune,* by disappearing down an alley and into a convenient tavern where he hid out under a table for a time.

Greeley's enemies remarked skeptically that the editor might not have been so ardent an abolitionist if he had ever visited the South, since he was inclined to change his mind after first-hand examinations. The South was the one section of America that Uncle Horace never visited, and his understanding of it was limited. But he knew that slavery was wrong, and he believed devoutly that secession would be fatal to the American idea. Southern travel, it may be said with certainty, would never have converted him from those beliefs.

When it came down to the nub of the day's issues, however, the beliefs collided head-on with Greeley's natural pacifism. He could not accept the idea of war. He was ready to let the southern states go, as Bennett was, if that were the only way, and in this his managing editor, Dana, agreed with him. Dana, who had started life as much of an idealist as Greeley, was becoming increasingly cynical about the world, but he still found himself in agreement with his employer on most large questions, except labor unions. Fort Sumter severed their relationship and changed their lives, as it did so many thousands of others. Greeley was profoundly against the war, and Dana was for it. Uncle Horace asked for his friend's resignation and got it. Thus the newspaper which had done more than any other to oppose the spread of slavery seemingly refused to take the final step.

Before he left, Dana had committed the *Tribune* to the war in Greeley's temporary absence and given the Union forces a headline which became a ringing battlecry, "Forward To Richmond!" Lincoln and his cabinet were so pleased with this kind of support from an important paper that when Secretary of War Stanton heard about Dana's resignation, he offered the editor a job in the War Department, and there Dana began a new and even more distinguished career. As for Greeley, he continued to give the President an uncertain support; Lincoln could not always be certain which side he was on.

In Raymond's case, he was having an even more difficult time with politics. The *Times* was doing well; in four years it had doubled the *Tribune's* city circulation, and Greeley was finding it his chief rival. But Greeley and Raymond were rivals in the political arena as well. Both were deep in the Whig politics of New York State, where Greeley found his ambitions blocked at every turn by his former assistant.

It was sad that these two men who had so much to give to the newspaper business should have ruined their lives for politics, a field for which they were supremely unqualified. Raymond was good at the practical side of politics—that is, getting elected—but once in office he was not politician enough to succeed. Greeley, on the other hand, might have done well in office, but in spite of his remarkable influence with the voters, he could not get himself elected. It was his curse that he suffered at an early date from that Potomac fever which, as Bernard Baruch would later remark, was enough to rouse a man from the grave and start him walking toward Washington.

In the Whig struggle between the northern free-soilers and the slaveholding southerners, Raymond won national attention at the convention of 1852 for his eloquent advocacy of the Northern cause. Nevertheless, Greeley hoped that Thurlow Weed, the Whig boss in New York, would get him the nomination for governor. When Weed ignored him, Greeley humbled himself enough to ask for the lieutenant-governor's job but Weed gave the nomination to Raymond. "No other name could have been so bitterly humiliating to me," Greeley wrote. The ticket was elected.

When Greeley came to the convention of 1860, he was determined to support anyone who was against Weed and Seward, and that is why Lincoln got the backing of the country's most influential newspaper, which was of considerable help in electing him. Newspapers had also played a vital part in securing the nomination for Lincoln, which had been engineered in large part by Charles Ray and Joseph Medill, entrepreneurs of the Chicago *Tribune.*

As for Raymond, he had been one of the founders of the Republican Party in 1856, and was the author of its first platform, but his inclination in 1860 was to compromise on secession. He actually opposed abolition until the war came, after which he supported Lincoln through the conflict, with few exceptions.

The Civil War, as has always been the case with wars, had a profound effect on the newspaper business in America. Every aspect of newspaper production was affected, and large questions were raised about the relation of press to government which had not been debated since the War of 1812. There were pro- and anti-war papers on both sides, all of them hotly partisan except for the *New York Times,* and the perennial problem which has never been solved plagued Washington and the editors: how to balance national security and the public's right to know.

In this struggle the press was in a far different position than it had been before. Thanks to Bennett and the other New York giants, it was much more powerful, and its ability to gather and disseminate news had been enormously enhanced by the coming of the telegraph and the railway post. Balanced against these factors was the nearly total ignorance of the military commands both North and South on the subject of censorship, with which none of them had had the advantage of experience. There were, in addition, the overwhelming tides of hate and bigotry washing over and nearly obliterating the national idealism which had prevailed since the Revolution.

The struggle was sharpened by the enterprise the newspapers demonstrated in covering the war. No war had ever been reported so freely and completely, and Bennett's genius made the *Herald* stand out above all the others—audacious as always, amazingly complete, and nearly always accurate. War coverage cost Bennett more than a half-million dollars, but the effort brought him to the peak of his success; one issue alone in 1864 sold 132,000 copies, unprecedented for those days. The *Tribune* constituted its most serious competition, but Bennett had the satisfaction of knowing that Lincoln himself read the *Herald*.

Bennett had forty war correspondents, known as "specials," in the field, including a young Bavarian immigrant, Henry Villard, who was considered the best of them. The battlefield stories were illustrated profusely with woodcuts, something new in war reporting—a kind of coverage which was even more outstanding in *Harper's Magazine*.

The *Herald's* correspondents, good as they were, found themselves matched by some unlikely "specials" from other papers. One was an unknown young reporter from the Cincinnati *Gazette,* Whitelaw Reid, who would one day carry on the *Tribune* from where Greeley left it. Reid's account of the Battle of Shiloh was the talk of the business, and his story of Gettysburg, from the vantage point of Cemetery Hill, the most exposed point, was considered a classic. Here is a paragraph from his eyewitness account:

> . . . Hancock was wounded; Gibbon succeeded to command— approved soldier, and ready for the crisis. As the tempest of fire approached its height, he walked along the line, and renewed his orders to the men to reserve their fire. The rebels—three lines deep— came steadily up. They were in pointblank range. At last the order came! From thrice six thousand guns there came a sheet of smoky flame, a crash of leaden death. The line literally melted away; but there came a second, restless still. It had been our supreme effort— on the instant we were not equal to another. Up to the rifle pits, across them, over the barricades—the momentum of their charge, the mere machine strength of their combined action swept them on. Our thin line could fight, but it had not weight enough to oppose this momentum. It was pushed beyond the guns. Right on came the rebels. They were upon the guns, were bayoneting the gunners, were waving their flags above our pieces. But they had penetrated to the fatal point . . .

An unknown reporter like Reid sometimes found himself in the distinguished company of no less a correspondent than the publisher of the *New York Times.* Raymond assigned himself to the field, where his speed and accuracy were soon legendary, and his stories of Bull Run and Solferino were acclaimed as masterpieces.

Dana saw as much of the war as any correspondent, but from a unique vantage point. Invited to Washington by Stanton after his resignation from the *Tribune,* he was assigned, in reality, to spy on Grant. Ostensibly his mission was to examine the pay service, but secretly he was ordered to join Grant at headquarters and provide Stanton with daily reports which would enable the Secretary to estimate what Grant was doing, and was capable of doing.

It was a superb piece of reporting, in which Dana used the talents which had made him a great managing editor on the *Tribune.* Sifting and analyzing thousands of facts, he made it clear at last in his reports what a commander the Union had in Grant, and ultimately resolved Lincoln's command problem. As a reward, after Vicksburg, the President appointed Dana Assistant Secretary of War. He was immediately assigned to do the same kind of reporting on General Rosecrans, and on the basis of these reports, Rosecrans was removed from his command. Afterward, as the Administration's personal reporter, so to speak, Dana traveled with Grant and Sherman through Chattanooga, Missionary Ridge, Lookout Mountain and other campaigns.

The correspondents, in general, enjoyed a freedom in their coverage they do not have even today. It was in keeping with the nearly complete freedom the press now enjoyed in its new prosperous, independent and aggressive state. Both sides tried to use its own newspaper supporters to influence public opinion, in the classic manner, and sometimes they were so successful as to influence actual military decisions. Politicians and generals sometimes found themselves in an undignified scramble for press support, and those who ignored or resisted newspaper power, like General McClellan, might find themselves removed.

One of the marvels of the war was the Press Association of the Confederate States of America—"PA," in its familiar logotype—to which all of the South's forty-three wartime dailies belonged. Astonishingly, its news of the conflict was a model of objectivity for the most part, sometimes more reliable than Northern reporting of the same events.

Not as much could be said for the press as a whole. The northern papers were in frequent conflict with military commanders, who took punitive action against correspondents in the field on occasion. Some newspapers were suspended. Others were wrecked by mobs, and these included both Copperhead and pro-Union papers. Much of this violence followed the shock of Lincoln's assassination.

Long before the fatal night at Ford's Theater, Lincoln was assassinated by the newspapers in a manner not seen since the darkest days of the partisan press after the Revolution. He was accused of all kinds of misconduct—drawing his salary in gold bars, drunkenness, granting pardons to get votes, needless slaughter of men for the sake of victories, even treason—the list sometimes seemed endless. No other President, not excepting Washington or Franklin Roosevelt, was subjected to an assault quite as venemous. It remains one of the darkest, most shocking chapters in journalistic history.

The leaders of the pack were men like Manton Marble, of the New York *World*; Wilbur F. Storey, of the Chicago *Times*; Samuel Medary, of the Columbus *Crisis*; Benjamin Wood, of the New York *Daily News* (unrelated except in spirit to the present newspaper of that name); Charles H. Lamphier, of the Springfield *Daily Illinois State Register*; and Marcus Mills "Brick" Pomeroy, of the La Crosse, Wisconsin, *Democrat*.

In these papers and others Lincoln was referred to by such common epithets as "a slang-whanging stump speaker," "half-witted usurper," "mole-eyed," "the present turtle at the head of government," "the head ghoul at Washington," and others even less complimentary. There was not a major paper Lincoln could depend on, except the *New York Times* and Samuel Bowles' Springfield (Mass.) *Republican*. Greeley was unpredictable. Bryant was offensively moral. Bennett could never be counted upon. The Springfield (Ill.) *Daily State Journal* was the only newspaper in the country, according to Robert S. Harper, the modern authority on the subject, which never wavered in its admiration for the President.

Lincoln did have what could be called an administration paper,

something in the manner of Jackson. He had suggested to John W.
Forney, proprietor of the Philadelphia *Press,* that he move to Washington and establish the *Daily Morning Chronicle,* which became a
loyal administration mouthpiece. Forney was constantly at the White
House, and as Harper says, "was as near to Lincoln as any man in
journalism or politics."

Through all the abuse, the President exhibited the greatest patience
and leniency, which his enemies mistook for weakness. Frequently
he used the papers as a sounding board, particularly through the New
York Associated Press, which he relied upon as unbiased. He often
spoke openly to reporters covering the White House, and thus in a
sense introduced the modern Presidential press conference, although
it was not a formal procedure.

Only once did Lincoln turn on an editor, but when he did his anger
was directed at the most powerful publisher and paper outside New
York, Joseph Medill and his Chicago *Tribune.* Medill had been
strong for the Union but lukewarm about Lincoln. The President did
not know it, but this man who had done so much to get him nominated
in 1860 had done his best to organize a stop-Lincoln movement in
1864. The *Tribune* had been useful nevertheless in fighting Storey's
Chicago *Times*—the two papers were once armed and barricaded
against an expected assault by the other—and in combatting Bennett's
assaults on the President. When the *Herald* boomed Grant as "the
People's Candidate" in 1864, Medill advised the paper that it could
not be "allowed to paw and slobber over our Illinois General, and if
it has any regard for its 'throat' or its 'fifth rib,' it will take warning and
govern itself accordingly." For the *Herald* to advocate Grant was "a
gross libel on him and an insult to his friends," the *Tribune* cried.
"Unless it keeps its unclean and treacherous hands off of him, it may
expect to get 'tomahawked.' "

Bennett could only mutter in reply that the *Tribune* was "the
sewer into which goes everything too dirty for its New York namesake
to print."

In the darkest hours of 1865, however, there came a crisis with
Medill which the President could not ignore. The draft quotas were
continuing to arouse widespread protest, especially in the cities. In

Chicago, Medill headed a committee of three to come to Washington and make a personal protest to Lincoln over the call levied on that city, which had already sent 22,000 men.

Lincoln heard the committee out quietly, and then, as Medill himself recalled later, he said: "Gentlemen, after Boston, Chicago has been the chief instrument in bringing this war on the country. The Northwest has opposed the South as the Northeast has opposed the South. You called for war until we had it. You called for emancipation and I have given it to you. Whatever you have asked for you have had. Now you come here begging to be let off from the call for men which I have made to carry out the war which you have demanded. You ought to be ashamed of yourselves. I have a right to expect better things of you. Go home and raise your six thousand extra men. And you, Medill, are acting like a coward. You and your *Tribune* have had more influence than any paper in the Northwest in making this war. You can influence great masses, and yet you cry to be spared at a moment when your cause is suffering. Go home and send us those men."

It may have been the only time in his life that Medill was abashed, and he had grace enough to admit it. "I couldn't say anything," he wrote later. "It was the first time I ever was whipped, and I didn't have an answer. We all got up and went out, and when the door closed, one of my colleagues said, 'Well, gentlemen, the old man is right. We ought to be ashamed of ourselves. Let us never say anything about this, but go home and raise the men.' And we did, six thousand men, making twenty-eight thousand in the war from a city of a hundred and fifty-six thousand."

The irresponsibility of the press during the war brought it into direct conflict with the government, out of which grew the most serious threat to its freedom it had known since the days of royal licensing. In dealing with a disloyal press in wartime, the government itself was guilty of highhanded infringements of fundamental freedoms in its gropings toward a relationship which finally worked, when the war was nearly over. During this process, writs of habeas corpus were suspended, and some Copperhead editors found themselves thrown into Fort Lafayette as prisoners, by both Secretaries Stanton and Seward.

Nor were these isolated instances. Censorship and suppression were imposed as soon as the war began. Postmaster General Montgomery Blair used his power to deny the mails to newspapers he deemed "subversive," and would not permit post offices to relay messages to enemy areas. Telegrams between North and South were seized, in the constant search for traitors. Stanton and General Scott compelled the telegraph companies, illegally to be sure, to stop sending any information of a military nature, which naturally affected the work of the correspondents. Congress somewhat redressed this summary repression by transferring such authority to Lincoln in 1862.

Censorship was first imposed in the field after Bull Run. McClellan, who understood the situation better than most of the other commanders, called the correspondents together in 1861 and offered them a plan of voluntary censorship, much like the one that prevailed in the second World War, but the papers could not be trusted, and in any case the direction of censorship was contested between the State and War Departments. The voluntary system lasted three months, after which Congress took away the control from State and gave it to War, where Stanton, just coming into office, succeeded in improving matters.

After his order of 1862, requiring correspondents to submit their copy to provost marshals who were instructed to delete only military information, the only trouble remaining lay in the administration of the order, which was interpreted variously by generals and their provosts, some of whom were more concerned with public relations than the problem of censorship.

General Sherman was the worst of the government's field problems. He was the kind of commander who attributed his own failures to information leaks in the newspapers, and never missed an opportunity to excoriate a correspondent or a newspaper. In reply, the kindly press circulated the story that he was insane. When one of Greeley's reporters did file a story which was a clear violation of censorship, thus proving Sherman's contention, the general had him arrested as a spy, and would have had him shot as well if Lincoln had not intervened.

This incident was serious enough to bring about a logical reform. Correspondents were thereafter accredited, as they are today, and had to be acceptable to field commanders in order to gain accreditation. Another step was to exclude British correspondents, who had been a difficult problem on the Union side because of Britain's sympathy with the Confederate cause. By 1864 these changes and a more relaxed attitude on both sides, government and press, led to such cooperation that Sherman was able to make his march to the sea without disclosure of his plans in the newspapers at any stage.

There is no question that freedom of the press was in serious danger through most of the war, but only apologists will argue against the proposition that the press brought its troubles upon itself. It had not developed more than the beginnings of a concept of responsibility in the 175 years which had elapsed since Ben Harris. It saw itself as dedicated to the pursuit of whatever principles its publisher might espouse, and resented the slightest infringement of its rights, but with a few isolated exceptions, these publishers of the Civil War era had no real concern for truth. They were interested in selling newspapers, electing candidates, and ousting those in power, and these ends were served with whatever means were available.

The war had increased circulations substantially, and because of the dependence of people on the day-to-day reports from the battlefields, the newspapers had created a reading public which lifted them again to first place among the print media, an advantage they were to enjoy for some time, as far as mass readership was concerned.

Technically, the newspaper had also made important advances during the war. In using the telegraph as the chief transmitter of news, correspondents had learned to write more concisely, since this transmission was expensive. There was much less florid writing and rambling opinion than before the war, although the stories still were far short of modern style. Most important, however, they were considerably more readable, and that would mean much to the masses who were now reading newspapers.

Another technical improvement was the invention of the summary lead—the first paragraph containing the who, what, when, where and why of a story, still a standard form. It came about because correspondents could not always be sure their entire dispatch would find its way through the precarious telegraph system, and so they tried to make sure that the essential facts would arrive if the rest of the story were cut off.

In the composing room, the invention by William Bullock in 1863 of the web perfecting press, which printed both sides of a continuous roll of paper on the rotary press, guaranteed that the new market created by the war could be supplied in quantity. This press, of course, was the prototype of the kind in common use today.

The Civil War era came to a close on that April night in 1865 when Lawrence Gobright, of the Associated Press, flashed from Washington the fateful first bulletin: "The President was shot in a theater tonight, and perhaps mortally wounded."

In New York the first era of giants was dying too. Henry Raymond, broken politically in the crucible of Reconstruction, when he had failed to guide Johnson's policies and allowed himself to be out-maneuvered by Thaddeus Stevens, died unexpectedly in 1869 at forty-nine, of a cerebral hemorrhage, presumably in the arms of his actress friend, Rose Eytinge. Greeley wrote an obituary editorial which was a flat contradiction of nearly everything the *Tribune's* editor had said about Raymond while he was living.

Uncle Horace himself was not far from the end. He had broken his heart trying to hurry social evolution and bring about the reforms he so desperately wanted for humanity. Now, in his old age, he pulled himself together for one more last fight to attain the greatest prize. Running against Grant for the Presidency in 1872, he placed his faith on the farmers of America, who had always been his closest allies. With their help, he thought, he would be elected and could then put into practice those true Republican principles he had fought for so long, on one side or another. But the people in whom he had always believed, the farmers and those others whom he referred to grandly as "humanity," betrayed him. They elected Grant by more than 750,000 votes, an added humiliation.

A few days before the election, Greeley's wife Mary had died, and five days after his defeat a distraught Uncle Horace wrote: "I am not dead, but I wish I were. My house is desolate, my future dark, my heart a stone . . ." In the house of a friend on Fifty-seventh street, he lay ill, in a physical and mental decline, while his associates on the

Tribune fought for control of the paper. Removed to a private mental hospital in Pleasantville, he sank into a coma and died on November 28, 1872.

He had wanted a simple burial. "Plant me in my favorite pumpkin arbor," he had written, "with a gooseberry bush for a footstone." Instead he got a Fifth Avenue church funeral, complete with three ministers and a solemn procession of prominent pallbearers and mourners, including Grant, the man who had defeated him, and the men who had been struggling for control of the *Tribune* even as he lay dying. He might have been consoled, however, by the thousands of plain people who lined Fifth Avenue and wept unashamedly as the funeral cortège rolled by. They were Uncle Horace's people, who loved him in their way, and knew instinctively that they were seeing the passing of a great editor, perhaps the greatest American journalism had ever known.

That would have been disputed by James Gordon Bennett, who had no doubt about who deserved to be called the greatest journalist. At the end of the war, he was at his peak. Rich and successful, this hard, calculating and strong-willed man had outlasted his enemies, and if he had few friends, at least there were fewer people who might betray him, as he would have said. He had no wish to serve anyone. When Lincoln had offered to make him Minister to France, possibly to get him out of the way, he had declined. There was really nothing left for him to fight for, and so in 1867 he turned the *Herald* over to his son and retired.

When he died in 1872, only a few months before Greeley, a good many of his enemies were among the pallbearers, including Greeley himself, soon to be accorded the same hypocrital resolution of animosities in the presence of death. Bennett had always sneered at Greeley and his concern for humanity, of whom he had once said: "The great mass of mankind, living in civilized society are happy. The suffering and misery are only exceptions to the general condition. The world is an excellent world. It is a happy world . . ."

If Bennett did not attain his fondest ambition, it was because it was impossible. "My ambition," he once wrote, "is to make the newspaper Press the great organ and pivot of government, society, commerce, finance, religion, and all human civilization. I want to leave behind me no castles, no granite hotels, no monuments of marble, no statues of bronze, no pyramids of brick—simply a name. The name of James Gordon Bennett, as one of the benefactors of the human race, will satisfy every desire and every hope."

Bennett had to settle for being a benefactor of the newspaper business, but that was enough to insure his place in history.

Only one giant remained. Charles Anderson Dana had left his government post on July 1, 1865, and after two unsuccessful years in Chicago as editor of the *Republican,* he returned to New York where he had dreamed of having his own paper. With the help of men like Roscoe Conkling, Cyrus Field and Alonzo Cornell, among others, he raised $175,000 and bought the *Sun.*

It had fallen on evil days. Moses Beach and his two sons had taken it over from Ben Day, but they were printers, not editors. When it began to fail, they had sold it in 1860 to a man named Morrison who had been converted in the great revival of 1858, and now wanted a paper to spread the good news. Under his editorship there was an incredible interval when prayer meetings were held in the city room and editorials urged the Union generals not to fight on Sundays. After a year of it, Morrison gave the paper back to Beach, who thought himself lucky to sell it to Dana.

At that juncture its circulation had fallen to a low point of 43,000. In less than three years, Dana brought it back to the top of the New York heap with an average daily circulation of 102,870, and in six years it had reached a peak of 131,000. Dana's dominance of post-Civil War journalism was challenged in the closing decades of the century, even before Hearst and Pulitzer arrived, by the growth of the newspaper business in other parts of the nation. Chicago was becoming a center second only to New York. There were excellent newspapers in the South, and sensational developments in the West. Personal journalism was no longer the property of the New York giants. Another phase had begun.

two

Public Service in the Middle West

FOR NEWSPAPERS THE PERIOD FROM THE END of the Civil War to the close of the century was a time of ascendancy over the other print media. Newspapers had enjoyed the most influence in colonial America and in the beginning years of the Republic, then had yielded to books and magazines in the first half of the nineteenth century. During the latter half, in spite of national crazes for book authors approaching the fan hysteria for movie and singing stars today, newspapers were once again the chief carriers of ideas.

It was a time which saw the era of personal journalism draw to a close in the gaudy struggle between Pulitzer and Hearst, and witnessed the concept of the newspaper as a business institution emerging naturally from the industrial expansion and turmoil which made institutionalized business the primary fabric of American life.

Preliminary changes in the transformation of the newspaper from personal weapon to business institution were already taking place in the post-Civil War era. If the papers of the time had a common denominator, it was the community service idea, which was in essence a turning away from the image of newspapers as reflections of strong publishers to their rôle as servants of the people. That rôle meant not only providing readers with news and information, but leading them toward civic reforms.

In the new era, as it developed, the emphasis began to shift from circulation to advertising as the lifeblood of the paper, and while newspapers were still free to attack the advertisers (as they have always been), the interests of businessmen and publishers, once poles apart, were beginning to approach each other.

Various factors were at work to bring about this rapprochement. The distribution of goods had moved out of local areas into regional and national patterns, brand names were proliferating, competition was keener, and there was an obvious demand for better merchandising methods. One of the best methods available was newspaper advertising, which could now be national and regional as well as local. Thus an important new source of advertising revenue, deriving from the growth of national big business organizations, was opening up to the publishers.

The cities were undergoing an explosive population expansion, which was being served by a growing number of retail outlets for goods and services, most of them advertisers, actual or potential. In the old days, the amount of local retail advertising had been helpful to a newspaper's income but not critical. In the new order, it would soon mark the difference between success or failure for some newspapers, no matter what they might do editorially.

All these complicated economic factors worked together like an intricate machine. Population growth stimulated business growth which created a need for better merchandising which stimulated the rise of advertising which became increasingly important to the life of newspapers, which were able to meet the advertising needs of business because their circulations were growing with the population and they were reaching the people the advertisers wanted to reach. This is such a commonplace fact of life today that it scarcely seems possible its real development began less than a hundred years ago.

From the publishers' standpoint, the rise of advertising could not have taken place at a better time. It was becoming more and more expensive to produce newspapers in the latter part of the century. The only way these costs could be met was through larger circulation and expanded advertising volume based on increased readership. Intense competition began to develop in both areas, and the papers which exhibited superior business talents were the survivors. In the end, as costs and competition mounted, a newspaper could not exist without efficient business management, and so in some respects newspapers began to resemble other businesses.

In this shifting of newspaper publishing patterns, personal owner-ship became more and more the property of the small daily and weekly, while the big city papers were increasingly corporate enterprises. Business, however, was good everywhere. Publishing opportunities bloomed in cities and villages, regardless of size.

Everything contributed to the growth of the mass media. The constant expansion of education and the consequent rise in literacy created more potential newspaper readers every year. The interests of Americans were being continually broadened and their cultural desires stimulated by the steady development of bookstores, libraries, art galleries, theaters and opera. These interests found their most popular expression in newspapers through reviews and articles.

The result of all this stimulation in the last two decades of the century was a startling growth of English-language daily newspapers. There had been only 850 of these dailies in 1880; by 1900 there were 1,967. Seven-eighths of this growth was in the evening field, represent-ing a greater home consumption, particularly by women; by 1890 two out of every three were evening papers. New York alone remained primarily a morning paper town, as it has to this day. And what was good for the dailies was equally good for the weeklies, which tripled in number during the same period.

As a result of Bennett's revolution and what followed, newspapers were now heavily concentrated on the news, which was written in the clearer style developed by the war correspondents. They were aggressive, as they had always been; corporate blandness would not overtake them for some time. On the editorial page there was as much diversity of opinion as ever; the editors had not yet developed the business viewpoint which would characterize the editorial page of the twentieth century. They were active crusaders for community interests, but as the readership base continued to broaden there began to occur the content popularization, the appeal to mass taste, however crude, which seems to be an inevitable process in the creation of mass media.

While New York was still trembling under the tread of giants—men like Dana, Pulitzer and Hearst—the center of gravity in the news-paper business had begun to shift out of the metropolis. Not that the nation's largest city was likely to stop publishing important, provocative newspapers. It was simply that such papers were now beginning to be published in other cities as well, particularly in brawling, exciting Chicago. All over the country were appearing editors whose voices were heard in the nation, and whose newspapers were celebrated for various reasons. The long dominance of New York, which had begun with Bennett, drew slowly to a close with the waning of the century.

The overwhelming voice outside New York after the end of the Civil War was that of the man Lincoln had chastised, Joseph Medill, in many respects the James Gordon Bennett of the Middle West. Medill had come to the Chicago *Tribune* in 1855 at the age of thirty-two, and for the next forty-four years he was its life. He was its managing editor during the first eight years, and editor-in-chief from 1863 to 1866, after which he made a brief excursion into public life as a member of the Illinois Constitutional Convention, the Civil Service Commission, and eventually as Mayor of Chicago. Returning to the *Tribune* in 1874, he took over complete editorial and business control of the paper, retaining it until he died in 1899.

If anything, Medill's *Tribune* was more uninhibited than Bennett's *Herald*. As an editor, Medill was more of a public figure than Bennett; he did not have nor need the New Yorker's infinite capacity for self-aggrandizement. Medill had his eccentricities too, but they were milder than Bennett's. He was, essentially, a fighter and a leader, and he unquestionably led midwestern journalism during his lifetime. No one could doubt that the *Tribune* was one of the most personal of personal journals. Like the *Herald* and other papers of its stripe, the *Tribune's* language was frequently out of the gutter. It was a paper which dealt in extremes, stopping at nothing either to attack an enemy or promote a cause.

Medill professed the usual lofty ideals common to the publishers of his day. A newspaper, he asserted, ought to be "the organ of no man, however high, no clique or ring, however influential, no faction, however fanatical or demonstrative, and in all things to follow the line of common sense." Medill's common sense had something of the same quality as Bennett's, who, it will be remembered, expressed the same pious thought in almost identical language.

As Bennett had been, Medill was a self-made man, the son of an immigrant Ulsterite who married an Episcopalian girl and settled on a farm near St. John, New Brunswick, under the mistaken impression that they were living in America. This strip of borderland eventually was given to Canada, rather than Maine, but that was after the family had migrated to Stark County, Ohio, when young Joe was nine. There, for the next dozen years on his father's farm, Medill got the kind of education which was available to young Americans who could not go to school regularly. He was an insatiable reader, particularly of history —Gibbon and Hume—and of travel and biography. As Lincoln was doing in nearby Illinois, Medill walked miles to get a book. On Saturdays he traveled nine miles to be tutored by a clergyman in Latin, logic and natural philosophy.

With this kind of preparation, he was able to study law in Canton at twenty-one, got himself admitted to the bar, and practiced for three years in New Philadelphia while he learned to set type in his spare time and wrote editorials for the local paper.

Once he had sniffed printer's ink, there was no longer any doubt about what he would do. With the money saved from his law practice, he bought the Coshocton *Whig,* ran it successfully for two years, then moved into Cleveland, where he established another Whig paper, the *Daily Forest City,* which became by consolidation the Cleveland *Leader,* a major factor in uniting that region's anti-slavery elements, and in making Medill a noticeable figure in the abolition movement.

As such, he came to Horace Greeley's attention. It was Greeley who urged him to go to Chicago in the spring of 1855 and start a penny paper, in collaboration with one of Uncle Horace's friends, Charles H. Ray, of Galena, Illinois, editor of the Galena *Jeffersonian.* Medill and Ray met in Chicago, then a city of 85,000, carrying letters of introduction to each other from Greeley. In the parlor of the Tremont House, where the proprietor introduced them, they made an agreement to buy into the *Tribune* rather than start a new paper. Medill had a third interest in the venture, Ray a fourth.

Abe Lincoln, a rising young Illinois politician, was one of the first to approve of the new ownership. "I didn't like the paper before you boys took hold of it," he advised them. "It was too much of a Know-Nothing sheet." His confidence was not misplaced. Even before the war, the *Tribune* was by far the most powerful voice in the Middle

West and was exceeded nationally in influence only by its New York namesake.

At the convention which nominated Lincoln in 1860, Medill found himself in direct opposition to Greeley, the man to whom he owed the fortunate start he had made in Chicago. It was characteristic of Medill's bold and arrogant nature that he did not hesitate to treat Greeley ruthlessly as his political enemy. By that time he had come to believe he was as much responsible for the Republican Party as anyone, not excepting Greeley and Raymond, who had done far more.

He had adopted Chicago as his own. "Chicago is the pet Republican city of the Union," he wrote, "the point from which radiate opinions which more or less influence six states." The Cleveland *Plain Dealer* answered sharply: "The principal productions of Chicago are corner lots, statistics and wind."

Medill had some admirable statistics to boast about before long. At the start of the Civil War, the *Tribune's* circulation had been only 18,000; by the end of it, the figure was 40,000 and the rise could not be entirely accounted for by the wartime upsurge in circulation figures everywhere. The *Tribune* was growing up with Chicago, and it was Chicago's favorite paper. After the great fire of 1871, it was the *Tribune* which appeared with its famous editorial, "Cheer Up!" containing the slogan which became at once the whole city's battlecry: "Chicago shall rise again!" Running on a "Fireproof Ticket" the following year, Medill was easily elected mayor.

After he returned to the editor's chair, he applied new vigor to his job, doubled the paper's circulation in a decade, and made it one of the best newspapers in the country, in the professional sense. In other respects, it was characterized by Medill's dogged opposition to every humanitarian or reform measure extant. In the bloody Chicago labor wars, Medill was for stringing up the leaders. His recipe for dealing with the unemployed, whom he equated with strikers, was set forth in an unbelievable editorial of 1884 in which the *Tribune* declared that "the simplest plan," provided "one is not a member of the Humane Society, is to put arsenic in the supplies of food furnished the unemployed or the tramp. This produces death in a short time and is a warning to other tramps to keep out of the neighborhood."

Medill had the confidence of ignorance, not only about the great forces which were shaping America, but about a good many other things as well. Sometimes it was hard to separate the ignorance from simple eccentricity. His passion for simplified spelling—"telegrafed," "infinit" and similar barbarisms—remain in somewhat modified form in the *Tribune* of today. Other fancies were transitory, as for example his conviction that most malfunctions of human affairs were caused by sunspots, until he became equally convinced that microbes were at fault. A reporter who had not heard about the change wrote a piece attributing the plague in Egypt to sunspots. Medill solemnly went through his copy and changed all the "sunspots" to "microbes."

Medill was an opportunist and an apologist for privilege and all its abuses. He made the *Tribune* a vituperative defender of big business, but he also made it a well-written, well-edited newspaper which was highly successful long after the time when its influence had declined to no more than the reinforcement of the convictions of a hard core element in the Republican Party's right wing. It was not only the *Tribune's* professional excellence in other departments than the political, but its devotion to the interests of Chicago which accounted for its success. It may well have been the first to introduce the community service concept as we know it today.

Whatever his faults may have been, and they were formidable, Medill was devoted to news—once more, like Bennett. As he lay dying on his ranch near San Antonio, the last words on his lips were, "What's the news?" If he had lived only three months longer, he would have delighted in one of the most splendid fruits of the *Tribune's* unquestioned news enterprise, its news beat on Dewey's victory at Manila. The *Tribune* beat the whole world with that one, even the President of the United States.

The *Tribune's* political intensity tended to overshadow its contribution to the new idea of public service which was developing in the Middle West. Better examples of what was happening could be seen in Kansas City, and in another part of Chicago, where one of Medill's rivals, Victor Lawson, was building a great community paper in the Chicago *Daily News*.

William Rockhill Nelson, who literally pulled Kansas City out of the mud by hitching it to his *Star,* was the apotheosis of the public service publisher. An Indianan, born in Fort Wayne of parents who had come west from New York and New Jersey, Nelson grew up inexplicably wild, since his father could hardly have been more respectable, a solid businessman and a prominent member of the Episcopal Church. The father, examining the situation, was not so dogmatic about Episcopalianism that he did not recognize the disciplinary values of the Roman Catholic Church. He sent young Nelson to Notre Dame. In two years the Fathers sent him back. Cross-fertilization had failed.

Apparently, William's difficulty was no more than an overabundant supply of energy which had not been channeled. He was not resistant to education; he simply could not sit in classrooms and study halls for very long at a time. When the Civil War came, he was practicing law, having disciplined himself enough to study and be admitted to the bar. His parents kept him out of the conflict, but as soon as it was over, he hurried to the South with a reconstruction plan of his own, inspired by the get-rich-quick schemes which were abundant at the time, and which were succeeding in making some people rich quickly. William was not one of them. His plan to establish a new cotton-growing empire was a dismal failure, and he came home again to Fort Wayne.

For a time he busied himself with the contracting business, building the wooden-block paved roads which were then threading the Middle West. At this endeavor he was more successful, accumulating a fortune of $200,000, immediately lost to him as the result of a partner's defection.

He was also in politics as a Democrat, and managed Tilden's campaign in Indiana. Through that experience he learned about the power of newspapers and was intrigued by it enough to buy a part of the Fort Wayne *Sentinel* in 1878. It took him only two years to conclude that newspaper publishing was what he had been looking for all his life, the one occupation which would absorb his energies. But he would need a larger scope than Fort Wayne provided, he knew, and casting about for the proper arena, he decided on Kansas City, where he founded the *Evening Star* on September 18, 1880.

In the customary manner, the *Star* announced itself as "independent but never neutral," which no one believed, the public having become cynical about the public pronouncements of publishers. Nelson meant it, however, and proved it in the following years by pursuing an entirely independent political course, backing men and issues as he saw them, without regard for party.

It was not its independence that made the *Star* successful, however, although that sturdy quality was not unappreciated by its readers. "Community service," the phrase Nelson used to express his philosophy, was the solid foundation. To him the words meant that in the news columns the *Star* would be predominantly local, a family newspaper for Kansas City families. Where the New York giants, and even Medill to some extent, had considered the editorial page the hard core of the newspaper, Nelson had little regard for it. He thought reporters were the most valuable men on the paper, and the use he intended to make of them was to investigate the deplorable state of Kansas City and, if possible, to bring some order into its lawless, violent atmosphere. It was a sprawling, reckless city, notorious for its corruption, at the mercy of unprincipled men.

The *Star* dug in. It attacked the fraudulent elections, the well-protected gambling and vice rings, the scandalous condition of public transportation, and the unpaved, muddy, shabby physical condition of the town, which looked more like a freshly settled frontier community than an important midwestern crossroads.

Naturally, not even a man of Nelson's energy, equipped with a paper as fearless and able as the *Star,* could hope to bring about complete reform. Kansas City corruption has remained a fact of life into our own time, although its shame has been no worse than that of other American cities, and not nearly as bad as some. But Nelson's campaigning made a substantial dent in the sorry conditions of his time by marshaling every last bit of good will and civic pride among the citizens. Corruption was brought under control, if not eliminated, and best of all, perhaps, the *Star's* program of physical rehabilitation made Kansas City the splendid place of parks and boulevards it is today.

Nelson had promised that the *Star* would be read in every Kansas City home and by the end of the century he had very nearly kept his promise. The *Star,* with its morning edition, the *Times,* was printing thirteen editions a week, including Sunday, for the bargain figure of ten cents. There was also a weekly bulldog edition which Nelson offered to farmers for only twenty-five cents a year.

The *Star* saturated its circulation zone with a completeness which gave Nelson an unprecedented control over his advertisers. Any one who had anything to sell in Kansas City had to use the *Star*, and the publisher knew it. He set his rates high—too high, a good many customers thought, but Nelson was adamant. Advertisers protested, and some tried to boycott the papers or do without them, but the *Star* was far too valuable to be ignored.

Nelson was something new in publishers, a man who stayed out of politics, remained independent of party, and devoted himself to his paper. He was not an accomplished writer; the editorial page was never his province, as it had been with the New York giants and most of the prominent editors elsewhere. As a man, consequently, he was much better liked by his readers and associates, to whom he was a somewhat formidable figure, with his large frame, heavy-set face, and calm dignity. He had a warm, friendly personality, however, and he was generally regarded with affection as well as respect. His closest friends called him "the Colonel."

Before Nelson died in 1915, he had the satisfaction of seeing Kansas City emerge as substantially the metropolis he had envisioned. It was significant of the different kind of journalism he represented that not only did his paper accomplish much for the community, but it did not falter and fail without him to guide it. In later years, the *Star* continued to be one of the best papers in the nation, a training ground for eminent reporters, editors, novelists, playwrights, and radio and television people. It continued to call itself independent, a fiction difficult to maintain when it was widely recognized as the authentic voice of Middle Western Republicanism.

Many of the men the *Star* trained went to the Associated Press, an organization in which Nelson was a director and the *Star's* other noted editor, Roy Roberts, was active most of his life. The man who made the AP the great newsgathering association it became was Victor Fremont Lawson, Nelson's counterpart in Chicago as an advocate of community service.

Lawson's rôle in newspaper history in thus a double one. To both the parts he played he brought an integrity which was an essential element in the public service idea. Bennett, Greeley, Dana, Medill, and even Raymond to a small extent, directed their newspapers along the lines dictated by their political purposes while professing to be acting in the public interest. Men like Nelson and Lawson were much more interested in the integrity of the news, and its use as a means of serving the public.

Lawson was a child of the new times. Born in Chicago of Norwegian parents in 1850, he contrived to get a good education at Phillips Academy before the fortune his father had accumulated in real estate was dissipated in the Fire. The father's death in 1783 brought Victor back to Chicago, where he assumed control of what inheritance remained, particularly a Norwegian daily called the *Skandinaven,* of which his father had been part owner.

The young man was already attracted to newspapers. During high school vacations he had worked in the circulation department of the *Chicago Evening Journal,* and he could not help observing what the *Skandinaven* accomplished in shaping the ideas of the substantial Scandinavian population of the Middle West, where its influence was strong.

But Lawson was not content to run a foreign-language newspaper. He kept his eyes open for a regular paper, one he could afford with his limited capital, and found it in 1876 when he learned that the *Daily News,* founded only six months before, was about to expire. When he offered to buy it from the three men who had started it, they fell on his neck and sold it at once.

The editor of this faltering property, which had been the first penny paper in the Middle West, was Melville Stone, who had gone to grammar school with Lawson. Stone came from Hudson, Illinois, the son of a Methodist circuit-rider and maker of tools for sawmills. He was a born newspaperman, who could set type when he was only ten years old and reported for the Chicago *Republican,* the paper Dana edited after the war, when he was still in his teens. At twenty he covered the convention of 1872 which nominated Grant and sealed Greeley's career.

There was a brief and largely unexplained interlude in which Stone left newspapering for a fling as part owner of an iron foundry and later as the founder of a theater ticket agency, but the Fire wiped out both these enterprises. It was then that he started the *Daily News* with his two partners, publishing it from the same job plant where the *Skandinaven* was printed. Consequently his old school friend Lawson had a first-hand opportunity to see the paper's pathetic decline until it was ready to fall in his lap.

Analyzing the publication's difficulties, Lawson thought he knew what was wrong. It was an old story, the one that had plagued the *Sun* after Ben Day sold it. Stone's partners were businessmen who knew virtually nothing about the newspaper business, and Stone himself had no talent for management. He was an editor and, as Lawson perceived, an exceptionally good one. Lawson was confident of his own ability to manage a newspaper property, but understood that he needed a man like Stone in the editor's chair. It seemed like a combination which would be eminently successful, and so it proved to be.

In acquiring the paper, Lawson was not simply gratifying a personal ambition. His family's immigrant background had given him a strong sense of duty to America; he intended to repay the nation, and Chicago especially, for all it had done for him. Looking at his native city, he saw what Nelson had seen in Kansas City—a shambles of crime and corruption, only on a larger scale. The moral and political climate of Chicago had resisted improvement since the city first rose on the Lake Michigan mud flats, but Lawson, an idealist, intended to try. He was not the first, and the last has not yet been seen.

In common with other publishers, Lawson had a set of principles on which the *Daily News* was to rest, and according to custom, he announced them to his readers. They were refreshingly free of the windy rhetoric which usually characterized these pronouncements. Lawson declared that the *Daily News* would be:

"Candid—That its utterances shall at all times be the exact truth. It is independent but never indifferent;

"Comprehensive—That it shall contain all the news;

"Concise—The *Daily News* is very carefully edited, to the end that the valuable time of its patrons shall not be wasted in reading of mere trifles;

"Clean—That its columns shall never be tainted by vulgarity or obscenity;

"Cheap—That its price shall be put within the reach of all."

Stone and Lawson between them carried out these high-minded principles with astonishing fidelity, and they made a profound impression on the crowded Chicago newspaper scene, where the papers were devoted largely to character assassination, of political figures and each other. Nor did it have the *Tribune's* provincial air, which led Medill to carry on a running warfare with the Eastern papers and everything they represented. The *Daily News* was local in a different way, devoted to reforming Chicago, if that were possible, without the flamboyant tactics Medill and the others used to sell newspapers. The method was much like Nelson's, and the result was in part the same— that is, the paper quickly numbered itself among the nation's best, although Lawson never succeeded in making the impression on Chicago corruption that Nelson did on Kansas City's. The job was too large for a mortal man.

For seven years Stone was the paper's brilliant editor, much liked by Chicagoans for his frank personality and constructive approach to the city's problems, and admired by other newspapermen for the distinction he gave to the news columns. Then ill health caught up with him. After two years of leisurely European travel, he returned to Chicago but not to newspaper life, which he considered too strenuous for him now. As president of the Globe National Bank, he planned to finish his career as a businessman, and to be active in Chicago civic life.

Lawson, meanwhile, was involved in a major battle, not with the *Daily News,* which continued its successful progress, but with the tangled affairs of the Associated Press.

He came into the struggle somewhat obliquely. As a publisher, Lawson was aware that the major economic news of the day centered in the phenomenal and often frightening growth of trusts, which were beginning to strangle American business life under the guise of improving it. One aspect of the day's frenzied financing was immediately under his nose. The New York wire carried the day's quotations from the New York Stock Exchange, along with other financial information, into the

Daily News city room, and Lawson was well aware that it was being manipulated to the greater profit of financiers in New York. Fortunes were being made and lost every week in those unregulated days, and thousands of small investors were ruined in the clashes between the titans.

Lawson had the uncomfortable feeling that the *Daily News* was contributing to the ruin of his readers by carrying these rigged wire reports, on which quotations, for example, might be delayed until the close of the Chicago exchange, when it would be too late for investors outside New York to react to closing prices. Sometimes, too, the financial news was specially phrased to convey particular meanings to those in the inner circles.

The trouble, Lawson realized, lay in the operation of the Associated Press. At the beginning it had functioned as two separate agencies, the New York Associated Press and the Western Associated Press, but in 1882 the divisions had come under the direction of a Joint Executive Committee, consisting of three New York men and two representing the West.

At the time when Lawson was beginning to concern himself with the problem, 1890, there was much dissatisfaction among the Western publishers about the arrangement, particularly because of the rising strength of the AP's rival, the United Press. The AP, as it is now, was a cooperative with elected members holding franchises and sharing the cost of gathering and distributing the news. The UP sold its news on a fee basis to anyone, as a purely commercial organization.

The unrest among the Western publishers was a confirmation of the suspicions Lawson already nourished, that the New York members of the AP's joint committee were engaged in some kind of underground chicanery with the United Press. The Western editors had observed that the UP appeared to be either stealing or otherwise acquiring AP news, a situation sometimes underlined wryly when an erroneous UP story would turn up inexplicably, and uncorrected, on the AP report.

At the 1890 meeting of the Western AP, the members appointed a three-man committee, with Lawson as chairman, to look into the matter. Lawson elected to do most of the committee's work. Working like a good reporter, he spent months in careful investigation. He was certain he was on the right track when some Eastern members of the AP tried to discredit and even abolish his committee. That convinced him, as a man brought up on Chicago corruption, that the evil went right to the top.

When the Western AP met in Detroit the following year, Lawson was able to unfold the whole sordid story. The nation's wire services, AP and UP alike, were actually in the hands of a three-man trust, consisting of Walter Phillips, director of the United Press; William Laffan, business manager of the New York *Sun;* and a financier named John Walsh. These men were the principal owners of the UP, but they had been able to gain control of AP news as well by means of a secret deal, negotiated through private gifts of valuable stock, with five of the AP's executives and members.

The assembled Western AP publishers could scarcely believe it when Lawson told them who these men were. The list began with no other than Charles Anderson Dana himself, who at the moment was chairman of the Joint Committee as well as the *Sun's* distinguished editor. Then came that enterprising battlefield reporter, Whitelaw Reid, now the highly respected head of the *Tribune,* and also the New York AP's representative on the committee. There were also two prominent Western publishers, W. H. Haldeman and Richard Smith, both representatives on the Western AP committee, and William Henry Smith, the combined AP's general manager.

What this highly placed combine had been able to do was shocking. It had, first of all, been giving the UP most of the AP's news without charge, thus reducing the UP's operation costs to a minimum. The resulting inflated profits were divided among the five. The agency's financial news report had been tampered with in several different ways, as Lawson had surmised, which further increased the income of the conspirators. After disclosing other unsavory details, Lawson produced the key document which completed his exposé, a formal contract among the five men legalizing their arrangement. It had been executed in 1888, because the fraud had grown so large and profitable that the partners no longer trusted each other.

If anyone expected the conspirators to wither and retreat in the glare of exposure, they underestimated the character of men like Dana, who brazenly proclaimed in a *Sun* editorial:

> These journals of the Associated Press that are distressed by reason of the superior and more accurate news that is regularly supplied by the United Press are hereby informed that there is no necessity for their remaining in such a state of unhappiness.
>
> The United Press is prepared to furnish the news, foreign and domestic, to any newspaper that is ready and willing to pay a reasonable rate for the same; and that without discrimination on account of race, complexion or previous conditions of servitude.

Dana was referring to the members constituting the Western AP, which had broken away from the New York AP and named a new Executive Committee, with Lawson as chairman. In his editorial Dana was, in effect, making a declaration of war. He and his fellow cabalists meant to wreck the Western AP, if possible, and secure their news-gathering monopoly.

It was a clear issue. If the Western AP members could not present a united front and preserve their organization, it quite obviously meant that the trust would control all wire news and sell it purely for profit. In that case business interests would always come before the integrity of the report, and the idea on which the AP was based would be lost.

To help him form the essential united front, Lawson called on his old friend and editor, Melville Stone, to come back to the news business as general manager of a reorganized AP. Stone could not resist the appeal. As he wrote later:

> A national cooperative news-gathering organization, owned by the newspapers and by them alone, selling no news, making no profits, paying no dividends, simply the agent and servant of the newspapers, was the thing. Those participating should be . . . all equally zealous that in the business of news gathering for their supply there should be strict accuracy, impartiality, and integrity. This was the dream we dreamed . . .

Stone made an immediate move to strengthen the AP by concluding a ten-year contract with Reuter's, the British agency, for exclusive

American rights to its reports, which also included use of Havas, the French agency, and CTC, the Berlin agency operating through Germany and middle and southern Europe. Then, with his hand strengthened, Stone led the battle with the UP for clients, a struggle which the UP was winning at first because it had more capital. But Lawson, Stone and James E. Scripps, editor of the Detroit *Tribune,* rallied the members at an emergency meeting and raised more than a half-million dollars to carry on what was eventually a successful fight. By 1894 the leading papers which had been the UP's chief strength in the midwest had switched to the AP. By 1896, Dana's *Sun* and Hearst's *Journal* were the only UP clients in New York.

In the end, Dana had to file a bankruptcy petition for the UP and the battle was over, at a nearly ruinous cost to the AP of a million dollars. There were some publishers who refused to join the AP, and these men organized the Publishers' Press, which eventually merged with the Scripps-McRae service to form the United Press Associations, now United Press International (UPI), since its acquisition of Hearst's International News Service. The UPI is still the AP's rival, but of course only in the normal business sense, as part of the Scripps-Howard empire.

There were no longer two APs after Lawson's exposure and the events which followed. The new Associated Press remained under Stone's management until he retired in 1921; he gave it the conservative, accurate tone which has been its hallmark. Lawson was the AP's president from 1894 to 1900 and remained as a director until he died in 1925, but most of his energies after the battle with Dana's crowd were directed toward the *Daily News,* particularly to building up a staff of correspondents in Europe and Asia which comprised, at its peak, the best foreign service of any newspaper outside the *New York Times.*

Lawson did not neglect community service. His paper fought hard for a system of postal savings banks, and could take some credit for the 1910 Federal act establishing them. In Chicago itself, the *Daily News* was in the van of every civic reform movement, and Lawson himself gave a great deal of his own time and money to various city organizations.

The monumental integrity and devotion to constructive reform which Lawson brought to the newspaper business contrasted sharply with most of what had gone before in the history of the American newspaper. He and Nelson were the first major figures in the business to demonstrate that a newspaper need be neither a propaganda organ nor a personal weapon, that it had even more power when it was used for unselfish ends. Bennett, Jr., Pulitzer and Hearst were fighting the old reckless fight in New York as the century ended, but in Chicago and Kansas City and other places as well the press was developing what it had never before possessed: a sense of responsibility. That had been the missing ingredient in its progress, and the addition changed the character of the business. Newspapers would soon be both free and responsible, but utopia was still far over the horizon. The questions about the nature of freedom and responsibility were yet to come.

three

The Voice of the South

NEWSPAPERS IN THE SOUTH were slow to mature, another result of a feudal economic system which imprisoned the southern states in an agricultural society while the industrialized North developed the institutions of a sophisticated urban organization. Yet, out of the ruin of the Civil War, there emerged from the South two of the finest newspapers the nation had yet seen, whose publishers did more to reconstruct the area and bind up the country's wounds than any of the Northern giants.

They were contemporaries, these men, whose lives were dedicated to the same basic propositions, but they represented two kinds of southerner. Henry W. Grady was a statesman who might have done as well in Congress as in the newspaper business. Henry Watterson was a newspaperman in his bones, of the same crusading variety as Greeley but with more emotional stability. They were alike in their intense feeling for the region, and their zeal to resurrect it from the disaster of the war.

It was hard for northerners to comprehend the totality of that disaster. After Appomattox the South was a desolated land, its pride crushed, its political and military leaders deposed. The mood was bitter, stunned acceptance; the outlook was bleak but not desperate. Rather it was a question: What next?

In a time of crisis the press normally provides a debating platform where the views of leaders and of the people can be heard and discussed before decisions are made. The postwar South did not have a press capable of such leadership. Many newspapers had been destroyed financially or physically in the war. Those that remained were invincibly provincial, as they had always been. In the agricultural prewar South, the newspapers had reflected the interests of individual communities rather than the region as a whole. Not a single newspaper with a national viewpoint had emerged, and while there were a few able editors, they were not heard in most cases beyond their own circulation areas.

From the misery and confusion of Reconstruction there emerged a young editor who gave a new cast to the journalism of the South and provided a solid answer to the question: What next? Henry W. Grady knew his people and he understood that it was not political guidance they were seeking so much as a philosophy, a direction to take, a constellation of ideas around which they could reshape their future.

Grady was of the South, southern. His father had never been farther north than North Carolina, from which he had emigrated to Georgia. His mother came from Athens, the quiet little Georgia university town where Henry was born in 1850, and she was as intricately related to a galaxy of other Athens families as a southern lady ought to be. Henry grew up with these aunts and uncles and cousins and traditions. When the war came, he was old enough to understand what it meant when his father rode off as a captain in the Highland Guards. The family heard from its absent head frequently. He had been made a colonel. He was marching with his men in the direction of Virginia. Then the official telegram of regret: Colonel William Grady was dead on the battlefield of Petersburg.

In the aftermath of the war, Henry pursued a quiet Athens life, finishing the local high school and going on to the University of Georgia, not many blocks from his home. Women considered him lovable. Men thought him highly talented, particularly in speaking and writing. He joined the Methodist Church during his freshman year at college, taking in with him the goodlooking girl, Julia King, to whom he had just become engaged. After graduation he went up north to the University of Virginia and studied law for three years, interspersing his studies with occasional pieces for the Atlanta *Constitution*.

Thus far the model young man had lived a model life, in the approved tradition. But sometime during his law studies he determined to go into the newspaper business, and as soon as he had his Virginia degree, he became editor of the *Courier,* in Rome, Georgia. No aspiring northern newspaperman could have taken such a large step, but it was not difficult for Henry. He came from a rich, well-known and well-connected Georgia family, he had the advantages of an excellent education, and he possessed the superb confidence which all these attributes in combination can give a young man.

His career on the *Courier* was brief. The publisher, his boss, told him to leave local politics strictly alone, and when Grady examined them, he understood why. The town's politicians were utterly corrupt, with the knowledge and connivance of all three local papers. As a young man with high ideals and no real knowledge of the world, Grady was not disposed to sit by idly. Disregarding the publisher's instructions, he made a start at exposing and denouncing the scoundrels, and found himself quickly out of work.

But Grady had resources other men in a similar position did not have. He went out and bought the other two papers, merged them, and resumed his attack. Like Greeley, he was betrayed by the people he thought he knew so well. The citizens of Rome were outraged to have the existing order challenged and threatened by a young upstart just out of college. They were happy with their local corruption; it was an old friend with good connections. Henry's paper was deserted by readers and advertisers in no time.

Taken aback momentarily, Grady went home to Athens and married Julia in 1871. He was by no means through with the newspaper business, and his idealism was only slightly dented. He meant to try it again in a larger town, and finding two partners with the same high-minded temperament, he established the *Herald* in Atlanta. Again, it was a miscalculation. Atlantans were not moved by the youthful high spirits of the *Herald* and it went out of business, taking with it the last of the money Grady had inherited from his father.

There ensued a period of amiable fumbling. Grady freelanced for such papers as the Atlanta *Constitution* and the Augusta *Chronicle,* turned down a job as editor of the Wilmington *Star* because he thought it wasn't good enough for him, and eventually came up to New York to look for work. There he fell into the hands of James Gordon Bennett,

Jr., a man as far from Grady in temperament as though he lived in outer space. Strangely, they liked each other. That may have been because nearly everybody liked Henry. In his earnest, boyish, idealistic enthusiasm, he still seemed somewhat the college sophomore but people were drawn to his warm personality. They were always wanting to help him, and the lean, dour junior Bennett was no exception. He gave Grady a job as Atlanta correspondent.

It was a pleasant assignment which Henry enjoyed, but he had not given up his dream of owning a newspaper and he waited only for a way to finance it. The way appeared in the person of Cyrus W. Field, whom Grady met in 1879 and charmed out of a $20,000 loan which he used to buy a quarter-interest in the Atlanta *Constitution*.

The opportunity brought out Grady's best qualities, which included a superb news sense, a gift for analysis, and an ability to write directly to the people. In a series of editorials and articles, he gave them his answer to the question, What next?

Southerners, he said, needed to diversify their crops and break the habits of the past. They should take an inventory of their local resources and find out the best means to develop them. Over and over he insisted that the South must attract and build industry to survive; it could no longer exist on agriculture alone. With a daring uncommon for the time, he told his fellow southerners bluntly that the Negro stood in a new relationship to them, whether they liked it or not, and somehow black and white must learn to live together.

His readers muttered about that one, and some wrote him the abusive letters and made the threats which are still common in the South now. Grady was ahead of his time, but the stand he took gave the *Constitution* a leadership in race relations which it has never lost. In his plea for a new, industrial South, Grady was selling another idea which would not be quickly taken up, but it was the seed from which the flowering is visible today. Grady was mistaken only in thinking it could be done with reasonable speed.

These ideas gave him a national prominence. In the South he was hailed as a man who was turning the eyes of southerners away from the lost past toward a hopeful future. In the North, his editorials were reprinted everywhere, welcomed by people who were weary of hatred and eager to make the Union stronger. A gap seemed to have been bridged at last on the December night in 1886 when Grady made a speech on "The New South" to a meeting of the New England Club in New York. He gave it with all the flourishes of southern oratory—indeed, of all oratory in that era—but what he said was considered to be one of the finest speeches ever made from an American platform, and it was declaimed for decades later in high schools and colleges.

It was a speech which enjoyed the widest possible distribution, and made Grady in demand everywhere as a speaker. He was a willing traveler, because it gave him an opportunity to spread what now amounted to a gospel with him. He had alternate speeches, variations of the same subject, and delivered them in opera houses, theaters, from club room platforms—anywhere he was invited to stand. It was a crusade which led to his death in a cold New England December. Speaking on "The Race Problem In The South" at Boston in 1889, he contracted pneumonia. He was able to travel home to Atlanta, and died two days before Christmas. The whole nation mourned for him.

After his death the *Constitution* carried on in his idealistic image under the leadership of two brilliant colleagues, Clark Howell and Joel Chandler Harris, whose superb talents as a newspaperman have been almost completely overshadowed by the fame of his Uncle Remus tales. Grady's own name and his principles have been perpetuated in the school of journalism at the University of Georgia named for him.

If Grady had not died so young, he might well have become an even larger figure in journalism and the nation's political life. As it was, he left the stage to the South's only other commanding figure on the newspaper scene, Henry Watterson, and "Marse Henry," as he was known, carried on in his own way Grady's effort to convert the Old Confederacy into the New South.

Watterson was another kind of man. By southern standards, he was barely southern, having been born in Washington, D.C. and brought up there and in the Tennessee home of his Congressman father. Moreover, his newspaper, the Louisville *Courier-Journal* was in the border state of Kentucky, and its office today is in fact no more than four blocks south of the Mason-Dixon Line.

Yet it would have been difficult to find a man more thoroughly

southern than Watterson. He was a commanding figure the like of
whose shaggy eyebrows were not seen again until John L. Lewis.
They overshadowed the one eye he had lost when he was growing up
and the bright blue right eye which had a peculiarly penetrating power.
His mustache and goatee, along with his string tie and frock coat,
made him look like the incarnation of the Kentucky colonel, and his
high, clear voice could fill a large hall. As Henry Villard wrote: "Whenever he appeared on a Southern platform, men and women beheld the
'Lost Cause.' . . ."

He was not, however, a professional southerner. Booker T. Washington, who knew him well, could testify to that. "If there is anywhere
a man who has broader or more liberal ideas concerning the Negro,
or any undeveloped, I have not met him," Washington said. Watterson
hated the cartoonists who depicted him as a stereotyped southern
Colonel, mint julep in hand, lounging picturesquely amid the magnolias
and white columns. It was true that he presided in patriarchal glory over
a splendid Southern mansion, Mansfield, whose verandas and green
lawns made it the Tara of the border states, but Watterson hated to
be called colonel and he drank champagne, still wine and beer, pre-
ferring them in that order.

His early years were as untypical as Grady's had been conventional.
Growing up alternately in the capital and in the family's ancestral
homes in Tennessee, he had the best of both worlds. He demonstrated
such remarkable musical talent at an early age that his parents thought
he might have a career as a concert pianist, but the loss of sight in
his eye and a weakness in his left hand ended that idea. Not,
however, before he had accompanied, at the age of twelve, a little
nine-year-old friend, Adelina Patti. Henry's formal education was
scant, no more than a brief session in the Philadelphia Protestant
Episcopal Academy, but he learned much from his insatiable reading
and from meeting and talking with his father's Congressional friends.

Watterson's playground was often the House of Representatives.
There he saw the aged John Quincy Adams stricken at his desk and
carried out of a shocked House to his death. He visited the Hermitage
with his father, and Jackson dandled him on his knee. "Marse Henry,"
indeed, knew every President from Jackson to Harding, and he knew

Coolidge, Hoover and Franklin Roosevelt before they reached the White House.

It was small wonder that young Henry grew up with a passionate interest in politics, but his career ideas were directed toward newspapers. There, too, he had the example of his father, who became a newspaper editor in Tennessee after he left the House. With the benefit of his father's connections, he had no trouble getting a newspaper job, first as a reporter on the *New York Times,* then on the Washington *Daily States* in 1853. He covered Lincoln's inauguration for that paper, and the new President had no more sincere admirer. Watterson was a Democrat but he was a Union man by profound conviction, and in his lifetime he never wavered in his devotion to Lincoln.

The coming of the war caught him, therefore, in a cruel dilemma. He was offered a lieutenant-colonelcy in the Union Army but turned it down, not because he was unsympathetic to the Union cause but because he thought the South could not resist long. He decided to go home to Tennessee and wait for the war to blow over, as he was certain it soon would. Such a course was impossible in a state where fervor for the cause not yet lost was at a high pitch. "The boys were all gone to the front, and the girls were . . . all crazy," Watterson recalled in his memoirs. The Union man had to join the secessionist army.

It was a peculiar service. He was assigned to General Polk's staff, but illness kept him from the field, and apparently it was decided in Richmond that, with his special background, he would be more valuable as a propagandist than a soldier. Sent to a busy newspaper propaganda mill in Nashville, Watterson was an editor in uniform until Union troops took the city. Not long after, he was placed in charge of the official paper in Chattanooga, which he called *The Rebel* and converted into an unabashed propaganda machine for the Confederate Army.

Driven out again by the Union advance, Watterson was on the staffs of several generals, including Hood and Johnston, until he was selected for a highly dangerous secret mission. He was instructed to try to reach Liverpool, England, and make a deal with the British in which the Confederacy would send cotton in exchange for badly needed cash loans. Fortunately, perhaps, he was unable to get out of the country, and the Confederate government made him an editor again, in Montgomery, Alabama.

After the war, Watterson went into the newspaper business in earnest, first for the Cincinnati *Evening Times,* where he became editor at $75 a week, then on the *Nashville Republican Banner* after a brief interval during which he got married and operated his own Nashville paper.

While he was on the *Banner,* he was the recipient of two offers from Louisville. One was from Walter N. Haldeman, publisher of the *Courier,* whom he had met while he was on *The Rebel,* inviting him to come in as editor. The other was from the rival *Journal.* Its aging owner needed help to run the paper. Watterson proposed to Haldeman what he thought was obvious, a merger of the properties, but when Haldeman showed no interest in the idea, he accepted the *Journal's* offer. There followed a six-month interval while the inevitable was postponed and the two papers engaged in polite warfare. The merger took place on November 8, 1868, and Watterson became editor of the combined *Courier-Journal,* a position he was to occupy with increasing distinction for the next fifty years.

Henry Grady was only eighteen at that time, and Watterson anticipated him in the *Courier-Journal* with an editorial campaign to regenerate the South and heal the breach with the North. But where Grady was to argue for social and economic principles, Watterson showed the effects of his political background by proposing a practical deal: in return for some of the rights and privileges it had lost to the victorious North, the South would guarantee civil and legal rights to the Negroes.

It was the kind of proposition not likely to satisfy anyone. Northern liberals like Greeley and Carl Schurz backed him, but other liberals argued that the Constitution already guaranteed Negro rights and it was the duty of the Federal government to enforce them. Abolitionists of the more extreme sort asserted that it would be a mockery to restore anything to the beaten Rebels. On the southern side, many unreconstructed Rebels wanted no deals at all with the North, particularly if it meant granting more than the irreducible minimum of freedom to the Negroes.

No deal could be made in any case, obviously, if the Washington climate was not favorable; consequently Watterson went to the Liberal-Republican nominating convention of 1872, in Cincinnati, determined to get the nomination for Greeley. He had the help of several other eminent editors—Carl Schurz, Samuel Bowles, Murat Halstead, editor of the Cincinnati *Commercial;* Whitelaw Reid and Horace White.

Watterson was disappointed by Greeley's crushing defeat at the polls in November, but he believed that the campaign had done something to bring North and South closer together, and with Greeley gone, he turned to Samuel J. Tilden as "the ideal statesman" who would realize Liberal-Republican ideals. For two years Watterson was one of the men who worked carefully behind the scenes to escort Tilden into the White House, but once more he was frustrated in the famous disputed election of 1876.

This second defeat did something to "Marse Henry's" political psyche. He abandoned party politics, declared himself independent, and never again found an occupant of the White House with whom he could agree for an entire term. His quarrels with Presidents and his stands on public issues were often hard to explain.

Of Cleveland, when he was nominated for the third time, Watterson asserted: "I will not vote for his nomination, if his be the only name presented, because I firmly believe that his nomination will mean the marching through a slaughter house to an open grave, and I refuse to be a party to such folly." For Theodore Roosevelt he used the phrase, "Man On Horseback," and called him "as sweet a gentleman as ever scuttled a ship or cut a throat."

These were not, it must be understood, the mutterings of an obscure writer in a small city. By this time Watterson was so noted as an editor that his editorial pronouncements were considered news by the wire services when they dealt with national politics. His feud with President Roosevelt attracted national attention, and by a curious coincidence, it duplicated the attacks on a later Roosevelt by other strongminded editors. There was a warning of things to come in Watterson's declaration that Roosevelt was a paranoiac who intended to be dictator of the country, and urged other members of the family to put this psychopath away.

When the first World War broke out in 1914, Watterson was perhaps the first American editor to exclaim, "To hell with the Hohenzollerns and the Hapsburgs!" He urged United States entry from the beginning, and his editorials on the subject won him the Pulitzer Prize in 1917. A year later he retired and went to Florida, where he wrote his two-volume autobiography, "Marse Henry," and died in 1921.

Watterson was a personality, and unfortunately he was more and more aware of it as he grew older. Much of the time he was playing himself. If he had been less of a personality he might have been more effective as a crusading editor, but even so the thousands of words he poured into his editorials did much to further the ideas about the South that he and Grady both believed in. Sometimes it seemed that he meant to drown his opponents in words. After the turn of the century, editorials were beginning to be much shorter in most major dailies—about the length they are today—but Watterson was incapable of saying anything in a short space. His editorials ran anywhere from two to nine columns in length.

Age mellowed him and he came to regard even editorials and the state of the nation with a wry disrespect. When Tom Wallace, a veteran *Courier-Journal* man, visited him at Mansfield during the old man's last illness, and mentioned that a serious discussion about the editorial page was going on at the office, Watterson remarked, "I do not see the slightest reason for anxiety. I read all of the editorials every day. I don't see anything in the paper that shouldn't be said, or anything that, without the slightest loss, might not be left unsaid."

His final opinion of the American newspaper was ascerbic. He wrote in his autobiography: "Neither its individuality, nor its self-exploitation, scarcely its grandiose pretension, remains. . . . There continues to be printed in large type an amount of shallow stuff that would not be missed if it were omitted altogether. But, except as a bulletin of yesterday's doings, limited, the daily newspaper counts for little, the single advantage of the editor—in case there is an editor—that is, one clothed with supervising authority who 'edits'—being that he reaches the public with his lucubrations first, the sanctity that once hedged the editorial 'we' long since departed."

What Watterson missed in newspapers, one supposes, was the kind of personal journalism he himself represented. The *Courier-Journal* was a one-man show while he edited it, and because of the force of his personality, it was a constantly entertaining and politically significant show. When he was gone, however, it went on being a distinguished newspaper, one of the top half-dozen in the nation today.

Together, Watterson and Grady exemplified a liberal, progressive element in southern journalism which persists today in the cities where they established great newspapers. It is to be found, too, in a few other southern cities, oddly enough, in a region where the general character of the press is still provincial, by and large. If one were listing a dozen of the best metropolitan dailies in the United States, four of them would be southern newspapers. Another four or five in smaller communities would have to be counted as not only well-edited and progressive, but courageous in the face of bigotry and extreme social pressures.

The progress the South has made in the past century toward the better industrial life Watterson and Grady dreamed for it must be attributed at least in part to the kind of leadership they provided in a period of crisis. The rôle their newspapers played, and are playing now, in the creation of a new South is one of the best examples extant of the press truly acting in the public interest.

four

The Sensational West

WHILE THE SOUTH WAS DEVELOPING A SENSE of responsibility in its newspapers, thanks to the two Henrys, Grady and Watterson, the West was exhibiting a kind of journalism consistent with its wide-open character.

The West of common usage in the latter half of the nineteenth century, it must be remembered, was not always what we know today as the Far West. By "West" people often meant the broad continent from Ohio to the Pacific. Thus the Western Associated Press was made up of what would now be considered midwestern newspapers. But Cincinnati, Chicago, Denver and San Francisco had one thing in common. They were inhabited by a people much closer to the frontier than those in the settled cities of the East Coast, and they liked their journalism raw. A few good, responsible newspapers did well, but most of them were as flamboyant as a saloon dance hall on Saturday night.

The contrast and the conflict could be seen in Cincinnati, a solid, cultured town settled by German immigrants. There "Marse Henry's" friend, Murat Halstead, had made the *Commercial Gazette* one of the finest newspapers west of the Alleghenies. Halstead's chief stock in trade was a sure instinct for news, and an extraordinary talent for developing it, like the Bennetts. Active in liberal Republican politics, he was also an excellent political writer whose convention stories helped to make him well known.

As good a newspaper as the *Commercial Gazette* was, however, it had an uphill struggle in Cincinnati against John R. McLean's

sensational *Enquirer,* the local Democratic organ. Halstead gave up
the battle in 1890 and went East to be editor of the Brooklyn *Standard-
Union,* at sixty-one, but was not nearly as successful in his new sur-
roundings. After his departure, the Cincinnati field was left to the
Times-Star, owned by William Howard Taft's half-brother, Charles
P., and his two-cent, eight-page paper (the others had been five cents)
became the high tariff Republican organ of the town. It was soon in
competition with E. W. Scripps' *Evening Post,* which took the circulation lead by virtue of a sensational and successful fight against a corrupt
city hall.

Similarly in Chicago, Victor Lawson's conservative, civic-minded
Daily News had to fight both Medill's aggressive, often loud-voiced
Tribune and Wilbur F. Storey's *Times.* The complicated and turbulent
story of Chicago journalism is replete with incredible tales, but "Old
Storey" and his *Times* may well be the hardest to believe. His kind
of newspapering accurately forecast what was about to happen in New
York with the advent of Pulitzer and Hearst.

He was an eccentric, like so many of the others, and in some
respects resembled the two Bennetts, but he had his own special driving madness. A dissipated tyrant, he nevertheless had the acute news
sense characteristic of all the great editors of the nineteenth century.
With his wild white hair and beard, he was a familiar figure in Chicago,
particularly in the courts, where he once had twenty-four libel suits
pending against him at the same time.

Chicagoans loved the kind of raw meat Storey fed them. The *Times*
led the *Tribune* in circulation, although not in advertising, as long as
Storey was editor. He gave his readers lottery drawings, plenty of
explicit sex, and gory stories about crime. The paper was most noted,
and quoted, for its headlines, in which alliteration and puns were
combined with unabashed editorializing. "Death's Debauch" read
the headline over a railroad wreck story; "The House That Vanderbilt" heralded a piece on a Vanderbilt will. Storey loved to collect
short, scandalous pieces from the wire copy and run them under
such blanket heads as "Sexual Skulduggery," or "Frail Females."

For some macabre reason, Storey and his chief headline writer,
Horatio W. Seymour, the telegraph editor, were especially fond of

stories about hangings. One was headlined "Feet First," with the next deck reading, "That's The Way They Shoved Bill Green Down Among The Fireworks." On another the head was, "A Drop Too Much." But the *Times* surpassed itself with the one it used on a hanging in which four repentent murderers were executed following last-minute prayers. "Jerked To Jesus," shocked Chicagoans read.

In his later years, Storey exhibited so many aberrations in his personal life, as in the *Times,* that it was no surprise when he was adjudged insane, and died soon after in 1884.

Nothing that happened in Chicago or elsewhere, however, could match the fantastic medicine show put on in Denver by Frederick Gilmer Bonfils and Harry Heye Tammen, or the struggle for dominance in violent San Francisco between men like the young William Randolph Hearst and Fremont Older. This was journalism which bridged the centuries not only chronologically, but in the mixture of old and new ways of making newspapers. It was personal journalism of the Bennett variety, carried well into a new century in which the business institutionalizing of the press was steadily going forward elsewhere. But it was also a forerunner of the "jazz journalism" of the Twenties, which in itself was only an extension of the "yellow journalism" of the Nineties. The bad old days disappeared from American journalism reluctantly, with as many farewell appearances as a retiring diva. In Denver and San Francisco they made a farewell flourish reminiscent of New York before the Civil War, making what had gone before and what was to come in the Twenties seem no more than prelude and postlude.

Only a taste of the strong brew provided by Bonfils and Tammen in Denver can be provided here. The whole gamey mess has been preserved with wit and affection by Gene Fowler in his classic "Timber Line," which records the happenings in Denver in vivid detail.

Frederick Bonfils, the real entrepreneur of the partnership, came from a background so respectable it could not possibly suggest the kind of life he was to lead. Born near Troy, Missouri, in 1860, his father was a probate judge and his mother a charming Virginia girl. He was one of seven children. His grandfather had been a modern language professor in the universities of Alabama and Transylvania, and his grandmother was a Boston girl directly descended from John Alden.

Bonfils went to public school in Troy, where his brief temper and restless nature marked him early as a problem to society. Deciding on a military career, he obtained an appointment to West Point, but he left the school without graduating. It was a short step down the Hudson to New York, where he worked for a time in a bank and married a girl from suburban Peekskill. Then he decided to try teaching, and got a job as drillmaster and mathematics instructor in a military school at Canon City, Colorado. For reasons not clear, but they were probably financial, he came back home again to Troy, where he worked in his father's insurance office and served as a clerk in the Missouri legislature.

Selling insurance disclosed to Bonfils that he possessed a talent for salesmanship and promotion which might be put to better use. Making a natural move from insurance to real estate, Bonfils sold parts of Texas to Missouri and Kansas emigrants, and he was present at the spectacular opening of Oklahoma Territory in 1889, where his subsequent dealings gave him enough money to get into something larger and illegal.

He moved into the Kansas City of William Rockhill Nelson, which the editor had not yet succeeded in reforming, and there, protected by numerous aliases, he began to operate the Little Louisiana Lottery. Bonfils was ideally cast for this part. Dark, trim and handsome, with a neat black mustache, he looked like Clark Gable playing a Mississippi River gambler.

Inevitably he came to the attention of Nelson and the *Star,* who were eventually successful in getting him arrested. But the authorities made no effort to keep him in jail. They escorted him to the city line and urged him to keep on going, understanding, if Nelson did not, that it was scarcely possible to confine Bonfils. If peace and sanity were preserved, he had to be eliminated.

Perhaps remembering the salubrious climate of Colorado, where he was unknown, Bonfils drifted out to Denver, and there in the long, mirrored bar of the Windsor Hotel he met the man who was to be his partner, Harry Tammen. The historic year was 1895.

Tammen had taken a more direct route to the outer limits of respectability. He was a Baltimore boy, four years older than Bonfils, the son of a German druggist who had come to America as an attaché of the Netherlands consulate. His father had died when he was eight, and Tammen was cast upon the world with only a few terms at Knapp's Academy to suffice for his education. His career began as pin boy in a bowling alley.

It was not long before Tammen discovered the occupation for which he was probably best qualified—bartending. Again, the casting could not have been better. To cite another modern instance, he looked like the character of Joe the Bartender created by Jackie Gleason on television. He was chubby and goodnatured, the kind of man to whom strangers found themselves giving confidences.

Coming to Denver in 1880, Tammen soon presided over the bar at the Windsor, where Bonfils found him, but he also had two profitable side ventures. One of these was a piece of Denver promotional literature called *The Great Divide,* which Tammen chose to call a newspaper. The other was a curio shop, where mementos of the West's glorious past were sold to unwary tourists. Tammen boasted that on a good day he could sell the scalp of a single famous Indian chief seven or eight times. Other items in the shop were of similar authenticity.

Bonfils had never met a confidence man abler than himself until the day he encountered Tammen, who talked him into investing $12,500 of his Kansas City money in a nearly extinct afternoon paper, the Denver *Evening Post,* established three years before. Bonfils and Tammen took it over on October 28, 1895, dropped "Evening" from the title and began what was to be the strangest career in newspaper publishing.

The partners knew nothing about journalism, but they knew a great deal about human nature and they understood the freewheeling nature of Denver. They had two policies. One was to proclaim as loudly and as often as possible that everything the *Post* did was for the Denver public's good. The *Post* cuddled up to its readers with slogans like "Your Big Brother," "The Paper With A Heart and Soul," and "So The People May Know."

The *Post's* second policy was to attack everything in sight with the biggest headline type and reddest ink in the shop, and with whatever other device came readily to hand. They began by exposing lotteries, a subject on which Bonfils was an authority. It was not a random choice. Bonfils had been in Kansas City long enough to see how successful Nelson was by concentrating on local news and crusading for the public welfare. Perversely adopting the ideas of his one-time enemy, Bonfils announced that the *Post* would operate on the principle that "a dog fight in a Denver street is more important than a war in Europe."

In carrying out this policy, the partners divided their talents. Tammen was recognized as the promoter, who thought up outrageous stunts to keep the paper under the public's nose—as though it could ever forget. Bonfils, the shrewd gambler, was in charge of the money drawer. By agreement he kept it shut tightly for thirteen years, plowing back the profits to put the *Post* in an unassailable financial position. By that time the circulation had jumped from 4,000 to 83,000, more than the combined circulations of the other three Denver papers.

After the *Post* was financially secure. Bonfils unlocked the safe. He put himself and Tammen on the payroll at salaries of $1,000 a week; they had taken only modest sums before. Then he moved the paper into one of the best locations in town, where he indulged his peculiar passion for red, which he had been able to express before only in the *Post's* screaming red banner headlines. He caused the walls of his and Tammen's office to be painted a flashing red. They called it the Red Room, but Denverites had another name for it—"the Bucket of Blood."

Bonfils and Tammen also moved the *Post* into high gear, now that they could afford to defend libel suits. No one in the city, or the state for that matter, was safe. The suits were not long in coming, but the partners took them in easy stride and went on to new outrages. Sometimes the victims, in the manner of the early days, came into the office to fight a few rounds with the owners.

One of these resistances nearly ended the partnership. Polly Pry, the paper's beautiful sob sister, whose real name was Leonel Campbell, had written a story about a man accused of murdering and eating his partner while they were hunting for gold. The supposed cannibal went to jail, from which the partners tried to extricate him with the help of a lawyer. Somehow a misunderstanding developed with the lawyer, who appeared in the Red Room one day and fired a volley at the proprietors with his side-arms. The counselor's aim was abominable, however, and he was further discouraged by pretty Polly Pry, who hurried in and seized him in her arms. The partners escaped with minor wounds.

On another occasion the *Post's* plant was not so fortunate. As a friend of the people, it had been presumed to be on labor's side during a violent strike against the Denver transit system, but it proved instead to be advocating the management cause. A mob of strikers, sensing an inconsistency in the paper's attitude, swarmed into the *Post* building and were taking it carefully apart until they were restrained. They did not stop to read the pious motto over the entrance: "Oh, Justice, when expelled from other habitations, make this thy dwelling place."

Sometimes, when it suited the proprietors, the *Post* did give shelter to justice. It fought for reforms in the child labor practices of the times, and in the management of prisons. It was always alert to the straying fingers of public officials. But it surpassed itself one winter when the cost of coal had reached what Bonfils deemed an unreasonable level. The *Post* would keep its readers warm and happy, he declared, and promptly leased some mines out of which he trucked coal around town and sold it to *Post* customers at considerably lower rates.

Bonfils was also a positive force in selling Colorado as the garden spot of America. Unlike Tammen, he was an outdoors lover who honestly loved his adopted state, if he could be honest about anything. Colorado was as much religion as he cared to have. Like a doting mother, Bonfils saw no evil when he looked at the Colorado landscape. If a cloudburst precipitated avalanches or flash floods in the state, causing severe damage and misery, it was never treated as a disaster in the *Post*. Bonfils only remarked calmly that the rain would be good for the farmers, who, as everyone should know, raised the finest crops in the nation.

Tammen produced endless promotion stunts for the paper, which were regarded amusedly by the public, except for the *Post's* enemies, as simply outbursts of its personality. Most of these were unexceptional —affairs like treasure hunts, planting an Eve in Estes Park Garden of Eden, or tossing pennies to Denver children from the *Post's* balcony. Others were more spectacular, as when Bonfils traveled all the way to Africa to meet his friend Theodore Roosevelt when the President emerged from the veldt after one of his safaris.

The most startling of the partners' idiosyncrasies, however, was not a promotion stunt but developed from the honest streak lying deep in Tammen. Bonfils honestly loved Colorado; Tammen was equally and sincerely devoted to animals, especially elephants. After he became a rich and prosperous publisher, he decided to satisfy this passion by starting a circus and operating it as a sideline. At first it was no more than a dog-and-pony show, which Tammen named for his sports editor, Otto Floto, but it prospered, like everything else Tammen touched, and in time it was the Sells-Floto circus, second only to the Ringlings and Barnum.

Somehow the circus became a crusade. There was a long legal wrangle with the Ringling combine, which Bonfils attacked with virulent editorials aimed at what he called the "circus trust." Sells-Floto, it seemed, was constantly involved in the courts, or else its employees were chasing escaped animals across the countryside. Tammen loved it all.

On two occasions the proprietors of the *Post* took on the United States government. In 1914, they were under the scrutiny of the Interstate Commerce Commission when an ICC hearing disclosed that the Rock Island Railroad had paid $60,000 to the *Post* for a purpose which it quaintly listed as "editorial advertising." Since the railroad was regulated by the government and the *Post* enjoyed—indeed, luxuriated in—freedom of the press, nothing came of it.

In 1924, however, a far more disturbing incident occurred. Bonfils was called before the Senate committee investigating the Teapot Dome scandal, which succeeded in extracting from him the information that the *Post* had been attacking Harry F. Sinclair, chief figure in the scandal, not out of an excess of virtue but through connivance with a man who had brought suit against Sinclair, whose payoff of a million dollars had stopped the suit and the *Post's* attacks simultaneously. The American Society of Newspaper Editors was sufficiently aroused by this episode to recommend through its Committee on Ethics that Bonfils be expelled from the organization, but he escaped on a technicality. Three years later, having saved face, he resigned.

Tammen died while this affair was going on, and Bonfils was left alone to carry on a battle of a different kind, which he regarded as much more serious. That was the first real challenge to his position in Denver from another paper, and it caught the *Post* financially unprepared. A personal quirk, perhaps a desire for revenge, had impelled Bonfils to buy the Kansas City *Post* in 1908 and fight the *Star,* but his Denver methods had been viewed with horror by Kansas City and the paper had been a constant drain on profits at home until the partners sold it in 1922 to the Kansas City *Journal* for a million and a quarter dollars. Considering that they had paid only $250,000 for it, the profit was handsome, but it had been an expensive fancy.

Now, in 1926, Bonfils found himself facing a competitor calculated to tax every resource he and the *Post* possessed. At the moment the paper was making a million dollars a year and its circulation was 150,000 daily and twice that on Sunday, but it was no more than enough to counter a bustling publisher named Roy Howard, whose Scripps-Howard League had just bought the *Rocky Mountain News.*

The *News* had never been a serious competitor. It represented an amalgamation of three papers which John C. Shaffer, publisher of the Chicago *Evening Post* and some papers in Indiana, had engineered, apparently believing in what the consolidation of Bonfils' opposition would do for him. Absentee ownership and the *Post's* hammer-and-tongs counter-warfare had discouraged Shaffer. As a result, Bonfils found himself facing the competition of chain journalism for the first time, and what was worse, an adversary who was more than a match for him.

Howard was also a bridge between the centuries, in a sense—that is, he was a personal journalist with an unerring news sense, but at the same time he was one of the new century's ablest business managers of newspaper properties.

For two years these men fought it out in an expensive, fantastic conflict which had the people of Denver bemused. It was a round-the-clock battle, because Bonfils started a morning edition and Howard answered with an afternoon edition. Every circulation stunt that had ever been seen in New York or Chicago was attempted, and the contestants produced some of their own invention. At one point the papers were locked in a contest in which they offered free gasoline in varying amounts up to five gallons for every customer who inserted a want ad in the Sunday editions. While it lasted, every Sunday was a Roman holiday in Denver as the citizenry went joyriding and the newsboys staggered under the weight of Sunday editions of more than a hundred pages, predominantly classified ads.

The competition might have gone on until either Bonfils or Howard were exhausted and possibly bankrupt, but the Chamber of Commerce intervened and negotiated a truce, to the relief of the participants and the exhausted public. The extra editions were dropped, and no one missed them.

It was not the last battle of Bonfils' stormy career. He was fighting right up to the end. In 1932, when he was seventy-two, he filed a $200,000 libel suit against the *News* for publishing a news story quoting a speech at a political convention by the publisher of the Grand Junction *Sentinel,* Walter Walker, who had said of Bonfils: "The day will come when some persecuted man will treat that rattlesnake as rattlesnakes should be treated, and there will be general rejoicing . . . Bonfils is a public enemy and has left the trail of a slimy serpent across Colorado for thirty years."

Preparing to prove the truth of the publication in court, the *News* lawyers drew up a forty-one point bill of particulars which would have been irreparably damaging to Bonfils if it had ever been heard in court. He knew it and kept postponing the actual joining of the issue by various legal subterfuges. In the midst of the maneuvering, Bonfils went to the hospital for a minor ear abscess operation. In less than a week he was dead of toxic encephalitis and pneumonia. Baptized a Roman Catholic on his deathbed, presumably at the wish of his wife, who was a member of the Church, he left behind him a bookful of legends and eight million dollars. Tammen had left two million. In their wills both men bequeathed much of their fortunes to good works of various kinds. These bequests must have been the result of conscience; they could hardly have resulted from a lack of imagination.

Something of the newspaper climate in Denver could be observed on a larger scale in San Francisco, where the bohemian, cosmopolitan atmosphere was even more friendly to journalistic mayhem. As in the case of Chicago, the story of San Francisco newspapermaking can hardly be encompassed in a few pages. Its full flavor can only be suggested.

For years after the Civil War, the Golden Gate scene was dominated by a single paper, the *Chronicle*. It had been started in 1865 by two young brothers, Charles and Michael H. De Young, St. Louis boys who were brought to San Francisco by their parents in the early Fifties. Noting the city's unusual interest in the theater, the De Youngs began publishing a free theater program sheet which they called the San Francisco *Dramatic Chronicle*. It was a brash, youthful effort, only four pages and not much bigger than a letterhead, but it contained short pieces by writers like Mark Twain and Bret Harte, along with brief paragraphs of San Francisco news. It was so popular with San Franciscans that it soon expanded into a regular newspaper, and was enterprising enough to be the only paper in town to get out extras on Lincoln's assassination. The word "Dramatic" was dropped from its title in 1868, when it became a regular two-cent newspaper.

For the next quarter-century the *Chronicle* led the field in San Francisco. It was a newspaper on the lines laid down by Nelson and Lawson, a community service paper which fought civic corruption, campaigned for civic improvements and extended its horizons to boost California. In fighting to reform the state constitution, and against land monopoly and the machinations of the powerful railroad barons who were building the Southern Pacific empire, the paper inevitably made enemies. Charles De Young was shot and killed in 1880 as a result of the *Chronicle's* battle against the Workingmen's Party. Earlier De Young had shot and wounded the Party's mayoral candidate, whose son was the editor's assassin.

Taking over from his brother, M. H. De Young gave the paper a more conservative cast, as the state's chief journalistic upholder of Republican principles. De Young was also a member of the Republican

National Committee for eight years. Active in civic and national affairs, he nevertheless kept a tight hand on the Chronicle until he died in 1925.

Long before that time, the *Chronicle* was challenged and had to share the San Francisco proceeds with other newspapers. The first of these invaders was George Hearst, W. R.'s father, who had made a fortune in the Comstock Lode and was using some of his money to further his political ambitions. He bought in 1880 the decrepit *Evening Examiner,* owned by Captain William Moss, who had erected it on the ruins of his *Democratic Press,* a Copperhead paper, which had been destroyed by the mob after the news of Lincoln's assassination had reached the city.

George Hearst converted his able lawyer, Clarence Greathouse, into an editor, and Greathouse revealed that he had exceptional talents for that occupation as well. Under his direction, and with the help of Hearst's money, Greathouse made the *Examiner* the state's leading Democratic newspaper, with a circulation of 20,000 in 1887. It helped to send George Hearst to the Senate that year, although it had failed earlier to elect him governor.

Safely in the Senate, and with no immediate use for the paper, Senator Hearst listened to the importunings of his son, Willie, who had failed to negotiate Harvard but thought he could make a success of the newspaper business. He had been observing closely Pulitzer's progress in New York with the *World,* and admiring that paper's sensational techniques, he believed he could apply the same formula to San Francisco, where many of the same readership elements were present.

At twenty-four, William Randolph Hearst became publisher of the *Examiner,* the start of his legendary career. He made the paper not only the most sensational San Francisco was ever likely to see, but perhaps the most enterprising and brilliant as well. Following the practice he would later use to establish his chain, Hearst achieved his results not alone through his own genius, but by surrounding himself with extraordinary editors and writers.

His first act was to replace Greathouse with Arthur McEwen, who is remembered today as author of the "gee whiz" definition of news: "It is anything that makes a reader say, 'Gee, whiz,' " or "My God!"

as the quotation is also sometimes phrased. As news editor he appointed the redoubtable Samuel S. Chamberlain, who had trained under Bennett on the New York *Herald* and later founded *Le Matin,* in Paris. One of his columnists was Ambrose Bierce, and Winifred Black Bonfils, who signed her work "Annie Laurie," was the *Examiner's* equivalent of Nellie Bly. With such writers and editors, the paper doubled its circulation in the first year. By 1893 it was up to 60,000 and had passed the Chronicle. Even after Hearst moved to New York to start the *Journal* three years later, it went right on growing, and by 1908 had reached 100,000 circulation. It has always been, to this day, one of the most profitable papers in the Hearst chain.

No publisher ever worked harder to establish a paper than Hearst did on the *Examiner.* Hearst had no need to fight at all; he did it for love of the game. He wrote to his mother in Washington: "I don't suppose that I shall live more than three or four years if this strain keeps up. I don't get to bed until two o'clock and I wake up about seven in the morning and can't get to sleep again, for I must see the paper and compare it with the *Chronicle.* If we are the best, I can turn over and go to sleep with quiet satisfaction, but if the *Chronicle* happens to scoop us, that lets me out of all sleep for the day . . ."

The kind of paper he created was best expressed by McEwen, its editor, whose "gee, whiz" definition was, in reality, taken out of context. That exclamation, he said, was uttered only when he saw the paper's first page. The second page elicited an astonished "Holy Moses!" and the third page an entirely irreverent "God Almighty!"

McEwen, a tall, blond Scotsman, of an exceedingly religious family, described the *Examiner's* star reporter, Petey Bigelow, as so "frail and pale" that once, when he walked down Market Street just after shaving his beard, a drunk sighting him cried out in awe: "Good God, the Holy Grail!" This "frail and pale" reporter was the man who pursued a pair of robbers who had held up a Southern Pacific train and calmly interviewed them in their mountain hideout.

Hearst's ideas which he put into operation in the *Examiner* were not particularly original. Essentially they were extensions and elaborations of what Bennett, Sr., had done in the *Herald* and Pulitzer in the *World.* The emphasis was always on mass appeal, on the sensational and the so-called human interest story. These were the prevailing methods at the time on many American newspapers, and Hearst simply improved on them.

They were methods which had properly begun with Bennett, and they consisted of professional and political techniques. The professional aspect was the employment of writers who could ferret out every exploitable piece of sin, crime and corruption in the daily grist of news and extract the last ounce of sensation from it. Hearst's improvements on the method were to get the best writers and reporters money could buy, and to add the new dimension of photography, done in the same sensational manner.

The political aspect was Hearst's technique of projecting his paper beyond the appeals of party politics and representing it as a St. George in search of dragons intent on devouring honest citizens and middle-class taxpayers. It was easy for Hearst to go beyond party politics, because he had no real political convictions of his own. Nonetheless, his crusades were among the most formidable in an era of crusading.

Hearst not only printed the news first if he could possibly get it, but he was first in everything else he could think of. Writers like Ouida, Anna Katharine Green and Gertrude Atherton appeared on newspaper pages for the first time in the *Examiner*. The first music ever printed by a daily paper in the West appeared in the *Examiner*. Hearst even went up in a balloon, accompanied by a flight of homing pigeons and a photographer, and while he stared down the sunburned gullets of his fellow natives, he sent the birds fluttering back to the *Examiner* office with exclusive descriptive stories and pictures of how the city looked from the air.

On Washington's Birthday in 1888, Hearst sent half the paper's staff to Washington, where it published a special edition of the *Examiner* in an attempt to persuade the Democratic National Committee, meeting there, to hold its next convention in San Francisco. The effort was an expensive failure, but Hearst had the satisfaction of being able to lay the *Examiner,* with a circulation already 47,526, at his father's doorstep on New Hampshire Avenue. Another special edition was published, printed in both German and English, to mark the death of Kaiser Wilhelm I. These and a thousand other curiosities came out of the madhouse which was the *Examiner's* city room.

If it seemed impossible to compete with a paper possessing the resources and staff of Willie Hearst's creation, the prospect did not dismay a man who was at the opposite pole from Hearst. His name was Fremont Older.

Older came from Wisconsin, of God-fearing farmer parents. His father died in a Confederate prison, leaving his pretty young wife to support herself and two sons, which she did in the beginning by selling books. One of these volumes was a biography of Horace Greeley. Reading it, young Fremont was so impressed that from the moment he turned the last page he was determined to be a newspaperman, if possible one like Greeley. The determination in time became fanaticism, which was fortunate, because no other editor had to endure so much to achieve his goal.

From the beginning he was driven by his ambition as he sought to find a place for himself in a hostile world—a tall, awkward youth moving from job to job, from one temporary home to another, after his mother married again and moved to California.

Following a brief country schooling and a few months in Ripon College, Older learned to set type. He fell back constantly on this trade while he worked at farming, as cabin boy on a riverboat, as a laborer in a carriage shop and anything else he could find to feed and shelter himself. He was one of hundreds of tramp printers, moving from one shop to another. But where the other tramps were likely to be motivated by some degree of alcoholism, Older's restlessness was the result of the inner drive that propelled him toward a goal he only vaguely understood.

When he was seventeen, his mother sent him enough money to come to San Francisco, where he supposed his progress would be easier. But it was Wisconsin and the Middle West all over again. Once more, and for the next ten years, he drifted from paper to paper. He was a good printer, good enough to be a foreman, but he was never given the opportunity to do editorial work, and that was all he wanted. Only when he reached Redwood City and its *Times and Gazette* did he have a chance to go out and get the news, as well as set type. He showed the publisher so much talent that he was made business manager, then editor. He could have made a career in Redwood City, but he could not stay away from San Francisco. Like so many other young men, before and since, he thought it the only place in the world to live. Returning there in 1884, he never left it again, except temporarily.

This time he found the city blooming with newspapers, as though they were saloons, and with his Redwood City experience behind him, it was not difficult to find an editorial job. After working on several of them, he had achieved the city editor's desk at the *Morning Call* in 1895 when he was hired to be managing editor of the *Bulletin,* a rapidly failing property in which R. A. Crothers had just purchased a half-interest.

The position crystallized Older's tremendous energy and talent and released these qualities. He was determined now to be a success, and as he wrote later in his autobiography, he meant to be ruthless about it, not caring whether his sensational stories and headlines "might make people suffer, might wound or utterly ruin someone."

Such a drive was certain to produce results, given Older's undoubted abilities. In a year he had increased the faltering circulation of the *Bulletin* from 9,000 to more than double that figure; it reached 100,000 before he left the paper. It took only a little longer to get enough advertising to make the venture profitable for Crothers, since the *Bulletin* had been losing $3,000 a month.

Older was a born crusader. In the beginning his *Bulletin* crusades did not stem from his convictions but solely from his purpose to increase the paper's circulation and thus help his personal fortunes. The first mouthful he bit off would have been enough to choke any man in the business. He decided to engage in combat the Southern Pacific Railroad, which virtually owned California through a system of widespread and utterly shameless bribery. Legislators, officials, and many of the state's newspapers were on its payoff list, including the *Bulletin* itself, Older discovered, which was down for $125 a month to guarantee its good will.

Moving against this giant network of corruption, Older first got his friend James D. Phelan elected as mayor of San Francisco. The intention was to set up a reform government in the city that could serve as an opening wedge to fight the railroad's political machine. Watching Phelan, a completely honest and fearless man, carry out his part of the bargain converted Older from simple opportunism. As he wrote later, he acquired his "first social sense."

Phelan's major battle was the obtaining of a new city charter, which meant exposing and checking the corruption of the city's public utilities. These had been returning regular subsidies to the papers, including the *Bulletin,* and Crothers was reluctant to give up his share. Older found himself opposing his boss as well as the machine.

In the subsequent conflict, Older was kidnaped by a gunman who lost his nerve before he could kill the editor. In turn, Older kidnaped a Chinese confederate of Abraham Ruef, the city's political boss. In the end, however, Older was victorious. Ruef went to prison for extortion in 1908, at the end of a trial in which the prosecutor was shot dead in the courtroom. A young lawyer politician, Hiram W. Johnson, succeeded him.

As soon as Ruef was in jail, Older began to have second thoughts. He decided it was the system and not the man which was to blame, and he began another crusade to get the boss out of jail, a move far more difficult than to get him in. Older was so obsessed with the idea of penal reform that he did not care whether people thought he was crazy or had "gone soft." He arranged the release of a San Quentin convict, printed his story of prison life in the *Bulletin,* then set him up as head of a bureau to help ex-convicts get a new start. He also fought capital punishment, and in an ever broadening scope, a good many other social evils. His crusading for the rights of labor leaders and their unions led him to embrace the extreme left wing of the movement, which brought down the fire of the conservative element. All these crusades produced circulation, however, and Crothers continued to let him use the *Bulletin* as a platform.

Older's *cause célèbre* was the Preparedness Day parade bombing in San Francisco on July 22, 1916. In the face of the prevailing fanaticism, Older declared his belief that Thomas J. Mooney and Warren K. Billings, the men convicted of the crime, had been framed. Their conviction, he said, was a monumental injustice, a mockery of the judicial process, and he kept up a steady fire of protest. A year after the bombing he was printing letters which charged perjury in the trial. This was too much for some of the paper's conservative advertisers, who complained to the publisher. Older was asked to resign.

It was logical at the time for Hearst, who had opposed most of Older's crusades, to offer him the editorship of the *Call,* which W. R. had bought as an evening companion for the *Examiner.* Hearst told him to "bring the Mooney case with me," Older recalled later. For Hearst it was a splendid deal. He acquired a first-class news executive, experienced in the crusading which was also a characteristic of Hearst papers in their constant push for circulation, and he assumed that a certain amount of Older's reputation would be reflected, thus adding to the Hearst public image as a friend of the masses. As a final touch of irony for Older, Hearst bought the *Bulletin* in 1928, and made him president and editor of the combined *Call-Bulletin.*

If Hearst made the complete circle of political beliefs, or pretended beliefs, in his lifetime, Older did much the same thing. He had started crusading in the belief that it was good for his paper's circulation and his career, but little else. Then he acquired the strong moral convictions which led him into prison reform and the Mooney case. Under Hearst, which may have been natural, he returned to his original conclusion. Crusades were good circulation builders, he said; they would never reform the social system.

The only crusade he maintained was the one for Hearst himself, who had won his unwavering admiration by taking in him and the Mooney case when he could have been shouldered out of San Francisco journalism. The years on the *Call-Bulletin,* where Hearst gave him free rein, were the happiest of his life. He became W. R.'s most vociferously loyal employee, even helping his second wife, Cora, to write an authorized biography of the publisher. Older died suddenly of a heart attack in 1935, after a pleasant afternoon writing an editorial about Montaigne's essay on death.

With his departure, the era of personal journalism ended on the West Coast, but not the rivalry among San Francisco newspapers. In the early 1960s the *Chronicle* and *Examiner* were engaged again in a circulation duel which splattered their front pages with sensational headlines and the inside pages with the blood let by columnists and editorial writers. But the years and frequent changings of the guard made the spectacle incongruous to readers with long memories. The *Examiner* had become with time the most conservative paper in the Hearst chain; at its advanced age, it appeared almost patriarchal, and the attempt to revive its earlier stridency seemed out of character. The *Chronicle,* on the other hand, for so many years the guardian of conservatism in the city, was apparently attempting to out-Hearst the Hearst method, something Joseph Pulitzer had failed to do in New York seventy years before.

As a brief reprise of the old days, it was entertaining journalism, but in the newspaper climate of mid-twentieth century it had an anachronistic air. As will be seen presently, they did it better before the turn of the century.

five

Pulitzer and Hearst:
The Last Great Duel

BEFORE HEARST AND PULITZER ended the era of personal journalism in New York with an exhibition which summed up its worst sins, the personalities who had survived the Civil War were adding to the record of the period in both its good and bad aspects.

To anyone who had witnessed the rise of the elder Bennett, it would have seemed impossible that anyone could have rivaled him in either eccentricity or enterprise, but his son demonstrated that he was his father's superior in the former and nearly his equal in the latter. During his career with the sound property he inherited, he made his own unique contribution to the development of the American newspaper, and having made it in a series of events as spectacular as any the city had seen, he threw away his opportunity to do more.

There were extenuating circumstances. By the time Bennett came into control of the *Herald* in 1867, when he was only 26, his personality had already been scarred by an abnormal childhood. From internal evidence it is reasonable to believe that he hated his father, saw little of him, and did not understand what he saw. In his early boyhood Bennett Sr. was far too busy creating the *Herald* to pay much attention to his son. Then he was embroiled in the Great Moral War against the paper, which made life uncomfortable for his family, if it did not for him, because Henrietta and her son were socially ostracized. If they were recognized in the street, people were likely to call insults after them, or vent their hatred of Bennett on these innocents in other ways.

Such humiliations, and Henrietta's fears of what effect the Moral War might have on a growing boy, led her to take him abroad when he was five, and they spent most of their time in Europe until the boy's mid-adolescence, quite literally refugees from their own country. The experience had a profound effect on young Bennett. He grew up without a father's influence, under the complete care of his protective, possessive mother, and with a strong feeling of alienation from America and its way of life. He learned to love European living, and it was no doubt with reluctance that he came home again to stay not long before the war. The final blow was his father's insistence that he join the Union Navy. Certainly he must have realized that patriotism and principle played no rôle in the move, that it was only part of the sop his father was throwing to the Abolitionists to save his paper.

How much damage was done no one can measure accurately. The first time young Bennett emerged as an individual in his own right was his appearance immediately after the war as managing editor of the *Herald,* after a brief tour of duty in other positions. His father was carefully grooming him to take over the paper, and apparently the son made no objection. Fortunately, he had inherited his father's keen sense of news and the elder Bennett indoctrinated him thoroughly with his own understanding of what had made the *Herald* pay off.

Otherwise, he must have been a disappointment to Bennett Senior. Outside the office he was a gay bachelor about town, inclined to be erratic and impulsive, an easy spender, given to fits of quick temper and jealousy. He did not have his father's driving, compulsive obsession with the paper. Nevertheless Bennett Senior retired and left the *Herald* to him in 1867, believing that it should stay in the family and trusting his son to grow up to his responsibilities.

In one way he did grow up, and no doubt that was a satisfaction to the older man in the five years of life he had remaining. The father had been a master at getting the news; the son proved himself a genius at making it happen. Bennett Senior lived long enough to see the first results of his son's talents.

The story was a dramatic one, but although the quotation it produced became a cliché, the details have long since passed from popular memory. David Livingstone, an explorer-missionary, had disappeared into the bush of East Africa early in 1866, on a search for the source of the Nile, during which he intended, idealistically, to put a stop to the slave traffic from which the Arab traders were getting rich. Other papers printed the stories of his disappearance. Bennett sent a reporter out to find him.

It was ironic that the man he sent to find and possibly rescue the high-minded enemy of the slave trade was Henry Morton Stanley, who switched from the Confederate to the Union side during the war because he had no sympathy with the ideology of either side. "I had a secret scorn for people who could kill one another for the sake of African slaves," he wrote later. "There were no blackies in Wales [his native land], and why a sooty-faced nigger from a distant land should be an element of disturbance between white brothers was a puzzle to me."

Joining the *Herald* in 1868, soon after young Bennett took command, Stanley had made his reputation by covering the war in Ethiopia. Four years later he was summoned to Bennett's Paris hotel room, and there the publisher told him his next assignment was to find Livingstone. Bennett added: "Draw a thousand pounds now, and when you have gone through that, draw another thousand, and when that is spent, draw another thousand, and so on; but find Livingstone."

Finding the missing man made Stanley as famous an explorer as Livingstone when his exciting stories of the search reached the *Herald's* pages. His story of the epic meeting concluded:

"There is a group of the most respectable Arabs, and as I come nearer I see the white face of an old man among them. He has a cap with a gold band around it, his dress is a short jacket of red blanket cloth, and his pants—well, I didn't observe. I am shaking hands with him. We raise our hats, and I say:

" 'Dr. Livingstone, I presume?'

"And he says, 'Yes.'

"Finis coronat opus." (The end crowns the work.)

Stanley was not above rewriting this story when he set it down in a travel book he produced later. In this later version, it appears that the doctor was wearing "a pair of gray tweed trousers." After the conversation reported previously, Stanley added,

"I replaced my hat on my head, and he replaced his cap, and we both grasped hands. I then said aloud: 'I thank God, doctor, I have been permitted to see you.'

"He answered, 'I feel thankful that I am here to welcome you.' "

The second version, it is hardly necessary to add, is of dubious authenticity.

Livingstone never spoke to a white man again. He set off on a new expedition into the interior, and died there. As for Stanley, the expedition had so convinced him of Africa's future that he remained there for nearly the remainder of his working life, sending back stories of the continent to fascinated readers. These stories are credited with awakening the great powers to the economic possibilities of Africa, and precipitating the scramble to establish colonies.

Bennett, after this success, began to surround himself with reporters at home and abroad who could dig out news—who could, in brief, make it happen. One of the best of these was Januarius Aloysius MacGahan, an Irish farm boy from Ohio who became the first noteworthy foreign correspondent in the American newspaper business. He began with the Franco-Prussian War. Then, in 1873, Bennett sent him after a Cossack expedition on its way into Central Asia to conquer Turkestan, the only country in the region still resisting Russian expansionism. Starting alone, with only an interpreter, a treacherous guide, a servant and six horses, MacGahan made an incredible march across wild desert country, only to be told when he caught up that he could not travel with the Russians, who in fact sent a detachment to catch him and arrest him after he started back. MacGahan eluded the hardy Cossack pursuers for six hundred miles until he reached the command post of a Russian General, and then had to talk himself to freedom.

After that he was permitted to follow the Russians into Khiva, the Muslim stronghold, which they took after a struggle. There, in the palace of the conquered Khan, he saw a dark-eyed beauty of eighteen who gave him such appealing glances that he crept into the palace that night after midnight and made his way to the harem, drawn revolver in hand. It was a perilous undertaking, during which Mac-Gahan nearly fell down a deep well and once sifted in his hands what he thought was black earth until he realized it was gunpowder, enough to blow up the palace. He found his beauty at last, made her understand by signs that she need not fear the Russians, and then with a kiss of the hands to him she disappeared down a corridor. Next morning she was gone with all the other harem women. They had escaped during the early morning hours.

Two years later MacGahan was on the bark *Pandora* which Bennett had chartered for him so that he might head a *Herald* expedition to find the fabled Northwest Passage. MacGahan again barely escaped with his life, and soon after he escaped from Bennett, later going on to his greatest exploits for the London *Daily News,* in reporting Turkish atrocities in Bulgaria, which so stirred the world's indignation that the Russo-Turkish War and an independent Bulgaria resulted. MacGahan, who was revered in Bulgaria as the country's liberator, died in Constantinople at thirty-four.

When one says the correspondent "escaped" Bennett, it was no more than the literal truth. For whatever Bennett's genius as a newsmaker may have been, he was a despicable human being, an arrogant, half-mad tyrant, a drunkard who needed only two glasses of his favorite champagne to carry his belligerency to insane lengths. He had outstanding reporters and editors working for him on the *Herald,* most of whom were afraid of him; the best men did not stay long.

Bennett was a tall, spare man, like his father, with a drooping mustache and a thin, aristocratic, saturnine face. He was the victim of too much money, from childhood onward, spending it with a reckless disregard for consequences, a good deal of it on his own extravagances. In the course of his mad life, he managed to spend nearly thirty millions. It was typical of his total lack of proportion that his idea of alleviating the misery brought on by the Panic of 1873 was to open a soup kitchen in the slums and dispense from it samples of the *haute cuisine* brought down from Delmonico's kitchens.

New York society accepted his gaucheries and arrogant manners tolerantly because he was, after all, "Jimmy" Bennett, a very rich young man, a *bon vivant* whose parties were memorable. He was accepted, that is, until New Year's Day, 1877. A few weeks before that time he had fallen in love for the first time in his life with the lovely, spirited daughter of a well-known doctor. Her name was Caroline May, and according to the custom of the period, she had invited him to make her drawing room one of his stops on New Year's Day, when everyone spent the afternoon calling on friends.

By the time Bennett reached Caroline's house, he had imbibed the slight amount of alcohol he needed to make him drunk. For once he was not in his usual belligerent mood; love had given his intoxication a jovial glow. Still he had managed to tax the patience of his friends and acquaintances in the room by slapping men on the back and telling crude jokes before the ladies, when suddenly he was seized by the urge to relieve himself. Making a befuddled estimate of the situation, he decided that he was unlikely to reach the bathroom, and making his way uncertainly to the fireplace, he urinated nonchalantly into the flames.

Next day, at high noon, Caroline's brother Fred confronted Bennett on the steps of the Union Club with a cowhide whip in his hand. Bennett took the first two lashes stoically, then his natural arrogance asserted itself and he leaped on young May. Fellow members separated them. When he was on his feet again, Bennett challenged the other man to a duel.

It was a harmless affair. May, who was over his anger by this time and ready to see some humor in the incident, fired into the air. Bennett, who had little sense of humor, would have killed his antagonist if he had not been so nervous. The two men shook hands, but Bennett was not ready to forgive. Something had happened to him which changed the course of his life and made him a bitter, disillusioned man who was resolved never to live in New York again. He gave up the old family home on Washington Heights, his villa in Newport and his town house at 37 West Forty-seventh Street, and lived the rest of his life in Paris, except for infrequent trips back home. When he was not in Paris, he was at his "lodge" in Versailles, or cruising on his yacht, the *Lysistrata,* with its hundred-man crew, or lounging in his villa at Beaulieu.

Wherever he was, he edited the *Herald* by means of a constant flow of cables, letters, and conferences with editors and writers whom he summoned across the Atlantic at the slightest whim. If he loved anything or anyone, it was France, especially Paris, where he established the *Paris Herald* in 1887. At home he started an afternoon edition of the *Herald,* the *Evening Telegram,* which Henry Villard called "that pink drab of lowest journalism." For years it drained the morning paper's profits, but in the end it was the sole support of the *Herald* in that great paper's declining days.

The stories of Bennett's remote editing of the *Herald* are legendary in the newspaper business, and often told. How the editor cabled Bennett in Paris that a man who had been summoned to the presence could not be spared because he was indispensable, and Bennett, asking for a list of the paper's indispensable men, fired them all when he got it. How he was met in New York harbor on an infrequent trip home by only one *Herald* reporter, whom Bennett in a fit of pique made city editor on the spot because a delegation had not been sent to meet him. How he became an international figure known to everyone as "The Commodore"—a spender, a sportsman, involved in mysterious, scandals, frequently drunk.

He made one more news sensation in 1879 by financing the expedition of the ship *Jeanette* on a voyage of discovery to the North Pole. It was crushed by the polar ice and sank with all hands.

Occasionally he did something constructive. In 1883, he helped John Mackay establish the Commercial Cable Company, whose interlocking financial arrangements with the *Herald* helped it keep one jump ahead of its rivals with the news. Later he was the first publisher to take up the cause of the airplane and auto, and his love of yachting made the *Herald* the best maritime paper in the United States for generations. The international outlook he acquired by his absence from the States helped the *Herald* to gain a clear superiority in foreign news. It was a *Herald* reporter who stood by Admiral Dewey in Manila Bay and heard him instruct Gridley, "Damn the torpedoes! Go ahead."

But these creditable endeavors were overshadowed by Bennett's increasing eccentricity as he grew older. For a time a reporter followed him around Europe secretly, canceling anti-Catholic cables denouncing the Pope which he was likely to send in his drunken states. Even sober, his instructions to the editors back in New York often passed credibility. One of his passions was the owl. On his orders, scarcely an edition of the *Herald* was printed without some kind of owl story in its columns, and eighteen huge bronze replicas of the birds perched atop the facade of the *Herald* building on Park Row. He was also preoccupied with dogs from time to time, and his paper fought the vivisectionists long before Hearst.

No one could have been more of a personal journalist than Bennett, yet living in an era when the editorial page was the most prominent weapon of his rivals, he had no faith in it. He was further handicapped in operating the paper by his absenteeism and his treatment of those who worked for him.

But the *Herald* had been a solid property when he got it, and the further excitement he contributed to it in the earlier days of his reign carried it a long way. When Pulitzer and Hearst arrived on the scene, however, Bennett could not compete with these resident wizards, although he made a desperate effort to do it by trying to accomplish the impossible and out-sensationalize the sensationalists. On a Sunday morning in 1896, for example, the *Herald* scored a smashing victory by printing what one contemporary historian called "an account of a prominent lady's linen with such detailed frankness that it may not be copied here."

Bennett went too far, however, when he started his famous "personals" column, which were really thinly disguised invitations to moral turpitude masquerading under such subdivisions as "manicure," "massage," "medical," "financial," and "business opportunities." Some of the more refined personals read:

YOUNG LADY, good figure, wants to pose for artists; references exchanged; positively no triflers.

A CATHOLIC maiden (28) worth nearly $5,000; musical, refined, good appearance, would wed.—Rosalie.

A HANDSOME young girl desires copying or some other profitable work.—M.P.

ANY person knowing of impending business failures or having other valuable information can make big money by communicating with smart lawyer.—Strict confidence.

In his peculiarly unprincipled way, Hearst adroitly maneuvered this circulation-getting effort into a means of possibly destroying the *Herald*. He pretended to take an indignant moral stand, echoing the protests of the shocked members of the electorate, who were astonished to see their protests echoed in the yellow *Journal*, and succeeded in getting Bennett, the *Herald* corporation and its advertising manager indicted for violating the postal laws. An able young lawyer in the Department of Justice, Henry L. Stimson, conducted the prosecution of the case. Bennett, accepting his defeat with angry frustration, pleaded guilty and paid fines totaling $31,000. Hating Hearst even more than he hated America, he retired deeper into his European retreats.

His last days were a *tour de force* of irony. In a reversal of everything he had clung to before, he deserted his bachelorhood for marriage with the widow of a French baron, and left the Catholic faith to become an Episcopalian. He heard with apparent indifference the news that his heavy spending had so weakened the *Herald* that it was being kept alive by the *Telegram*.

Bennett died of a heart attack at his Beaulieu villa in 1918. His will left the *Herald* in the hands of his executors, notwithstanding that he had promised all his life to leave it to whatever veteran employees remained on the paper. Presumably in an effort to mitigate this reversal, he left a large bequest to establish a shelter for indigent New York newspapermen, in memory of his father, whom he recognized at last. But there was so little money remaining in the estate when his obligations had been paid and the other provisions of the will were carried out, that the home remained no more than a belated good intention.

In 1920, to carry the melancholy story to its end, the *Herald* fell into the hands of Frank Munsey, the "grand high executioner" of the newspaper business, who treated papers as pieces of business property, to be merged, sold, suspended, or whatever else would make a profit. Munsey sold the *Herald* in 1924 to the burgeoning *Tribune*, to create the *Herald Tribune* familiar in our time as the standard bearer of New

York, and to some extent national, Republicanism. The long rivalry between the two papers was over. Uncle Horace, in effect, had had the last word.

Bennett's competition in New York during the closing decades of the century came, with one exception, from strong-minded personal journalists who, in their own fashions, were nearly as eccentric.

In the earlier years, the strongest of these figures was Charles Anderson Dana, whose beginning career and involvement with the chicanery of the New York Associated Press have already been related. Dana is widely credited with bringing the principles of sound business management to the American newspaper's development. It was true. Dana had a keen business mind, well attuned to the ruthless, unprincipled practices of the day, and without devoting himself to extremes of truth and honesty, he made the *Sun* a paper operated on the general business lines laid down near the turn of the century. But he also made it a superb editorial product, by and large, a "newspaperman's newspaper," so well done that its excellence persisted until its death.

By the time Dana bought the *Sun* in 1868, under the circumstances described before, he had already gone through two different phases of his life. In his early days he had shared the adversities of other editors, growing up in New Hampshire as the son of a country storekeeper whose business failed. His mother died when he was nine. Put out to work as a clerk in his uncle's store in Buffalo at twelve, he was cast into the world again at eighteen when this enterprise, too, went bankrupt.

Fortunately, Dana was not unequipped to get along in the world. As a farm boy he had studied Latin by himself, and in Buffalo he had gone on with the self-study of Greek and read his way through the classics of literature. A truly self-educated man, he was able to get into Harvard without conditions at nineteen. Hard study there nearly ruined his eyesight, and he had to leave at the end of his junior year.

He got a job immediately teaching Latin and Greek at the co-operative experiment in "plain living and high thinking," Brook Farm, in West Roxbury, Massachusetts. Its transcendentalist philosophy had already made Horace Greeley its strong supporter. At Brook Farm, Dana had his first taste of journalism, writing for its paper, *The Harbinger,* during the five years he spent there. Inevitably he met

Greeley, but when the Brook Farm experiment ended in 1846, he did not immediately approach Uncle Horace for a job. Instead, he went up to Boston, where he became assistant editor of a Congregationalist organ, the *Daily Chronotype*.

Unfortunately for all concerned, Dana approached this paper with the viewpoint of a Unitarian, and when he was in charge while the editor was away, he came out "mighty strong against hell." The editor had to apologize to every minister in the state, and Dana lost his job. It was then that he approached Greeley and became almost at once city editor of the *Tribune* at a salary of $10 a week, later raised to $14.

In his fifteen years on the paper, as city editor and managing editor, Dana perfected his writing style, which was epigrammatic and concise, if a little pompous, and he acquired an encyclopedic knowledge of the business that made him one of the best managers of a newspaper property in his time. When Greeley was away, he made all the editorial decisions and edited everyone's copy, including the publisher's. He was in more or less complete control of the paper's business side.

The most important event of those fifteen years, however, did not take place in the *Sun's* city room. In 1846 and 1847, Dana made a long European trip and it is not too much to say that it completely reshaped his life. Until that time he had been an idealist, the result of absorbing the ideas of Brook Farm and of Greeley. But in Europe he saw at first hand the appalling results of power politics and political chicanery. It was a time of crisis everywhere on the Continent, when mighty tides of revolution and unrest were changing the fate of nations. Dana documented many of these changes in correspondence for the *Sun* which was a model of analytic reporting.

It was a disillusioning experience, during which the Brook Farm idealist lost his idealism. He came home with the beginnings of a corrosive cynicism about men and events which deepened as he grew older. Idealism was replaced with the practical principles of nineteenth-century business management. His split with Greeley was inevitable after that journey.

There followed the period of his war service, when he was the administration's spy, and the brief post-war years in Chicago before he returned to New York as a publisher in a city whose newspaper scene was dominated by James Gordon Bennett, Jr. That fact undoubtedly conditioned the kind of newspaper Dana made the *Sun,* although there was no hint of it in the usual opening declaration which heralded his ownership. The *Sun* would, he said, "study condensation, clearness, point, and will endeavor to present its daily photograph of the whole world's doings in the most luminous and lively manner." In later promotional advertising he declared that the *Sun's* news was "the freshest, most interesting and sprightliest current, and no expense is spared to make it just what the great mass of the people want."

Behind these persuasive words lay Dana's real problem, which was how to compete with the *Herald,* at the moment doing a superb job of getting the news. The *Sun* got the news too, and Dana made sure it was "what the great mass of the people" wanted—that is, murder, scandal, gossip and interviews. The tone of the two papers was much alike, sensational and flip. Dana added two improvements to the news content, however. One was the "human interest story," which he virtually invented in its modern form. The other also became a cliché. It was expressed in the immortal words of city editor John B. Bogart's advice to a young reporter: "When a dog bites a man, that's not news; but when a man bites a dog, that's news."

Dana gave his readers one thing they could not find in the *Herald,* and that was a brisk, well written editorial page. Bennett's lack of interest in editorials made the *Herald's* page perfunctory. The editorials Dana wrote were meant to be read, and no doubt he knew they would make people angry. In them he expressed his cynical, perverse view of life, which included a conviction that no confidence could be placed in any man in public office and a pervasive skepticism about all human loyalties.

In expressing these beliefs, Dana was honest, at least. He practiced what he preached. Thus in 1872 he turned on his old friend Grant without compunction, and coined the famous campaign phrase, "Turn the rascals out," but in the same campaign he gave only lukewarm support to his own candidate, another old friend, Greeley, whom he always referred to sarcastically as "Dr. Greeley." When Greeley died after the campaign, Dana turned his self-righteous editorial guns on those who had attacked Uncle Horace while he was alive.

Again, in the disputed Hayes-Tilden election of 1876, Dana took Tilden's side and refused to recognize Hayes as long as he was in office by any title except "the fraudulent President." To Dana, Garfield in 1880 was little better than a common thief, and his opponent, General Hancock, was described as "a good man, weighing 240 pounds."

Dana opposed Cleveland for no better reason than the refusal of a political favor, and he had an even worse opinion of the other party's candidate, Blaine. When he was not attacking Presidential candidates, successful and unsuccessful, Dana wrote biting denunciations of labor unions and strikes, and civil service reform. He came out strongly for the annexation of Cuba, Santo Domingo and Canada. In New York, he supported some of the most fragrant of Tammany candidates. The McKinley Tariff Act, to which he gave his unqualified approval, is now considered one of the most damaging pieces of legislation ever enacted. One had to admit that Dana's editorials on all these subjects sparkled and demanded to be read, but they were devoid of any moral content.

With his talent for management, Dana surrounded himself with good writers, an essential if he meant to compete with Bennett's stable of virtuosi. One of his editorial writers, Francis P. Church, achieved fame with a single line in one editorial: "Yes, Virginia, there is a Santa Claus." Among his reporters were men like Julian Ralph and David Graham Phillips, one of the best investigators of the century, whose stories of corruption in city, state and national government made him a celebrated figure. Jacob Riis was a *Sun* reporter of distinction, and abroad there was the beau ideal of foreign correspondents, the handsome Richard Harding Davis, who went on to earn $3,000 a month working for Hearst.

For all his oposition to organized labor and his almost total lack of principle, Dana's relationships with the talented men who worked for him were the opposite of Bennett's. Whatever he might be away from the office, or however he might connive in the plundering of the Associated Press, he was an encouraging and helpful boss in the *Sun's* city room. Those closest to him said he was at home and most human when he was working, and he endeared himself to these intimates. Watterson, who was not a particularly good judge of human character, called him "the most scholarly and accomplished of American journalists."

However that may be, there was no doubt Dana stood foremost among the editors of the post-Civil War period until Pulitzer came on the scene. Raymond and Greeley were dead. Samuel Bowles had turned over the Springfield *Republican* to his son, a lesser figure; and the second Bennett was too eccentric to be a serious challenge.

There was, indeed, only one man among the New York editors who approached Dana as a leader, or at least a provoker of public opinion. That was Edwin Lawrence Godkin, editor of a small paper called *The Nation*. Dana despised him for the same reason he had Greeley, because Godkin was an idealist, an unabashed and undiscouraged fighter for the rights of man. Of Godkin, William James wrote: "To my generation, his was certainly the towering influence in all thought concerning public affairs, and indirectly his influence has assuredly been more pervasive than that of any other writer of the generation, for he influenced other writers who never quoted him, and determined the whole current of discussion."

Both in career and personality, Godkin was a man apart from the mainstream of nineteenth-century newspaper making. A transplanted Anglo-Irishman, he was devoted to America and spent his life trying to correct the evils of democracy, but with an approach markedly different from all the other publishers who professed themselves as friends of the people, whether they meant it or not. Godkin fought hard for the masses, but he disdained to mix with them, or even to write for them. His paper and his editorials were addressed frankly to intellectuals, which accounted for its small circulation. He even remained aloof from his professional colleagues, and indeed from nearly everyone else. He was a strange, lonely man whose energies were directed toward liberal, progressive causes, of which he was the best and most effective advocate in America.

As Villard wrote of him: "Almost every one of the reforms in government of our day, Godkin championed, and always by going to the root of the thing, by seeking the underlying principle and setting it forth."

The organs he chose for this task were unpromising by conventional standards, but they represented a new element among American newspapers—the specialized paper directed to a non-mass audience.

The *Nation,* which Godkin edited from 1865 to 1899, was a brilliant but highly unprofitable paper, eventually rescued from oblivion by its fortunate sale to the *Evening Post.*

The *Post* had come a long way since Hamilton founded it and Coleman was its fiery editor. For nearly forty-nine years William Cullen Bryant had been its editor-in-chief, serving with such distinction that, as Parrington remarked, he was "a power for sanity in a scurrilous generation." In 1870, Bryant retired to translate Homer, and his son-in-law and associate editor, Parke Godwin, took over with the help of a succession of brilliant managing editors. After Bryant's death in 1878, however, Godwin found himself in irreconcilable conflict with the paper's business manager, Isaac Henderson, who had a half interest, and the quarrel led to the paper's sale to Henry Villard.

Villard, too, had come a considerable distance. After his career as a Civil War correspondent, he had turned to finance and made a large fortune in the new railroad enterprises of the Northwest. In expanding his interests in 1881, he bought not only the *Post* but the *Nation* as well, and in doing so he acquired Godkin. The *Nation* became the *Post's* weekly edition.

For a time the paper operated under a troika arrangement in which Carl Schurz was editor-in-chief, with Horace White and Godkin as his associates. White had been editor of the Chicago *Tribune* for a brief period, during which it had taken on a tone of independent liberalism never seen there before or afterward. No paper was likely to exist long with three editors, however, and the *Post's* triumvirate lasted only two years. Schurz and Godkin quarreled over a telegraphers' strike, and Schurz retired, leaving Godkin as editor with White as his associate. Godkin held the post until 1899.

During all these vicissitudes the *Post* never reached a circulation of more than 35,000 and sometimes it fell below 10,000, but its influence was out of all proportion to its circulation figures. Its editorial viewpoints penetrated to the farthest corners of the country, and in New York State, Governor David B. Hill once expressed the opinion of his fellow politicians when he complained, "I don't care anything about the handful of Mugwumps who read it. The trouble with the damned sheet is that every editor in New York reads it."

Every editor read it, ministers read it and quoted it in sermons, college presidents did the same in their public addresses, and indeed most men of prominence in public life were bound to read the *Post*. Its opinions trickled down from this top layer of intellectualism to the masses, most of whom had never heard of Godkin, and so the paper's influence was pervasive.

The reason, of course, was Godkin. He was not a great editor like Dana or Greeley or the senior Bennett, but he was an editorial writer of the most exceptional talent, an intellectual of extraordinary integrity who taught the country, as Henry Holt once said, more than any other man in it. Villard wrote of Godkin's prose style: "His English was clear and straightforward, wonderfully powerful, free from all unnecessary verbiage. No one else, no Bowles, or Watterson, or Raymond, has approached that style in our press except occasionally. For one thing, it was the writing of a completely educated man, polished by travel and the society of intellectual leaders everywhere, who wrote only with profound conviction, who till the last of his long career burned at injustice with the ardor of youth. To this he added a power of irony and sarcasm never equaled by anyone else, almost too great at times."

In the content of his editorials, Godkin opposed everything Dana stood for, with a moral austerity at the opposite pole from Dana's cynicism. He battled for civil service reform and against high tariffs, for sound currency and against corruption in government. Day after day he pursued his adversaries with such cold, witty irony, such penetrating shafts of intelligence that it was sometimes too much even for the *Post's* readers. A story was circulated about the old lady who lived alone in the country, but was not afraid because, as she said, a carrier boy threw her copy of the *Evening Post* on the porch at dusk, and "It just lay there and growled all night."

As a single example of Godkin in action, perhaps none would serve better than his frontal assault on James Fisk, the financier who looted the Erie Railroad in company with Daniel Drew and Jay Gould. On July 20, 1871, when Fisk was at the height of his fame as a gambler, financial manipulator and man-about-town, Godkin employed his editorial space in the *Nation* to flay him mercilessly in an editorial titled "Notoriety." It read, in part:

This man came to New York a few years ago, a smart, impudent and ignorant pedlar, without morals or manners, and with a good deal of animal spirits, and in search of two things—physical enjoyment and notoriety. The physical enjoyment he might have had with a little money, but notoriety he could only get with the help of the newspapers, and this help they gave him to his heart's content.

He went incontinently to work to do strange, indecent, and outrageous things, and they went to work to chronicle them and denounce him for them. This was natural enough when he first showed himself on the scene as a swindler and blackguard, but when it was discovered that he was really indifferent to public opinion, that he had no shame and no sensibility, and really enjoyed his bad reputation, liked to be thought lewd and smart and knavish, the press at once began to treat him as a curious phenomenon, and laugh over him, chronicle his movements, record his jokes, give him pet names, and devote an amount of time to the consideration of him as an entertainment simply, which proved the best advertisement any charlatan ever had, and gratified his dearest ambition. To be "in the papers" every day, to be thought smart by brokers and drygoodsmen and railroad men, are what he of all things most desires.

The treatment he received, too, helped all his speculations. It advertised his theatre [the Grand Opera House], his steamboats, and his railroads; it made the box in which he sat, and the carriage in which he rode with his strumpets the objects on which all eyes were fixed. His fame, in short, filled the continent, and has now filled the civilized world.

At last, too, the jocose treatment of him resulted in making him look less disreputable than he was at the beginning; from laughing over him a good deal, people got to think him "not such a bad fellow after all"; and, finally, we came to see business suspended at midday in the principal thoroughfare of the commercial capital of the country, whose courts and legislature he had corrupted, in order to see him ride down as elected Colonel at the head of a regiment nine hundred strong, composed of respectable young Americans. As colonel of this regiment, he asked for a municipal invitation for himself and it from the city of Boston, and, amongst other things, expressed a desire to have "divine service" celebrated for his benefit on Boston Common. The newspapers, thereupon, took this up, and discussed it, and joked over it, and showed the absurdity of it in article after article, and paragraph after paragraph, as if Fisk was really trying to play the hypocrite, and was trying to pass himself off as a religious man, the fact being that he was merely gratifying a showman's love of making a sensation, and by the newspaper exposures of him as an impudent dog got all he wanted, and probably far more than he looked for . . .

We cannot make Fisk a person of importance and fill everybody's mind every morning with his doings and sayings, without making Fisk's career an object of secret admiration to thousands, and making thousands in their inmost hearts determine to imitate him. The newspapers ought to remember that, while for some offenders against public decency and security denunciation may be a proper and effective punishment, the only way of reaching others is not to mention them.

Only a year later the newspapers were giving Jim Fisk more front page space than he had ever enjoyed before, as he lay dead in the lobby of the Grand Central Hotel, shot by Edward Stokes for love of the actress Josie Manfield.

Unfortunately, Godkin failed to be a leader of anything but opinion. He could never speak directly to the people, and he failed wholly to understand the tidal rise of labor unions in the latter part of the century. Nevertheless, he was a powerful, constructive force in the country, standing in sharp contrast to Dana, who in the end was only a rich man able to vent his prejudices in a daily newspaper—the personification, in that respect, of personal journalism.

Dana and Godkin died within five years of each other, and of the two, oddly enough, it was Dana who made the best use of his later years. Before he died in 1897, he had learned most of the European languages, conducted classes in Dante, raised rare foreign trees, shrubs and flowers, and regarded himself as a connoisseur of wines. He spent much of his time with musicians, writers and artists, and in short, died quite unlike the way he had lived. His editorial enemies pursued him to the end, but when he died, the *Sun* did not carry an obituary. None was necessary.

As for Godkin, the health of this thin, intense man broke in 1900 and he had to retire and sail for England in the following year. Depressed and unwell, he lived only a year longer, contributing a few pieces to the *Post* before he died. He did not know it, but he represented

the climax of a period in which the editorial page spoke with conviction, strength and authority. It was never again so influential.

The only paper in New York to approach the integrity of the *Post*
under Godkin was the *Times,* which was quietly pursuing, under some
difficulties, the line laid down for it by Henry Raymond, a line from
which it would never deviate.

After Raymond's death, the paper was directed for a time by his
friend, George Jones, the business manager. He made the final decisions, but he had the inestimable help of three outstanding editors:
Louis J. Jennings, John Foord and Charles R. Miller. It was Jennings
and Foord who directed the exposure of the Tweed Ring, one of the
Times' finest hours.

William Marcy Tweed was one of the most accomplished plunderers
of a city which, like Boston and Chicago, had suffered from corrupt
city governments almost since its founding. Tweed began his remarkable career of corruption as a member of the Common Council in 1852
and amassed a fortune through the common route of streetcar franchises, city-land sales and other such devices. In 1868, he and a gamey
cast of municipal scoundrels were swept into New York's chief public
offices by a Tammany landslide and the most gigantic frauds in the
city's history began.

On July 8, 1871, the *Times* broke its exposé story, basing it on
documents provided by one of Tweed's rivals, an ex-sheriff named
James O'Brien, who had thoughtfully purloined some of the City
Controller's records before he left office. Hearing of this defection, an
alarmed Tweed sent the Controller, Richard B. "Slippery Dick"
Connolly, to offer Jones a bribe of five million dollars if he would
withhold the documents.

"I don't think the devil will ever make a higher bid for me than that,"
Jones remarked, refusing.

Connolly could not understand such honesty. "Why, with that sum
you could go to Europe and live like a prince," he exclaimed.

"Yes, but I'd know I was a rascal," Jones said.

Once the lid was off, the revelations followed rapidly, not only in
the *Times* but in *Harper's Weekly,* where Thomas Nast's savage cartoons so aroused the public that Tweed tried to buy off the cartoonist

with a half-million-dollar bribe. Tweed's Tammany machine tried to strike back at the *Times* by attempting to oust it from its building, but the other papers came to its defense, except for those which had been on Tweed's payroll and now stood exposed. They had to suspend.

The *Times* followed its July 8th story with one on July 22nd under a front-page banner: "The Secret Accounts: Proofs of Undoubted Frauds Brought To Light." These accounts, said the paper, were "copied with scrupulous fidelity from Controller Connolly's books." When the entire fraud was disclosed, it appeared that the Tweed gang had gotten way with a sum estimated at somewhere between $75 million and $200 million, only a fraction of which was restored. Tweed was arrested, escaped from jail, and was captured in Spain by an official who recognized him from one of Nast's cartoons; he died in Ludlow Street Jail. Connolly got away with enough money to spend the rest of his life in luxury in Paris.

Everywhere in the country newspapers were leading the fight against plundering politicians. During the year after Tweed's exposure, the *Sun's* Washington man uncovered the corruption in the Post Office Department involved with the star-routes, in which mail carriers were paid for mail that was never delivered. The *Times* aided in that clean-up. In St. Louis, the *Democrat* exposed a whiskey ring organized there to cheat the government of its alcohol revenues. These were only two of hundreds of crusades in a crusading era.

Miller, the third of Jones' editors, was more literary and less a crusader, but he was a man of exceptional talent. He led the *Times* in a revolt from the Republican Party in 1884, although Jones himself was for Benjamin Harrison.

These editors gave the *Times* its continuing editorial distinction, but it was Jones' shrewd management which kept the paper prosperous, a fact that became painfully clear after 1891, when he died. The paper lost ground rapidly. Miller and other executives of the *Times* bought it in 1893, but in 1896 it had dropped to a circulation of 9,000 and was losing a thousand dollars every day it published. It was barely alive that year when Adolph Ochs, the 38-year-old publisher of the Chattanooga *Times,* a mid-South equivalent of its New York namesake, managed to raise $75,000, most of it borrowed, and bought what everyone thought was a property too near death to be recovered.

Ochs was a Cincinnatian who had gone to work at eleven on the Knoxville *Chronicle* as an office boy. By the time he was twenty he had learned so much about newspapering that he was emboldened to buy the Chattanooga *Times* with a borrowed $2,500. His formula for making newspapers was a simple one. A paper should be "clean, dignified and trustworthy," he said, at a time when the character of journalism in general, as we have seen, could not have qualified on any of these counts. But that was the kind of newspaper Ochs published in Chattanooga, and when he bought the New York *Times,* no transplanting was necessary. The *Times* was already clean, dignified and trustworthy, and had been since the day Raymond founded it.

There were hard times at first, but Ochs beat off unscrupulous advertisers and politicans, lowered the price of his paper to a penny in 1898, and in a year the circulation had tripled. The *Times* was never in trouble again.

One reason for Ochs' success was the overheated climate of the newspaper business in New York at the end of the century as the era of personal journalism closed with the bizarre struggle between Pulitzer and Hearst. The excesses of the *World* and *Journal* in that contest led Ochs to coin his famous slogan, "All the news that's fit to print," an implicit slap at the two competing giants. A good part of the New York readership turned to his honest newspaper with relief.

They were turning from a struggle which surpassed ordinary credibility. Young W. R. Hearst had descended on the town, fresh from his triumphs with the San Francisco *Examiner* and determined if he could to put the paper on which he had modeled it, the *World,* out of business. Pulitzer by that time was ill-equipped to fight him. He had already gone through an exhausting struggle with Dana, and the acute nervous disorder from which he suffered compelled him to edit the *World* from his apartment.

Pulitzer was a strange, complex personality, whose life is still not well understood today in spite of all that has been written about it. Like so many of the nineteenth-century giants, he was contradictory and eccentric. There was a shocking gap between what he professed and what he did with the *World;* the paper achieved most of its real distinction after his death. Yet his contributions to the newspaper business were substantial, and some of them were lasting, which was more than most of his rivals could say.

Born in 1847 of a good Jewish-Hungarian family, Pulitzer left his native Mako, Hungary, at seventeen because he could not abide the man his widowed mother, whom he idolized, had married. He had been given a good education by private tutors, but he was not fitted for anything in particular. His ambition was to be a soldier. This "tall, scraggy youth with long, thick black hair, large head, and oversized nose," as one of his biographers has described him, wandered about Europe looking for an army to join.

He was a strange sight, "about six feet two and a half inches tall, ungainly in appearance, awkward in movement, lacking entirely in the art of human relations." Even in a world torn by wars and revolutions, he could not find a recruiting sergeant who wanted him. He was told he had weak eyes and an unpromising physique. There may also have been some indications of his approaching nervous disorder.

After being turned down by the Austrians, the French Foreign Legion, the British Army, and even by the old sea captains in Hamburg where he tried to ship as a common seaman, Pulitzer would have gone home from the North Sea port except that he fell in with an agent of the Union Army in America, busy hiring promising young men who would get their passage while he pocketed the $500 bounty given for these recruits, who would then be substitutes for men who did not want to be drafted. Pulitzer signed up immediately.

Later he told several stories about his voyage to America. For a man whose watchword on his newspaper was "accuracy, accuracy, accuracy," Pulitzer was extremely vague about the details of his early life. One story, the best, said that he found out about the bounty on the way over, jumped ship in Boston Harbor, and collected the $500 himself. In any case, he enlisted for a year in the First New York (Lincoln) Cavalry, which had been organized by Colonel Carl Schurz.

Once in the army, he found its life intolerable. Pulitzer's most prominent characteristic was his incessant asking of questions, and he despised anyone who withheld information. These were admirable qualities for journalism, but hardly useful in the military. His skirmishes on the battlefield were far outnumbered by those he fought on the barracks and on the parade ground. Once he was nearly court-martialed when he struck a noncommissioned officer.

Out of the army in 1865, he was alone and broke in New York, sitting in City Hall Park with the other unemployed and staring out at the formidable façade of Park Row, where the offices of the *Times,* the *World,* the *Tribune,* the *Herald* and the *Sun* were clustered. At the moment Pulitzer had no yearning to inhabit them. He only wanted to get a job and learn English. When a man with a crude sense of humor told him the best place to learn the language was in St. Louis, he made his way there—to the city which had the largest concentration of Germans in the country.

At least he could use his native tongue in St. Louis, and he was soon working on the *Westliche Post,* the leading German-language daily. In less than a year he was the city's leading reporter, whose furious energy made him well known to everyone, particularly to the political leaders at the State House, where he spent a good deal of his time. Impressed with his vivid, knowledgeable reporting, these leaders decided he ought to run for the State House of Representatives. In that first year, it should be added, he had mastered English and obtained a certificate of naturalization.

As a legislator, Pulitzer was the same explosive human being he had been as a reporter. Only a year after he was seated, he shot and wounded a well-known lobbyist, but his numerous friends saved him from serious trouble. From the legislature he became one of the city's three police commissioners, worked hard for the Liberal Republicans and helped nominate Greeley in 1872. Pulitzer was one of those several newspapermen backers of Greeley who was profoundly disappointed by Uncle Horace's failure. He turned to the Democrats and became a lifelong member of the Party.

Now he began a series of intricate movements in the newspaper business, during which he acquired a part interest in the *Post,* sold it at a profit, bought the bankrupt *Staats-Zeitung* for next to nothing and sold its AP franchise to the *Daily Globe* for a substantial profit.

With the profits he studied law, was admitted to the bar, married a distant cousin of Jefferson Davis, and in 1878 stood at a crossroads in his life. He could have gone on to become a successful politician; all roads were open to him. But he chose journalism instead, and bought the *Dispatch* for $2,500. He had enough additional resources, $2,700, to operate the paper for seventeen weeks, he estimated. Merging it with his first love, the *Post,* to form the *Post-Dispatch,* he was making $45,000 annually with it after the first three years.

From the first day the *Post-Dispatch* attacked corruption, inspired by Pulitzer's slogan, "Never drop a big thing until you have gone to the bottom of it." As usual, it was dangerous crusading. The paper survived a major scandal when Pulitzer's chief editorial writer killed a prominent lawyer in an argument rising out of an attack on the lawyer's firm, but in spite of this and a few other incidents somewhat less sensational, the *Post-Dispatch* won public acceptance and respect as a fearless newspaper of unblemished integrity, and so it has remained to this day.

Pulitzer was soon a rich man, ready to conquer New York if the opportunity offered. On his way to Europe in May 1883, seeking escape from his growing nervous restlessness, he stopped off in New York, where Jay Gould's representatives sold him the New York *World* for $346,000. Gould thought he had concluded a shrewd deal, since the *World* had been struggling for life ever since its founding as a penny religious daily. He knew Pulitzer could afford it. The *Post-Dispatch* was netting its publisher $85,000 a year by this time, and in any case the *World* purchase was to be paid in installments. Pulitzer believed he knew what to do with his acquisition.

On the first day of publication under its new owner, the *World* printed something more than the usual grandiloquent statement of purpose. It was perhaps the finest expression of journalistic idealism ever written, and it is still carried today on the editorial page of the *Post-Dispatch.* The statement declared the purpose of a newspaper to be as follows:

> An institution that should always fight for progress and reform, never tolerate injustice or corruption, always fight demagogues of all parties, never belong to any party, always oppose privileged classes

and public plunderers, never lack sympathy with the poor, always remain devoted to the public welfare, never be satisfied with merely printing news, always be drastically independent, never be afraid to attack wrong, whether by predatory plutocracy or predatory poverty.

The *World* also announced a ten-point platform: It was for the taxing of luxuries, inheritances, large incomes and monopolies. It advocated abolishing all special privileges possessed by corporations. It demanded tariffs for revenue only, civil service reform, severe punishment for corrupt officials, and punishment for employers who tried to coerce employees in elections.

On the front page the formula was different. It was the mixture as before, brewed by the elder Bennett and improved upon by Dana. The *World's* news columns specialized in sex, scandal and corruption. Its total idea was now clear: a front page for the workingman and the editorial page for the idealistic intellectual. The contrast was marked, and it did not please either class. The workers didn't know what Bennett was talking about on the editorial page, and the intellectuals deplored the *World's* sensationalism.

At this point Hearst arrived in town and started the *Journal* in 1896. He had no idealistic illusions. The *Journal* was frankly and unabashedly for the masses, exploiting them in every possible way, introducing new techniques in words and pictures which gave birth to the phrase "yellow journalism," derived from Hearst's introduction of the comic strip, in which cartoonist Richard Outcault's "Yellow Kid" appeared in monochrome color.

Pulitzer had already been providing a steady diet of sex and crime, but now he understood that he would have to fight Hearst on his own ground if he were to survive. He must have had little heart for it. A general physical failure had compelled him to retire from on-the-spot management of his paper in 1887, perhaps induced by his knockdown fight with Dana and the *Sun* for circulation, during which Dana had proclaimed, "I have never published a falsehood," and Pulitzer responded, "That's another lie."

By this time Pulitzer was going blind, and his nervous affliction had half-crippled him. The worst manifestation of it was an extreme sensitivity to noise. He had made his apartment soundproof, and found he could edit his paper from there in relative comfort, unless some thoughtless editor consulting him should drop something, or crumple a piece of copy paper in his hand. That was enough to send Pulitzer into a pitiful attack of nevous frenzy.

As the disease developed, the restlessness it produced in him kept him traveling constantly. Like Bennett Junior he became a voluntary exile, moving about constantly for nearly twenty years, editing the *World* from wherever he happened to be. If he stopped at a hotel, he had to rent the rooms above and below and on both sides to insure the quiet which was essential. Sometimes he crossed and recrossed the ocean without stopping. In spite of it all, he continued to edit the *World* closely, with incredible tenacity and intelligence. His curiosity never wavered for a moment.

Facing Hearst, ill as he was, he fought back with courage but with the mistaken idea that he could beat the young man at his own game. He had established the *Evening World* in 1887, and the revenue from this extra edition helped in the morning battle, but the profits which Pulitzer had been able to build up through sound management could scarcely match the millions in family fortune which were Hearst's resources. Pulitzer dropped the price of the morning *World* to a penny, so that he would at least be fighting on even terms in that respect. The difference, however, was not only a financial one. It lay in Hearst's genius for mass journalism, and Pulitzer's mistaken determination to hold that market no matter what it cost.

The *World* had made the *Herald* seem pale, but the new *Journal* outdid everything that had gone before in pure sensationalism, and its success was immediate. It was particularly galling to Pulitzer that this success was due in part to the talent Hearst had hired away from the *World* staff—men like Arthur Brisbane, Morrill Goddard, Solomon Solis Carvalho and William H. Merrill. With his virtually unlimited bank account, Hearst hired the best men he could entice from all the papers in town, including the *Sun's* best reporter, Julian Ralph. To write his features, he hired such literary figures as Julian Hawthorne, Bob Davis and Stephen Crane. Then there was a cluster of outstanding executives and writers he had brought along with him from the *Examiner:* Samuel Chamberlain, Winifred Black, Arthur McEwen and Homer Davenport, the noted cartoonist.

Hearst's art department was full of talented men, turning out the comic strips which were new to journalism and which would be read, some of them, for generations to come—one, at least, down to the present day. Richard Outcault drew the first of them, the "Yellow Kid," but then came Rudy and Gus Dirks and their "Katzenjammer Kids"; Jimmy Swinnerton, and the creators of "Foxy Grandpa," "Happy Hooligan," "Alphonse and Gaston," and a dozen others. The art department also employed a young artist who frequently had to be rescued from neighboring bars. His name was John Barrymore.

These were the visible evidence of Hearst's genius, and money, which the public could see. What they did not see was the *Journal's* composing room, where Hearst's good friend and mechanical wizard, George Pancoast, also imported from the *Examiner,* had set up the first press capable of printing four to sixteen color pages. It turned out the first Sunday comic section in color, a revolutionary development which added considerably to the *Journal's* circulation. The *Sunday Journal* was also the first newspaper to use halftone photographs printed on newsprint. That was in 1897, when Hearst further solidified his position by acquiring the dying New York *Morning Advertiser,* for the sake of its Associated Press franchise.

On the front page of the daily, whose makeup was much like the *World's,* which Hearst had always admired, the *Journal* carried on crusades which Pulitzer and his staff had never even thought of. It was a muckraking paper, attacking the "criminal corporations" in a manner that would give Hearst readers fatal convulsions today. Hearst even hired Ella Reeve "Mother" Bloor, later a Communist party heroine, to expose the evils of the packing industry, in the style of Upton Sinclair's *The Jungle.*

The *Journal's* editorial page was far distant from the intellectual appeal of the *World's* editorials. With short, shocking paragraphs— again, something new—Hearst addressed the same people who read the front page, and came out strongly for the eight-hour day, the direct election of United States senators, woman suffrage, Federal income taxes (they were considered a blow to the rich in those days), the rights of labor, and municipal ownership of public services.

Surveying Hearst's gyrations from the Olympian height of the *Post* editorial page, Godkin growled: "A yellow journal office is probably the nearest approach, in atmosphere, to hell existing in any Christian state, for in gambling houses, brothels, and even in brigands' caves there is a constant exhibition of fear of the police, which is in itself a sort of homage to morality or acknowledgment of its existence."

The worst was to come, but it was not quite as bad as it has been depicted. The Spanish-American War is sometimes described as a conflict started by Hearst, part of the violent circulation war between the *Journal* and the *World*. As proof, there is the often quoted pre-war telegram from Hearst to the noted artist, Frederic Remington, who had asked to be relieved of his Cuban assignment: "Please remain. You furnish the pictures and I'll furnish the war." Hearst was even charged at the time, and since, with having conspired to blow up the battleship *Maine* in Havana harbor.

It is quite possible Hearst believed his jingoism was a major factor in precipitating United States entry into a revolution which had already started, but the *Journal's* voice was merely the loudest, seconded by the *World's*, in a journalistic outcry emanating from most of the nation's newspapers. Indeed, Hearst's name is scarcely mentioned in present-day histories of the United States.

At the time, however, to those who lived in New York it must have seemed that the war was the joint invention of Hearst and Pulitzer, with the *Journal's* publisher getting most of the credit. He had started beating the propaganda drums in the first few months of his ownership, hiring no less a correspondent than Richard Harding Davis to go down to Cuba and report the rebellion of 1896. It was that move, no doubt, which convinced Pulitzer he must fight for this obviously tremendous circulation prize.

In their attempt to influence the foreign policy of the United States, in which they were joined by a majority of the nation's press, Pulitzer and Hearst concocted a series of news stories, editorials, pictures and headlines which constituted the most depressing display of unabashed jingoism in the history of American journalism. It shot the circulations of their newspapers well past the million mark, and it helped to stir the people into an emotional response which pushed a reluctant President McKinley into a war that should not have happened. The propaganda of that conflict, and the part American newspapers played in it, is not one of which the business can be proud.

Amidst the clamor, the cold scorn of Godkin dripped from the editorial columns of the *Evening Post,* soon after the sinking of the *Maine* had resulted in the worst excesses of the two papers.

"Nothing so disgraceful as the behavior of two of these newspapers this week has been known in the history of American Journalism," Godkin asserted flatly. "Gross misrepresentation of the facts, deliberate invention of tales calculated to excite the public, and wanton recklessness in the construction of headlines which even outdid these inventions, have combined to make the issues of the most widely circulated newspapers firebrands scattered broadcast throughout the country . . . It is a crying shame that men should work such mischief simply in order to sell more papers."

Once the war started, both the *Journal* and the *World* spared no expense to cover it. The cost of the entire circulation war between Hearst and Pulitzer has been estimated at figures varying from a half-million to eight million dollars. It is certainly higher than the lowest figure, because Hearst spent that much covering the war itself.

Even though its resources were considerably less, the *World* was not without its distinguished coverage. Pulitzer sent Stephen Crane, whose *Red Badge of Courage* had appeared in 1895, as a correspondent, and Crane, who had been living from hand to mouth doing pieces for the *Tribune* and the *Herald,* responded by filing some of the war's best stories. They were not tales of battle, but of soldiers and soldiering— the kind of reporting Ernie Pyle was to do in the Second World War. Crane did, however, cover the fight at Guantanamo Bay in June 1898, when the first American casualties were recorded, and his detailed, informative story appeared on the *World's* front page. He was cited later for his bravery under fire. Later, he made the mistake of describing too accurately the behavior of New York's Seventy-first Regiment in the charge up San Juan Hill, which brought down the patriotic wrath of Hearst, who charged that Pulitzer was slandering the heroism of New York's own sons. Crane came home soon afterward, broken in health; he had only two years to live.

Hearst's coverage of the war was accomplished in his usual magnificent style. He chartered a tramp steamer with a printing press and small composing room in its hold, big enough to print an edition of the *Journal,* and set sail for Cuba himself with a crew of reporters and photographers.

The *Journal's* men not only covered the war, they fought in it on occasion. Early in the conflict a Hearst reporter named Karl Decker had recued the beautiful Evangelina Cisneros, daughter of a Cuban insurgent leader, from a Havana prison in an incident straight out of a bad movie which Hearst inflamed to the proportions of an international incident. At the battle of Guantanamo Bay, Hearst himself headed a foray in a steam launch, in which he landed on the beach and captured twenty-six frightened Spanish sailors stranded there, delivering them as prisoners of war.

As the unlikely climax of the *Journal's* personal war effort, James Creelman, the paper's dignified chief correspondent who was always "Mr. Creelman" even to the other reporters, personally led an infantry charge at the battle of El Caney, during which he was wounded. Creelman wrote about what followed in his book, *On The Great Highway,* published in 1901:

> Someone knelt on the grass beside me and put his hand on my fevered head. Opening my eyes, I saw Mr. Hearst, the proprietor of the New York *Journal,* a straw hat with a bright ribbon on his head, a revolver at his belt, and a pencil and notebook in his hand. The man who had provoked the war had come to see the result with his own eyes, and, finding one of the correspondents prostrate, was doing the work himself. Slowly he took down my story of the fight. Again and again the tinging of Mauser bullets interrupted. But he seemed unmoved. That battle had to be reported somehow.
>
> "I'm sorry you're hurt, but"—and his face was radiant with enthusiasm—"wasn't it a splendid fight? We must beat every paper in the world."

No wonder Governor Sadler, of Missouri, half-seriously proposed that Hearst send down five hundred of his reporters to free Cuba. If he had thought of it in time, no doubt Hearst would have done it.

The cost of the war was more than financial for Pulitzer, although that was serious in itself, since he had been compelled to reach deeply into his reserves. But his precarious health was worse than ever, and he had seen his newspaper so lowered in public esteem during the battle with Hearst that it had been banned, along with the *Journal,* from a good many homes, clubs and libraries. Taking on two such opponents as Dana and Hearst in succession had nearly wrecked both Pulitzer and the *World.* In the years remaining to him, he tried to repair the damage, and succeeded with his paper; his health was beyond repair.

The ceaseless flow of memoranda issuing from him, through the corps of administrative assistants who followed him about, guided and controlled the *World* as completely as though he had been in the building. These instructions were studded with aphorisms, since much quoted, as, "Accuracy is to a newspaper what virtue is to a woman." Always he fought against his abnormally taut nerves. If a guest at dinner so much as cracked a nut unexpectedly, he would suffer a paroxysm of pain, anger and fright. After an attack, one of his respiratory ailments would appear—colds, coughs, bronchitis, asthma. He had, in addition, chronic indigestion, and by this time he was blind. That a man in such condition could control a great newspaper with so much authority is one of the most formidable facts in the history of journalism.

Pulitzer brought the *World* back from the Hearstian depths. He no longer aimed it at the working-class audience which his rival now dominated, but edited it instead as a liberal, democratic organ. It spoke courageously, even passionately, for free speech, personal liberty and Constitutional government. It fought hard against privilege, and attacked relentlessly what Pulitzer always called "the money power."

In its new respectability, the *World* had reached a circulation of 300,000 morning, 400,000 evening, and 600,000 on Sundays before Pulitzer died in October 1911, on his yacht as it lay anchored in the harbor of Charleston, South Carolina. The restless genius left behind him a splendid newspaper, perhaps the best ever published in New York, and the prizes and School of Journalism at Columbia University by which his name is still familiar today.

As for Hearst, he went on to establish the most remarkable newspaper, magazine and real estate empire the country had ever seen, of which more will be said later. He was, however, a survival of the past. For all practical purposes the era of personal journalism, which had begun with Bennett, ended with the end of the century. It had been an era of strong men and strong newspapers, but except for isolated cases like the New York *Times,* the *Evening Post* of Godkin, the Chicago *Daily News* of Lawson, the Kansas City *Star* of Nelson, and the Atlanta *Constitution* of Grady, it had not developed a sense of responsibility. The tone of the press remained strident and barely restrained by the libel laws. In the growing dominance of advertising, however, appeared the first indication that another change was about to take place, and in less than a half-century the American newspaper would emerge as a sober business institution.

THE NEWSPAPER
as
BUSINESS
INSTITUTION

one

Passing of the Old Order

AMERICAN NEWSPAPERS IN LARGE CITIES were already big business as the twentieth century began. They were physically larger, their circulations and advertising volumes were constantly rising, and the total investment each represented had attained figures which put them in a class with other large business enterprises. Bennett had started the *Herald* for $500 in 1835; by 1900, it would have taken at least a million dollars to launch a new newspaper in New York.

The transition was complete by 1914, and the business was beginning to see the fulfillment of Arthur Brisbane's gloomy observation of 1904: "Journalistic success brings money. The editor has become a money man. 'Where your treasure is, there will your heart be also.'"

In the decline and fall of two great newspapers, the *World* and the *Sun,* could be seen the transition from propaganda and personal journalism to the conservative newspapermaking of a new generation of businessmen publishers soon to rise. It was a change in attitude which went beyond the facts of business growth.

The *World,* in 1897, was the largest newspaper in America, with a full-time staff of 1,300 men and women and an annual budget of $2,000,000. Its combined morning and evening circulation was about one million copies, and its regular size of sixteen to twenty-four pages was expanded on Sunday to anywhere from forty-eight to seventy-two pages, approximately half of it advertising. At a conservative estimate it was worth $10,000,000, and was reported to be making a 10 per cent profit. Only thirty-four years later it was sold for $5,000,000 and disappeared forever as a newspaper.

What happened during those thirty-four years was instructive. There was, initially, a passing of the reins from Pulitzer's failing hands to an extraordinary new editor, Frank I. Cobb. Pulitzer had sent one of his personal secretaries on a recruiting tour across the country to find a successor to William H. Merrill, who had been editor of the editorial page for fifteen years, and the emissary had discovered Cobb in Detroit, where he was chief editorial writer for the *Free Press*. After a most careful examination of the candidate—"Search his brain for everything there is in it," Pulitzer instructed his secretary—he was hired, and then was compelled to undergo a daily examination by the publisher so intense he was often tempted to go back to Detroit. Satisfied at last, Pulitzer gave him full control of the editorial page, with the understanding that he would be editor when Pulitzer died.

Almost at once Cobb helped initiate the most famous of the *World's* crusades, its revelation that officers of the Equitable Life Assurance Society were using company money for their own investments. As the inquiry broadened, the New York Life was involved as well. The resulting investigation by a legislative committee not only substantiated everything the *World* had charged, but brought to full public attention the committee's counsel, a young attorney named Charles Evans Hughes who vaulted to the governorship in 1906.

Cobb's enterprise soon involved the *World* in a public quarrel with the President of the United States, in which the issue of freedom of the press was once more argued. The issue rose from the *World's* determination to find out what happened to the $40,000,000 paid by the United States for the rights of the defunct French company which built the Panama Canal. Cobb suspected that some, at least, of this money had gone to government insiders, particularly to William Nelson Cromwell, a promoter, attorney and mystery man of the Roosevelt Administration.

As the 1908 campaign neared its end, the *World* charged that blackmailers were trying to get a part of the Panama millions out of Cromwell and his friends. On the eve of the election, the Indianapolis *News* published an editorial which strongly attacked the whole deal and demanded again to know the whereabouts of the money. This editorial was based on the *World's* story. When it was brought to Roosevelt's attention by a friend, he replied with a letter released to the press which attacked Delavan Smith, publisher of the *News,* and William M. Laffan, the New York *Sun's* publisher. He did not mention Pulitzer or the *World.*

Cobb's editorial on the following day, titled "The Panama Scandal —Let Congress Investigate," was perhaps the strongest editorial aimed at a President since Lincoln's day. It charged Roosevelt with "deliberate misstatements of facts in his scandalous personal attack" on Smith. It called on Congress to make "a full and impartial investigation of the entire Panama Canal scandal." In effect, it charged the President with lying in four separate statements, and added that Roosevelt "must have known they were untrue when he made them." Finally it raised the old cry: "Who got the money?" and ended: "The inquiry was originally the *World's,* and the *World* accepts Mr. Roosevelt's challenge."

The President was angered beyond the limits of good judgment. No real friend of the press in any case, he particularly disliked the *World,* a prejudice no doubt dating from the day of Stephen Crane's San Juan Hill story. Two of the other major New York papers were in little better odor at the White House. "He [the President] takes only the New York *Herald* and the New York *Tribune,*" Major Archie Butt reported. "He knows he will not find anything in them to upset his digestion. 'I could not stand the *Evening Post* or the *Sun* after a hearty meal,' he said."

Roosevelt's response to the *World's* challenge was a special message to Congress, denying any wrongdoing. He called the stories "scurrilous and libelous in character and false in every essential particular," and he said of Pulitzer:

> It is idle to say that the known character of Mr. Pulitzer and his newspaper are such that the statements in that paper will be believed by nobody; unfortunately, thousands of persons are ill informed in this respect and believe the statements they see in print, even though they appear in a newspaper published by Mr. Pulitzer . . . While the criminal offence of which Mr. Pulitzer has been guilty is to form a libel upon individuals, the great injury done is in blackening the good name of the American people. It should not be left to a private citizen to sue Mr. Pulitzer for libel. He should be prosecuted for libel by the governmental authorities.

It was more tirade than message. The result was a governmental criminal libel suit filed in District of Columbia Criminal Court. Indictments on five counts were returned against Pulitzer, his managing and night editors, and the Press Publishing Company. A seven-count indictment was returned against Delavan Smith and his associate, Charles R. Williams. The law on which the indictments were based had been written in the time of Charles II.

No legal justification existed for the bench warrants which went out immediately for the defendants, since they would be taken out of their own jurisdictions and transported to Washington for trial. Pulitzer avoided trouble, because of his health, by staying offshore on his yacht, aptly named the *Liberty*. The others stood their ground.

A federal judge in Indianapolis dismissed the case against Smith and Williams, soon after the United States district attorney resigned rather than be a party to the action. The federal court declared: "If the history of liberty means anything—if constitutional guarantees are worth anything—this proceeding must fail." In Washington, the Attorney General agreed; he had the indictment against Pulitzer and the others dismissed.

That was not the only action, however. Roosevelt had written to Henry L. Stimson, then U. S. District Attorney for Southern New York, saying, "I do not know anything about the law of criminal libel, but I should dearly like to invoke it against Pulitzer, of the *World*." Stimson invoked it, on the technical grounds that twenty-nine copies of the *World* had been circulated at West Point, a federal reservation, thus violating a law intended to protect harbor defenses from malicious injury "and for other purposes." Pulitzer was not indicted, but the *World* and its managing editor were. The court dismissed this indictment on the ground of jurisdiction, and on appeal the United States Supreme Court upheld the *World* unanimously.

The whole affair had been, from the beginning, one of the President's worst misjudgments, about which little that was kind or tolerant could be said. Its practical effect was to establish that the federal government could not sue newspapers for criminal libel in its courts. Cobb called it "the most sweeping victory for freedom of speech and of the press in this country since the American people destroyed the Federalist party more than a century ago for enacting the infamous Sedition law."

The *World* was no more popular with William Howard Taft than it had been with his predecessor in the White House. Archie Butt told this amusing and revealing story to document the fact:

Last night after dinner, when he asked if the New York papers had come, Mrs. Taft handed him the New York *World*.

"I don't want the *World*," he said. "I have stopped reading it. It only makes me angry.

"But you used to like it very much," said Mrs. Taft.

"That was when it agreed with me, but it abuses me now, and so I don't want it."

"You will never know what the other side is doing if you only read the *Sun* and *Tribune*," said this wise woman.

"I don't care what the other side is doing," he answered with some irritation.

When Woodrow Wilson was elected in 1912, the *World* and other crusading newspapers in the nation believed momentarily their troubles in Washington were over. Wilson had declared himself in favor of "pitiless publicity" for public business, and he backed this conviction by instituting the first formal, regular White House press conferences. But the new President, perhaps because of his academic background, only believed in the theory of freedom of the press. He had little confidence in newspaper publishers, and not much more in reporters. A shy and sensitive man, he could not tolerate the idea of personal publicity for himself or his family. The inevitable collisions resulted and it was not long before Mr. Wilson was writing to a friend:

"Do not believe anything you read in the newspapers. If you read the papers I see, they are utterly untrustworthy. They represent the obstacles as existing which they wish to have exist, whether they are actual or not. Read the editorial page and you will know what you will find in the news columns. For unless they are grossly careless the two always support one another. The lying is shameless and colossal."

The President did not, in general, do battle with individual publishers or newspapers, as other presidents had before him. His quarrel was a broader one: he disapproved of the way newspapers operated, and he never understood their practices. Yet no other president ever exercised such power over newspapers as was given to him by the wartime acts governing censorship, espionage and sedition. It must be said he used them wisely for the most part, in spite of the cry raised by some publishers, the same one heard from Washington's day to our own, that the government was interfering with the people's right to know.

Taft believed Wilson was a better manager of the news than most people imagined. Eight months after he retired as President, Taft wrote to Elihu Root: "The use of the Washington correspondents by this administration has been masterly and . . . moves me to say that Theodore is not the only pebble on the beach in the use of the press. It shows a keenness of the use of political instruments and an ability in this direction that rouses my very great admiration, however much it may break the idea that so many people have formed of Woodrow's character."

The *World* performed brilliantly through the Wilson years, under Cobb's direction. It had before it the admonition of Pulitzer as set forth in his long, complex will: "I particularly enjoin upon my sons and my descendants the duty of preserving, perfecting, and perpetuating the *World* newspaper, in the same spirit in which I have striven to create and conduct it, as a public institution, from motives higher than mere gain."

Pulitzer's three sons had been trained carefully to succeed him, but as is the case so often, they were quite unlike the father and had gone into newspaper management only because of Pulitzer's virtual bullying. He had never consulted them about what they might want to do with their lives; as far as he was concerned, it was the *World* or nothing. He supervised their professional schooling himself, and it was rough training. All of them resented it, particularly Joseph, a proud, rebellious young man who had inherited some of his father's temperament. Pulitzer seemed to place more confidence in the other two, Ralph and Herbert, but it was Joseph to whom he gave his closest attention. Apparently he meant to make him the editorial director of the paper, while the others tended to its management.

Joseph's training under his father had been harsh, but his work on the evening *World* as a reporter under the redoubtable Charles E. Chapin was worse. Chapin was a sadistic news executive who gloried in his reputation as the toughest man who ever sat at the city editor's desk. Of the many stories told about him, a large share of them apocryphal, the enduring one was his command to a reporter who had been beaten up and kicked out by a reluctant news source: "You go back and tell that ——— he can't intimidate *me.*"

Chapin may have been "the ablest city editor who ever lived," as Stanley Walker called him, but the price of his competence was too high for most of those who knew him. As Allen Churchill describes him, "He was granitefaced, and under a close-clipped military-type mustache, his mouth seemed a tight, straight slash. On the bridge of his thin nose perched a tortoise-shell pince-nez, anchored to his buttonhole by a dignified black ribbon . . ." A contemporary wrote of him: "His face was a graying paving block, with jaws as square as a lynx's jaws, and as tight. His snake eyes were dull and empty. The shallow light from those eyes never seemed to come from within but from without. His voice seemed to match the rest of him. Big game hunters say that a hostile leopard has a voice like that."

When the excursion steamer *Slocum* sank with an appalling loss of life, Chapin "capered about the city room," as Churchill tells it, "with every trace of enjoyment, to make him seem a figure of jerking, hysterical life in a ballet with a background of morbid death. He would run up and down, peering over shoulders to read the nauseating details of the tragedy as they were typed out. Then, standing erect, he would shout, 'Women and children jumping overboard with clothing afire! Water full of charred bodies!' And between these jackal outcries he would strut exultantly up and down, humming a simmering, happy, tuneless tune."

Of this iron-handed despot, his star reporter, Irvin S. Cobb, coined the memorable phrase, on hearing that "Hard–boiled Charlie" was ill: "Let's hope it's nothing trivial."

Chapin had the consummate bad taste to be proud of his loathesome personality. He wrote: "In twenty years, I never saw or spoke to a member of the staff outside the office or talked to them in the office about anything except the business of the moment. I gave no confidences, I invited none. I was myself a machine, and the men I worked with were cogs. The human element never entered into the scheme of getting out the paper. It was my way of doing things."

Although Chapin has been held up in newspaper memoirs as a man whose total devotion to the news excused everything else, it may well be doubted that he deserved his reputation. There were other city editors similarly devoted who got the news without sadism or self-dramatization. The *World* was not celebrated for the news Chapin obtained. His specialties were sex, crime and disaster, run-of-the-mill spot news. He had no sense of humor, not the slightest understanding of human beings, and for a man to whom news was life, he had little respect for the truth.

It was Frank Cobb who gave the *World* its brilliance and style, which commanded so much respect, and Cobb who gave it direction and meaning with his uncompromising editorial attacks on privilege and corruption. (Walter Lippman succeeded Cobb as editor and carried on in a more subdued way.) The news columns under Chapin were very much as they had always been in the *World's* history—sensational and sometimes offensive. What distinction they possessed came from the work of such first-class reporters and writers as Irvin S. Cobb, Heywood Broun and Franklin P. Adams, and cartoonists like Rollin Kirby, all working under a managing editor, Herbert Bayard Swope, who was by all odds the best in the business, barring Carr van Anda.

Chapin had come to the *World* in 1898 as successor to a city editor, Ernest Chamberlain, who had gone mad. During his tenure on the paper, Chapin's own sanity showed signs of deterioration. Megalomania led him to a frantic speculation in the stock market, disdaining all advice, which led to his imminent financial collapse. In this crisis he planned to kill his wife, Nellie, and himself. He accomplished the murder but failed to turn the gun on himself. Through his personal political influence, he was permitted to plead second-degree murder and was given a twenty-years-to-life sentence in Sing Sing.

There his curious career continued. He edited a prison paper so successfully it had to be taken away from him. He carried on a strange love affair by correspondence with a young girl from Cleveland, who aspired to be a writer, and their letters were published in book form. They met in prison and she appeared to be, inexplicably, in love with him. His personality changed, and he became more human during these prison years. With Warden Lawes' help, he raised roses and built a splendid prison garden. When he died in 1930, it was, in effect, from a broken heart over the removal of his garden to make room for prison expansion.

Chapin fired more than a hundred men while he was city editor of the *World,* and one of them was said to be young Joseph Pulitzer, who later denied it. In any case, Pulitzer went to the St. Louis *Post-Dispatch,* where for many years as president and publisher he carried on the paper's own reputation, as well as the *World's,* for liberal journalism. Under his direction, it became known as the *Manchester Guardian* of America, won many Pulitzer Prizes, and remains one of the best newspapers in America.

Ralph and Herbert, left to manage the *World,* had neither the ability nor the interest essential to guide the newspaper through a period of rapidly changing conditions in the business. Mistakenly, they raised the price of the paper to three cents in 1925, while the competing *Times* and *Herald Tribune* remained at two cents. Tabloids, a new phenomenon, were cutting into circulation, and operating costs were rising. There were desperate maneuvers. The two-cent price was restored, economies made, and high-pressure methods employed to get advertising, but it was too late. In 1930, the Pulitzers lost $1,900,000 on their properties, and at this juncture Roy W. Howard appeared with a $5,000,000 offer for the three papers. He intended to suspend the morning and Sunday editions, and merge the *Evening World* with his *Telegram.*

The *World's* founder had appeared to forbid explicitly any such transaction. His will declared unequivocally: "Nothing in this my will shall be taken to authorize or empower the sale or disposition by the trustees of any stock of the Press Publishing Company, publisher of the *World* newspaper." A hearing had to be held in Surrogate Court to determine whether his sons had the power to sell. It took place in an atmosphere of tension and suspense. *World* employees were trying frantically to buy the paper for themselves; protests over the paper's imminent death were rising everywhere. But the Pulitzer sons' lawyers found a way to make legal the sale which the father's lawyers had tried to prevent, and the surrogate approved. There was an added satisfaction for Roy Howard. He had tried to get a job on the *World* a quarter-century before, but had not been given the courtesy of an interview.

The passing of the *World,* its earlier sins now forgotten, was mourned by people in and out of the newspaper business. But its fate was symbolic of what was happening to newspapers in this transition period. Business methods and the climate of business were beginning to prevail. The man who epitomized the new order was Frank A. Munsey, the telegraph boy from Augusta, Maine, who came to New York in 1882 with $40 in cash, a bundle of children's stories he hoped to make into a magazine, and an overwhelming determination to make money. After establishing himself successfully as a magazine publisher with *Golden Argosy* and *Munsey's,* Munsey ran his various ventures—grocery stores, hotels, banks, magazines—into a million-dollar-a-year income by 1905.

Turning his attention to the newspaper business, Munsey viewed it with a cold but nevertheless calculating eye. It was, he thought, a chaotic and disorganized industry, running counter to every sound management practice in business. "There is no business that cries so loud for organization and combination as that of newspaper publishing," he said. "For one thing, the number of newspapers is at least 60 per cent greater than we need." He described what he intended to do about it with characteristic megalomania, reminiscent of the first Bennett:

> Think of the possibilities involved in a chain of 500 newspapers under a single control! Such a faculty could be so maintained as no college could support; the greatest authors, artists, engineers, essayists, and statesmen could write with authority on every question of importance, each of the 500 papers getting the benefit of these great minds, while maintaining their individuality on purely local matters. There

could be a $100,000 or $200,000 a year man at the head of the editorial force and another God-made genius in charge of the business end . . . and the combined genius of the men in control would be the most uplifting force the world has ever known.

Munsey had no doubt that he was the God-made genius who could make this dream come to pass, but in his subsequent career he was scarcely an uplifting force. He began by buying the New York *Star,* with which he lost $40,000 in four months before he sold it to Hearst, as the *Morning Advertiser.* In 1901 he tried again, this time planning to start his chain with the old New York *Daily News,* Benjamin Wood's Copperhead organ of Civil War days, and the Washington *Times.* To these he added the Boston *Journal,* the Baltimore *Evening News* and the Philadelphia *Evening Times,* which he founded. But he lost $750,000 on the *Daily News* alone; he had to sell the Boston paper; and the one in Philadelphia was suspended. Those in Baltimore and Washington were successful, but Munsey, disappointed, sold them anyway.

He remained unconvinced that there was any other answer to the ills of the newspaper business than consolidation, of the kind that was already taking place in industry and retailing. Using the single newspaper he still owned, the New York *Press,* he looked about for a paper he could combine with it and decided on the *Sun,* which he bought in 1916 for $2,500,000. Edward P. Mitchell, who had been editor of the *Sun* since Dana's death, stayed on as editor, and for a time the accomplished staff he directed made the *Sun* one of Munsey's more profitable ventures. Keats Speed, its managing editor, was regarded as one of the best, surpassed perhaps only by Swope and the legendary Van Anda, of the New York *Times,* who had been night editor of the *Sun* from 1893 to 1904 before he joined Ochs in re-establishing the *Times* as the leader in conscientious and intelligent handling of the news.

The *Sun* also had the advantage of an excellent reporting staff, led by another remarkable figure, Frank Ward O'Malley, whose talents as a feature writer were so much admired that the phrase, "O'Malley of the *Sun*" became a part of the New York mythology.

Munsey cut the price of the *Sun* to a penny and spent two million dollars on it, but the expenses of covering the first World War sliced sharply into profits, and by 1920, the Grand High Executioner was looking about for new victims to merge with the *Sun*. There were, at the moment, fourteen newspapers of general circulation in New York, not including the foreign-language press: the *Times, World, Tribune, Herald, Sun, American,* and the new tabloid *Daily News* in the morning field; and the *Post, Evening Sun, Evening World, Telegram, Evening Journal, Mail* and *Globe and Commercial Advertiser* comprising the evening papers. These newspapers had ten different owners.

Then Munsey set to work. He bought the *Herald*, the *Telegram* and the Paris *Herald* for four million dollars from the Bennett estate. Merging the morning *Sun* with the *Herald*, he passed on its name to the evening edition, which he operated in competition with his own *Telegram*. Next he bought the *Globe*, in 1923, primarily to get its AP franchise, and merged it into the *Sun*. That cost him two million dollars. A year later another two million got him the *Mail*, which he merged with the *Telegram*.

To Munsey it was logical that his morning *Herald*, running perilously close to the margin, should acquire the *Tribune*, then at the bottom of the morning heap in circulation. Here, however, he encountered the determined opposition of the *Tribune's* owners, Ogden Mills Reid and his talented wife, Helen Rogers Reid. The *Tribune* was a proudly and closely held family newspaper, and the only Republican paper left in the morning field. The Reids refused to sell, whereupon Munsey offered to sell them the *Herald* and its Paris offshoot for $5,000,000. This transaction enabled the new *Herald Tribune* to continue on its editorially successful, if occasionally financially rocky course until its sale in 1958 to John Hay Whitney, the present owner.

Death ended Munsey's fantastic career in 1925 before he could make any more drastic changes in the New York newspaper scene. In 1931, however, the *Telegram* he had left behind was acquired by the Scripps-Howard chain and merged with the *World*, thus setting the stage for the passing of the last of the grand old newspapers, the *Sun*, when Roy Howard bought it in 1950 (it had for several years been a staff-owned paper, directed by William T. Dewart) and merged it into his *World-Telegram* to make the present-day *World-Telegram & Sun.*

Although Munsey was blamed for the shrinkage of the New York newspaper field, he only hastened a process which was, in any case, inevitable. Munsey was a businessman, a very good one, who had an unsentimental attitude toward the newspaper business which profoundly irritated members of the profession. Their opinion was expressed by William Allen White's famous obituary in his Emporia *Gazette:* "Frank A. Munsey contributed to the journalism of his day the talent of a meatpacker, the morals of a money-changer and the manners of an undertaker. He and his kind have about succeeded in transforming a once-noble profession into an eight per cent security. May he rest in trust!"

What Munsey had begun was going on in all the major urban centers of the country. In Philadelphia another successful magazine publisher, Cyrus H. K. Curtis, was busy demonstrating that he had much less talent for managing newspaper properties. There had been thirteen dailies in Philadelphia in 1895, but there were only eight when Curtis came on the newspaper scene in 1913. At that time the *Evening Bulletin,* owned by William L. McLean, was in command of the field.

Curtis reduced the field. He bought the *Public Ledger* from Adolph Ochs and made it an evening paper, in competition with the *Bulletin.* To obtain an AP membership in 1918 he bought the *Evening Telegraph,* a paper founded in 1864, and killed it; the same fate befell the *Press,* started in 1857, which Curtis bought and suspended in 1920 to get its newsprint contracts. His third victim was a distinguished magazine, the *North American,* a crusader since 1839. He also bought the New York *Evening Post* in 1923 and temporarily interrupted the liberal course it had pursued since its founding.

Out of these maneuverings Curtis succeeded in building a formidable property in the *Public Ledger.* Pouring money into its plant and personnel, he created a newspaper with a foreign service rivaled only by the Chicago *Daily News* and the New York *Times,* a paper well written and edited which he intended to make a national organ, like the *Times*. In 1930 he bought his only morning competition, the *Inquirer*.

But the financial underpinnings of this empire were unsound, and shortly after Curtis died in 1933, it came apart. The *Inquirer* and *Public Ledger* were merged, and this paper went back to its former owners, who in turn sold it to Moses L. Annenberg in 1936. The *Evening Public Ledger* expired in 1942. J. David Stern, the liberal "maverick" publisher of the *Inquirer's* morning rival, the *Record*, rescued the New York *Evening Post* and restored it to a liberal course. Of Curtis's seven papers, only one remained.

Similar shiftings were going on in Chicago, which in 1904 had four morning papers (*Tribune, Inter Ocean, Record-Herald* and *Examiner*) and four evening (*Daily News, Post, Journal* and *American*). By the time the consolidators, led initially by Herman Kohlsaat, were through in our own time, there were only four newspapers under two ownerships.

Everywhere in the nation the story was the same, particularly in the morning field, which was being hit hard by the developing preferences of readers and advertisers for afternoon papers. The number of morning dailies dropped from 500 to 388 between 1910 and 1930. By 1933, there were forty cities in the nation with populations of more than 100,000 which boasted only one morning daily. The growth of the two largest chains, Hearst and Scripps-Howard, was also hastening the consolidation process. Sixteen papers succumbed to the Hearst ax between 1918 and 1928, while the Scripps-Howard interests accounted for fifteen more between 1923 and 1934.

Not all the victims deserved to live, judged strictly on merit, but it was sad to see such traditional papers of real excellence like the Boston *Transcript* go under. In Boston, the eleven major newspapers of 1900, under seven ownerships, were reduced to eight newspapers under five ownerships. The story was the same in Baltimore, Milwaukee, Detroit, San Francisco, Los Angeles and other cities.

Chain journalism and the trend to consolidation together constituted one of two major phenomena characteristic of the old order's passing. The other was the advent of tabloid journalism and its companion, "jazz journalism," a manifestation primarily of the Twenties. A distinction is made because not all "jazz" journals were tabloids.

The tabloids reflected the times and rising costs. Jazz journalism was the last flowering of nineteenth-century sensationalism, transplanted to another century and destined for a short but effulgent growth. It was as much out of context as those two anachronisms, William Randolph Hearst and Colonel Robert R. McCormick, who carried on personal journalism in an era which had outgrown it.

In 1835, Bennett had introduced sensationalism to a mass market waiting for it. In 1920, a war-weary generation about to embark on the gaudiest decade in the nation's history, embraced jazz journalism, producing a new mass readership added on to existing circulations. New ingredients were now added to the old formulas of sex and crime: the tabloid format, and photography. Not that either ingredient had never been used before. Tabloids had been seen in America since 1873, and Alfred C. Harmsworth, Lord Northcliffe, had operated a highly successful tabloid in London since 1903; his *Daily Mirror* already had a circulation of more than a million by 1909, against two similar competitors. All these papers, abroad and at home, were richly illustrated.

The proper combination of ingredients was not achieved, however, until two grandsons of Joseph Medill, Joseph Medill Patterson and Robert R. McCormick, held their historic meeting on a manure pile in France in 1918, where in effect they launched the New York *Daily News*. These disparate cousins had been co-existing as proprietors of the Chicago *Tribune* since 1910, but their partnership was wearing thin. They could not have been more unlike. Patterson considered himself a man of the people, possibly a socialist, and he had already written two novels of social protest. McCormick thought of himself as an aristocrat, and behaved as though he were the last of the Bourbons.

They were as unlike in war as in peace. In the Mexican episode of 1916, Patterson had enlisted as a private and traveled with the cavalry; McCormick was an officer on General Funston's staff, and had been horribly embarrassed when his cousin, visiting him and smelling like a stable, had ridden in the same hotel elevator with him and the General. In the first World War, which both men had violently opposed until six months before American entry, Patterson again had enlisted, working his way up from the ranks to a captaincy, while McCormick began as an officer on General Pershing's staff, living in Paris a good part of the time and ultimately became a colonel. Their meeting in France, transferred from a farmhouse to the aromatic pile outside because of the noise in this field headquarters, resulted from a conversation Patterson had just enjoyed with Northcliffe, who urged him to try the *Daily Mirror* formula in America.

The cousins agreed that after the war they would end their uneasy Chicago relationship, although Patterson would, of course, retain his family financial interest in the *Tribune*. Then the Captain would establish in New York a tabloid paper, which would remove him from Chicago, satisfy his restless urge to be his own boss, and as far as the Colonel was concerned, create an enterprise which might well be unprofitable enough to help the highly solvent *Tribune's* tax situation. Both men were pleased with the idea. They shook hands on the agreement and parted.

As a result, the *Daily News* began publishing on June 26, 1919. Patterson divided his time at first between Chicago and New York but the new paper was soon claiming all his attention and he moved permanently to Manhattan.

The going had not been as easy as he anticipated. Other publishers and editors called the *Daily News* the "servant girl's Bible," and Patterson found it difficult to attract able newspapermen from other dailies to work for him. But then, overnight, the formula Patterson had developed found its audience. Circulation, which had been as low as 26,000 at the start, passed the million mark in December 1925. It had taken the *News* just five years to jump from last place to first in New York. Its Sunday edition moved even faster. Started on May 1, 1921, it climbed to fourth place in a year, and in four years more it was first, with a new Sunday circulation record in the United States of 1,234,189.

Sex and sensation were the stock in trade of the *News*. Observing its phenomenal success, the old master of the art, Hearst, launched a competing tabloid in 1923, the *Mirror,* but it was never more than a dim reflection of the *News,* which went on to become the largest daily in America. Other imitators were no more successful. Bernard Macfadden attempted to out-sensationalize Patterson with his *Evening Graphic,* known in the trade as the "Pornographic," but the numbing effect of its daily assaults on sense and sensibility made it impotent in a short time. It ultimately went insane and was committed to the history books.

The *News* was described accurately as "by turns sobby, dirty, bloody and glamorous," covering the news in a manner that would "appeal to the more elementary emotions of a truck-driver, and to the truck-driver in everyone." When the crash of 1929 changed the emotional tone of America abruptly, Patterson astutely altered his formula. "We're off on the wrong foot," he told his staff. "The people's major interest is no longer in the playboy, Broadway and divorces, but in how they're going to eat, and from this time forward we'll pay attention to the struggle for existence that's just beginning."

Patterson's decision resulted in the paper's passionate support of the Roosevelt administration for nearly eight years, while the Chicago *Tribune* became the President's principal enemy. The cousins were united again, however, when the issue of isolationism or intervention found them in the same camp. By that time, too, Patterson was rich and successful enough to have lost his enthusiasm for socialism. In a short time the *Daily News* was quite as far to the right as the *Tribune.*

A proud man, six feet tall, with gray, bristling hair, a square face heavily seamed, lips straight and thin, eyes deepset, hands large and thick, Captain Patterson walked with a heavy, decisive step. In sharp contrast to the Colonel's sartorial elegance, the Captain dressed casually; at his best, he was no more than baggily orthodox. With all his faults and virtues, he was a dominant personality, perhaps a genius in his special field, the mass tabloid, and these facts were recognized even by his enemies. When he died in 1946, no one doubted that the *Daily News* would continue successfully in other hands; it was in complete command of its market. But it was equally clear that Patterson himself would be irreplaceable.

Not all tabloids were like the *Daily News* and the *Graphic.* Even in the jazz age there were attempts to establish newspapers in the newly popular format which would purvey news and pictures in a more conventional way. Cornelius Vanderbilt, Jr., started crusading, respectable tabloids in Los Angeles, San Francisco and Miami in the early 1920s, but the chain died because it never commanded advertising support to back its circulation. In Los Angeles, too, there was Manchester Boddy's liberal, Democratic *Daily News,* and in Chicago, the Chicago *Times,* founded in 1929, was another well-edited tabloid. Marshall Field bought it in 1947 and combined it with his standard-sized *Sun,* but retained the tabloid format for the new *Sun-Times,* which his son publishes today. The Scripps-Howard interests also employed the tabloid idea in Washington with the *Daily News,* and in Denver with the *Rocky Mountain News.*

Perhaps the most interesting of the tabloid experiments was in New York, where Marshall Field III launched the newspaper *PM,* a liberal, experimental daily, without advertising, on June 18, 1940. *PM* was the child of Ralph Ingersoll, a mining engineer who found himself in 1936 as vice-president and general manager of Time, Inc., and a year later as the entrepreneur of *Life Magazine,* which he had conceived. *PM,* another outgrowth of his amazingly active brain, was backed by Marshall Field III and a board of directors which included some of the best-known names in publishing and business. Its prospectus was so exciting, and its promise of a frankly liberal policy so entrancing, that it attracted thousands of applications from some of the best newspapermen in the country.

Certainly few papers have ever been launched with such a distinguished staff, and such promising prospects. Few, too, have ever lived up to their promise as well. Yet *PM* was, in the end, a failure. The liberals did not support it, as Field and the others had expected they would, in spite of the fact that American liberals had never really supported any of the publications addressed to them. The decision not to take advertising was a mistake, rectified in 1947 when it was too late. General readers were attracted by *PM's* outstanding art work, superlative departments, good writing, excellent editorials and investigative reporting, but they were disappointed by the inadequacy of its news coverage, which was often as biased on the liberal side (although never pro-Communist, as some of its more excitable enemies charged), as Colonel McCormick was on the opposite side. After suffering losses estimated at as much as $5,000,000, and failing to achieve a circulation of even 200,000, *PM* was sold in April 1948 to the late Bartley Crum, a noted lawyer, and Joseph Barnes, foreign editor of the *Herald Tribune*. It had a brief reincarnation as the *Star*, before it suspended in January 1949.

Earlier in New York the jazz journalism of the city's tabloids during the 1920s had created the impression that the worst excesses were committed there. They were no worse, however, than the wild days of the Twenties in Chicago, where the *Tribune* and the *Examiner* fought a bloody circulation war, with gangsters allegedly driving the delivery trucks on occasion; and where the *Tribune's* noted crime reporter, Jake Lingle, was mysteriously murdered (in 1930), presumably because of his underworld connections.

Those Chicago days were chronicled by Ben Hecht, who had been a reporter there, and his friend Charles MacArthur in their famous play, "The Front Page," an account theatrically exaggerated but nevertheless conveying the spirit of a time when newspapers came closest to being the kind of madhouses they were later depicted as being in motion pictures and television. That image, in fact, derived principally from the Hecht-MacArthur characterization of life on the Chicago police beat. A fuller, richer flavor was embodied in Hecht's reminiscent "A Thousand and One Afternoons In Chicago," and later in his autobiography, "A Child of The Century."

Certainly they were days that would not come again. The Great Adjustment of 1929 and the Great Depression which followed it marked the end of a kind of American newspapering which had existed since James Franklin's *Courant*. The transition period itself had been a long one, from the turn of the century through three decades of crusading, war and tabloidism, but it was now complete. Hearst's career was well past its prime, and McCormick, the last of the personal journalists, was a curious anachronism. The world began to change radically in the Thirties, and the second World War created in its aftermath a wholly new environment for the newspaper business.

What could be said of the first 240 years of the American newspaper as it came to this dividing line in 1930? Its freedom had been established and certified by the Constitution and by subsequent court decisions, but it would never be free enough to satisfy those publishers who regarded every effort at reasonable control, particularly on the part of government, as infringement of a sacred right. It was a press which frequently proclaimed its responsibility, but generally speaking was only beginning to develop a sense of it after more than two centuries. It had progressed from partisan propaganda to private one-man ownership control, to a status as large-scale business institution, operating within the framework of the national business structure. Thus institutionalized, it was rapidly taking on the characteristics of institutions, becoming by and large a conservative defender of the status quo, although professing independence and progressivism.

The men who had made the nation's newspapers in those first 240 years had been a curiously mixed bag. The strain of creative eccentricity had run strongly through them all. The political connivers and slanderers of the first period had given way to the egocentric editors of the second era, and these had been succeeded by the businessmen publishers of the twentieth century, although traces of the strong-minded editor and the personal crusade still survived. It could be said fairly that the newspaper had made the slowest adjustments to changing times in its long history than any of the other print media.

This slowness and resistance to change was much more evident in physical aspects. Changes in printing technology had been traditionally slow, and were more or less forced by cultural and population pressures. Makeup and writing styles had changed, also slowly; newspaper techniques in 1930 were not substantially different than they had been sixty years before. The rise of advertising and its supplanting of circulation as the newspaper's chief source of revenue had been the outstanding development of the new century, and would continue to play an increasingly important role in newspaper development.

Newspapers and the other print media had been threatened successively by the bicycle, the automobile, motion pictures and radio, each one of which, it had been freely predicted, would mean their death, but they had survived and prospered. These inventions, to which television would soon be added, were to create a new era of mass media competition, and again the newspaper would be slow to adjust.

When the debits and credits were balanced, the American newspaper in 1930 stood clearly in the black. It had become the primary source of news and information in America, indispensable as an advertising medium and as a community bulletin board. It had come a very long way since James Gordon Bennett had devised its modern concept in 1835. The worst trials were ahead.

two

The Rise of Chain Journalism

CHAIN JOURNALISM, WITH ITS CONCOMITANT TREND toward monopoly, has been one of the most significant journalistic developments of the twentieth century. For the more than sixty years that chains have been a fact of life in the newspaper business, they have been dominated by two men and their successors—W. R. Hearst, and Edward Wyllis Scripps, the self-styled "damned old crank." They were strong, colorful men, but the organizations they created were larger than life and in the end tended to submerge them.

Scripps did not invent the chain idea, but he was the first American publisher to make it work. He made it work so well that he left behind him one of the richest legacies in journalism: the Booth Newspapers of Michigan, the Scripps League of Newspapers in the Northwest, the John P. Scripps papers on the Pacific Coast, and the Scripps-Howard chain, with its allied United Press International, and three feature syndicates.

This empire resulted from the genius of a single man, who was accurately measured by Lincoln Steffens, one of the greatest of all reporters, in a letter he wrote to Jo Davidson when he learned that the sculptor had been commissioned to do a bust of Scripps.

> You must do a great thing with Scripps. He is a great man and an individual. There is no other like him: energy, vision, courage, wisdom. He thinks his own thoughts absolutely. He sees straight. He sees the line he is on and his thinking sticks to that. I regard Scripps as one of the two or three great men of my day.

He is on to himself and the world, plays the game and despises it. He is sincere and not cynical. Really he should be done, but as a full-length standing figure so as to show the power of the man, the strength he took care to keep from being refined; he avoided other rich men, so as to escape from being one; he knew the danger his riches carried for himself, for his papers and for his seeing.

Rough, almost ruthless force, but restrained by clear, even shrewd insight; an executive capable of fierce action, restrained by the observation that a doer must not do too many things himself, but use his will to make others do them. And he did that all right. Read some of his letters to editors, the young fellows he was driving so hard and letting alone.

The man Steffens described in such glowing terms was once called "the laziest boy in Schuyler county," although it is hard to understand why. Born in 1854, he grew up the youngest of thirteen children, an awkward, redheaded farm boy who worked the dawn to night schedule of other farm children and seldom had time to play. The "laziest boy" appellation may have stemmed from the fact that Ed, when he was only fourteen and his brothers had all left home, was compelled to run the farm himself when his father fell ill, and in doing so conceived the idea of hiring town boys to work with him at twenty-five cents a day, and encouraged them to race with each other down equal rows which he divided off, while he watched from a fence rail or read in a shady spot.

That was part of his philosophy, a principle he outlined later in "Some Outlandish Rules for Making Money." On the farm and afterward, he wrote, his idea was: "Never do anything that you can get someone else to do for you. The more things that someone else does for you the more time and energy you have to do those things which no one else can do for you."

Most of Ed's education came from his half-sister, Ellen Browning Scripps, who was eighteen years older and had graduated from Knox College. He had an elder brother James, of whom he stood in awe as a child and later disagreed with violently. It was James who founded the Detroit *News* in 1873 and thus laid the foundations of empire. It was there Ed went to work when he left the farm at eighteen. Ellen and another brother, George, were already working on the *News*.

The chain itself was born in Cleveland, where Ed founded the *Penny Press* in 1878, with $10,000 borrowed from his sister and brothers. Like so many other publishers of the day, he announced himself as the enemy of the "interests," of power and privilege. Ellen contributed short paragraphs which he printed as "Miscellany," and these pieces inspired the creation of the Newspaper Enterprise Association (NEA), to distribute syndicated features.

With the *Press* making a profit, Ed persuaded his brothers to buy the St. Louis *Chronicle,* but there he found himself opposed by Joseph Pulitzer and the competition was too much. In 1883, he bought the *Penny Paper* in Cincinnati, changed its name to the *Post,* and attacked municipal corruption. Scripps himself led an unconventional life, as unorthodox as his ideas, but he saw no inconsistency in that; he was his own man.

The split with his brother James came in 1887, when Scripps took advantage of James' absence abroad to revolutionize the Detroit *News* by expanding it into a major newspaper, with a staff he trained himself. Instead of being impressed, James was frightened and angry. He fired his brother as president of the Detroit News Association, and as president of the Scripps Publishing Company. George, too, was involved in the quarrel. He had promised in writing to turn over control of the Cleveland *Press* to E. W., but now he was prevented by James from doing it. George and E. W. remained friends, but Ed never forgave James; the break with him was complete.

He still had the Cincinnati *Post,* which he had put in charge of Milton McRae, a cautious but shrewd businessman who had come from the Detroit paper. With McRae, Scripps formed a partnership in 1889. It permitted Scripps to take two-thirds of the profits and to "go where he pleased, live where he pleased and do as he pleased" without being hampered by business details. McRae took the other third of the profits and served as the front office man. Scripps preferred to stay out of the public eye.

In 1890, then, at the age of thirty-six, Scripps retired. He was driven to it, according to his granddaughter's husband, Charles R. McCabe, by "a combination of misanthropy, raw nerves and family exacerbations," which "drove him as far away from his kind as was possible without loss of nationality." He moved with his wife and three children to Miramar Ranch, his windswept mesa home sixteen miles from San Diego, in the farthest southwest corner of the United States.

From Miramar he became another long-range publisher, like Bennett and Pulitzer, managing his enterprises and expanding his chain. As he expanded, he chose promising young men as editors and business managers of his new enterprises, giving them the opportunity to buy 10 per cent of the stock, and lending them money at 6 per cent to buy it if they were not in funds, which was ordinarily the case.

The papers he established were often grubby affairs, operating on next to nothing, published in shabby quarters, but they all had the inestimable advantage of Scripps's managing genius, and their editors had the opportunity to sit at the publisher's feet in Miramar, sometimes for weeks at a stretch, and absorb his ideas and iconoclastic philosophy. He was like a lord of the manor, holding court in feudal splendor, but quite unlike that other lord, Hearst, who would someday reign at San Simeon farther north in California. Scripps was a striking figure in this rôle, with his bushy red beard, balding head covered with a skullcap, trousers tucked into white kid boots.

He wanted his papers to be autonomous, but at the same time he wanted his editors to feel and think as he did, and he thought and felt about any number of things. "I have one principle," he said, "and that is represented by an effort to make it harder for the rich to grow richer and easier for the poor to keep from growing poorer." Of his own papers, he said: "We can hold together, having supporting us the army of our followers, so long as we fight hard and fight and win our battles for them; so long as we fight against privilege and success, by degree transferring some of the privileges from the few to the many.

Scripps summarized his philosophy in his much quoted "Letter To A Young Editor," who happened to be Paul Edwards, then entrusted with the Scripps paper in Houston. He wrote,

> I would advise you to begin your course as editor of this paper with one object and only one object in view, and that is to serve that class of people and only that class of people from whom you cannot even hope to derive any other income than the one cent a day they pay for your paper. Be honest and fearless with them, always without

regard to the goodwill or the ill will of the so-called business community . . .

Be diplomatic, but don't be too damned diplomatic. Most men fear to speak the truth, the bald, bold truth, to any man or community because they fear that the man or the community is not prepared to endure such franknesses. I think this is a mistake. It is rare indeed when the circumstances are such that a conscientious man can lose anything by fearless, frank speech and writing.

These words, it must be remembered, came from a man who was living on a 2,100-acre ranch, in a lovely Spanish-style house, with fountains and thousands of trees around it, shouting at the servants, living like a lord. He made no secret of this discrepancy, often remarking that he would sacrifice anything in the world for the common people but he was damned if he would live with them.

"The loneliness of my life is great," he wrote. "I am hated by the rich for being a renegade, and I am hated by the poor for being rich. I am not wise enough or learned enough to be an acceptable member in the highbrow club. I have learned too many things to make me a comfortable companion of the man in the field, on the street and in the shop."

In the reorganization of the Associated Press, the Scripps papers were told that they would have to join up at once without reservation, or be left out in the cold. E. W.'s answer was to combine his Scripps-McRae Association with two other news distribution agencies in 1907 to form the United Press, at a cost of several hundred thousand dollars more than it would have cost the papers to join the AP. Scripps made this move against the considered opinion of most other publishers that it would be a flat failure. He only remarked that it would have to be a large venture to succeed.

Behind the creation of the United Press was Scripps' resentment of the franchise idea which was the basis of the AP. To him it smacked of the private club and the monopoly. He wanted every man founding a newspaper to be able to obtain a wire service. The UP, he said, would "disseminate news that is of value to the public and that is against the interests of the plutocrat band . . . Perhaps my greatest reason . . . was that I knew that at least 90 per cent of my fellows in

American journalism were capitalistic and conservative. I knew at the time at least that unless I came into the field with a new service, it would be impossible for the people of the United States to get correct news through the medium of the AP."

While this was taking place, George Scripps died and left his share in the Detroit *News* to E. W. An out-of-court settlement of a suit by James contesting the will gave him the Detroit paper while the remainder of the Scripps properties went to E. W. James and his descendants continued to develop his paper successfully, while a son-in-law, George Booth, left the *News,* bought the Grand Rapids *Press,* and founded the Michigan chain of eight Booth newspapers. As for Scripps, he retired once more after the UP was under way, remarking, "I like to play dead and watch the property I've built."

He was, of course, incapable of real retirement. Secretly he commissioned one of his editors, Negley Cochran, to found an experimental adless tabloid paper, anticipating *PM* by some thirty years. His paper was the Chicago *Day Book,* which began publishing in 1911, with its expense budget arbitrarily set at $2,500 a month, including everything but paper. The other Chicago papers reacted exactly as the New York *Daily News* did when *PM* appeared. They tried to get it thrown off the stands, and only an influential alderman was able to get it back on sale. The *Day Book* lasted for six years before Scripps decided, in 1917, that Cochran was more important to him in Washington than Chicago. The paper's suspension was certainly not for lack of talent: its outstanding staff included Carl Sandburg, among others.

E. W. trained his sons to succeed him, keeping them out of college so that they would not, as he said, acquire a sense of superiority through buying knowledge and training which the common people could not afford. His oldest son, Jim, was so like James Scripps that a break between father and son was inevitable, and it occurred in 1920, leaving the son in control of the five Scripps papers on the West Coast. These were continued by his widow and sons as the Scripps League, after Jim died suddenly at thirty-four. A grandson of E. W. and Milton McRae, John P. Scripps, later established a small group of papers in Southern California.

Until nearly his last breath, E. W. was busy in his retirement. In 1920 he founded *Science Service*, the first attempt to translate the burgeoning activities of the nation's scientific community into stories the untrained reader could understand. A little later he endowed the Foundation for Research in Population Problems, at Miami University in Ohio, and with Ellen, established and financed the Scripps Institute of Biological Research at La Jolla, which eventually became the Scripps Institute of Oceanography, part of the University of California.

Like Bennett and Pulitzer, Scripps was a yachtsman, and at the end of his life he retreated to sea, as they had, to escape the pain of life ashore, roving from place to place, proud and alone. One night in March 1926, he died suddenly of apoplexy at seventy-two, on his yacht as it lay anchored in Monrovia Bay, off Liberia. According to his wishes, he was buried at sea.

Robert Paine Scripps, his only surviving son, was left with the controlling interest in papers in fifteen states, plus the UP, the NEA, Acme Newsphotos, United Features Syndicate, and mechanical and supply properties. Robert was at the editorial helm, and Roy W. Howard was business manager of the Scripps interests. It was an arrangement which did not last long. The name of the organization had already been changed in 1922 from Scripps-McRae to Scripps-Howard, and after E. W.'s death, the emphasis changed too from Scripps to Howard.

It was an inevitable change. Roy Howard was a qualified genius in his own right, a natural reporter and a born manager of newspaper properties. He had begun life in a tollhouse on the Dayton turnpike near Cincinnati in 1883, and started his newspaper career as high school correspondent for the Indianapolis *News*. After reporting for papers in Indianapolis and St. Louis, where he was assistant telegraph editor on the *Post-Dispatch* under another noted editor, O. K. Bovard, Howard came up to the Cincinnati *Post* and entered the Scripps realm. He went to New York as correspondent for the Scripps-MaRae News Service, and when the UP was formed, he was made its first vice-president and general news manager.

Until this time he had never met Scripps. The historic confrontation took place at Miramar in February 1908, and Scripps later set down his impression. He found Howard ". . . a striking individual, very small in stature, a large speaking countenance and eyes that appeared to be windows for a rather unusual intellect. His manner was forceful, and the reverse from modest. Gall was written all over his face. It was in every tone and every word he voiced. There was ambition, self-respect and forcefulness oozing out of every pore of his body . . . However, so completely and exuberantly frank was he that it was impossible for me to feel any resentment on account of his cheek."

Two months after this meeting, the UP's first president, John Vandercook, died and Howard was appointed to succeed him. He was a spectacular success at it, traveling the world, interviewing great men, hobnobbing with international celebrities.

After the first World War, Howard turned his attention to the chain. In the year following E. W.'s death, he satisfied a long-held desire by buying the *Telegram* and establishing the Scripps-Howard banner in New York. Less and less was heard of Robert P. Scripps. Curiously, he too retired to Miramar, and again like his father, died on his yacht, at sea, off Lower California, when he was only forty-two. Until the founder's grandchildren were old enough to take over, Howard ran the empire under a trust agreement.

It was a contracting empire in the Thirties, following the general trend to consolidation, but the papers still carried the Scripps stamp, as they do today, as crusading, community newspapers, although their politics swung around in time to the opposite point of the compass from the founder's view.

Scripps's chief rival in the business of chain journalism was Hearst, and the contrast both in methods and personalities could not have been greater. Where Scripps ran his papers on little money, made them relatively autonomous and trained the editors himself, Hearst spared no expense to establish his empire, and hired editors to run his newspapers but gave each one of them his daily personal attention.

The Hearst empire began to form in 1904, when he added a Boston paper to those in San Francisco and New York, and started another *Examiner* in Los Angeles. Then there was a lull until 1912, when he purchased the Atlanta *Daily Georgian*. In the following year he bought the conservative San Francisco *Morning Call,* converting it into an evening paper.

In the years of the first World War, most publishers abandoned expansion temporarily to meet the circulation demands generated by the battles, but Hearst took advantage of their preoccupation to buy three more newspapers, the Washington *Times* and the Boston *Daily Advertiser* in 1917, and the Wisconsin *News* (Milwaukee) in 1918. Again, in the depression that followed the war, he ran counter to the tide by adding three more in 1921: the Boston *Record,* the Detroit *Times* and the Seattle *Post-Intelligencer.* The Boston acquisition was merged with the *Advertiser,* whose Sunday rights and features were combined with the Sunday *American* and reissued as the tabloid Sunday *Advertiser.* Its name was changed to the *Record* in 1929.

In 1922, on his fifty-ninth birthday, Hearst remarked in his usual philosophic statement to the press: "I never plan any extensions, but newspapers seem just naturally to keep coming to me to be taken over. I am not as young as I was once, and the older we get the less likely we are to set out to conquer the world."

That was the same year the reluctant world conqueror bought five more newspapers: the Washington *Herald,* the Rochester *Journal,* the Oakland *Post-Enquirer,* the Los Angeles *Herald,* and the Syracuse *Telegram,* which three years later was merged with the Syracuse *Journal.* For good measure, in 1922, he founded the New York *Mirror.* A year after these wholesale operations, he acquired the Baltimore *News,* and the year after that, the Albany *Times-Union,* the San Antonio *Light* and the Milwaukee *Sentinel.*

When at last he rested on his oars, he commanded an audience of more than three million people for his Sunday morning papers, and perhaps twice that on weekdays. The California papers alone earned more than five million dollars a year. For a man who talked about the end of desire and the lack of worlds to conquer, it had been a fairly active three years of labor—and it did not include the excitements in Chicago, where his morning *Examiner* had taken over the *Record-Herald* in 1918 and become the *Herald-Examiner,* whose circulation pusher was the noted mobster, Dion O'Bannion. It was a thoughtful appointment, because the other papers were attempting to keep Hearst off the newsstands and out of Chicago by the usual strong arm methods.

When O'Bannion turned his talents to illegal liquor in 1922, Hearst put Max and Moses Annenberg in charge of his circulation department, and these able men organized a crew of persuaders so frightening and effective that they quickly equalized the situation. Colonel Mc-Cormick found their performance so impressive that he hired away the Annenbergs and their entire capable staff, reversing the usual procedure where Hearst was concerned.

There appeared to be no end to Hearst's appetite for newspapers, as in the other things he collected—real estate, objects of art, men, animals, trees. In 1927, it was the Pittsburgh *Sun-Telegraph;* in 1928, the Omaha *News-Bee;* in 1929, the San Francisco *Bulletin,* which he combined with the *Call* to corner the evening field. Then, in 1931, at the bottom of the depression, he took over the Los Angeles *Express* and merged it with the *Herald* to make the *Herald-Express* the Los Angeles equivalent of the *Call-Bulletin.*

That, however, was the end of expansion. At this point the Hearst empire began to decline, until it was consolidated at a somewhat lower level.

In the operation of this powerful chain, the key word was "crusade." Hearst carried on where the nineteenth-century battles left off, but in a different way. His were not the high-minded crusades of the *World,* or the personal crusades of Colonel McCormick. Often they were frankly for circulation, but sometimes they were on behalf of ideas which, at the moment, he happened to believe in and he might believe in exactly the opposite a few years later.

"Crusade" had its own peculiar meaning to him. He told a convention of Hearst executives at San Antonio in 1929 that it must not be considered necessarily an attack. "Attack is the easiest form of crusade," he said, "but it is the least advantageous to the community, and the least beneficial to the newspapers. It is easy to pull down and difficult to build up. It takes more thought and more knowledge, more conscientious sense of public duty, to outline and develop a constructive campaign than it does to be merely critical of conditions which may be unsatisfactory.

"I feel that it is desirable for the papers not to make enemies by violent attacks: but it is essential for the papers to conduct constructive campaigns for the benefit of the community with which they are associated . . . Make crusades, but take enough interest in the affairs of your community and give enough thought to the situation existing to be able to make constructive crusades and accomplish results of actual, acknowledged value."

Hearst may have honestly felt that way, but the record shows that his crusading was fanatical, unyielding and ruthless. The unremitting attack he made year after year on the most eminent captains of industry baffled and profoundly irritated these fellow-capitalists. He used them and their banks and services when he needed them, but he had little in common with them and let them know it. They had spent their lives in the acquisition of money through the hard discipline of business; Hearst had spent his having fun, working as hard as they, but always at what he liked best and with no particular regard for profit or loss, except at the beginning and end of his career.

His crusades reflected his shifting opinions; at one time or another, he was on both sides of nearly every major issue of our times. A former associate once remarked ruefully: "The bankers fought him for years, then he turned around and kissed them. They couldn't figure it out."

But the crusading, the maneuvering, the shouting and the exposé led relatively nowhere in the end. In 1936, when the Hearst papers had been particularly loud in their attacks on the Administration, and again in 1939 and 1940, when they renewed the isolationist policies of *circa* 1916, there were boycotts here and there of Hearst papers, or of his newsreel, which faithfully followed the propaganda line, but these were shadowy reflections of the public rage Hearst had once generated with his policies. As Oswald Garrison Villard noted wryly in the *Nation,* "It is amazing . . . to hear Wall Street men now praising Hearst when they themselves, or their fathers, in 1898 and again at the outbreak of World War I were violently denouncing Hearst and having his newspapers thrown out of their clubs and libraries."

The truth was that the constant reiteration of Hearst policies in his papers for nearly half a century had produced a kind of acceptance.

He had become something of an institution, as safe and reliable as the Republican Party. Those who opposed him were no longer particularly afraid of him. Those who agreed with him found him a dependable reassurance in troubled times. A sign of those times was the New York *Journal-American,* whose pages presented the largest menagerie of extreme right-wing writers ever gathered under one journalistic tent. They were the chief solace of a great many of the people Hearst had spent most of his life attacking.

In all, Hearst had either bought or established forty-two daily newspapers. Fourteen of these were merged with other Hearst papers, seven others were sold, and four suspended. By 1940 there were only seventeen remaining in the Hearst chain.

After Hearst's death in 1951, his newspapers and other properties were managed by his five sons, with William Randolph Hearst, Jr., as president of Hearst Consolidated Publications, later president of the Hearst Corporation. For some time the Hearst empire, under a trust arrangement, had been trimming and consolidating, with the result that the chain was on a much sounder basis. Although the trust had ended, the maneuvering has continued to the present, with unprofitable papers sold or otherwise disposed of as circumstances required. By 1960 only thirteen dailies and nine Sunday editions remained, but the Hearst papers still led all the other chains in circulation.

The chain circulation figures for 1960 were impressive proof of the strong hold this kind of management has on American journalism. Total daily circulation of the Hearst papers was four million; of the Scripps-Howard papers, three million: of Samuel I. Newhouse's chain, two million. Although not a chain in the conventional sense, the Chicago Tribune Company's three papers totaled nearly three-a-half million circulation.

By 1950, it must be noted, the entrepreneurs of the newspaper business had shuddered away from the word "chain" and referred to themselves as "groups." This change was said to be motivated by a desire to express the fact of autonomy of papers within a "group," but there was far more public relations than truth in this claim. There was no single case on record of a newspaper in a "group" being in violent opposition to the policies or political beliefs of the group owner or owners. Obviously, in the curious semantics of business, "autonomy" had acquired a different meaning.

In 1960 there were more than a hundred chains, but slightly more than 60 per cent of them were organized within the boundaries of single states. Hearst, Scripps-Howard and Newhouse were the only important national chains. It was a further significant fact that nearly 30 per cent of the nation's dailies were chain-owned in 1960. At least sixty newspapers were serving two or more suburban communities under hyphenated names, reflecting the shifts in population from city to suburb.

Of the new chain proprietors, the major figure was Samuel Irving Newhouse, a retiring, publicity-shy man who had quietly built up an empire of thirteen dailies and eight Sunday papers, along with four television and three radio stations, and eleven magazines. Newhouse, the son of Russian immigrant parents, was cut to the nineteenth-century pattern in some respects. His formal education had been confined to grammar school, although he later studied law at night, and his beginnings were modest. He started out to be a lawyer, but his fascination with journalism led him to start making investments in newspapers when he was only twenty-five, mostly in small papers in the circulation area around New York City.

His expansion to Portland, St. Louis, Birmingham, Harrisburg, Jersey City and other communities, sometimes buying no more than a percentage of ownership, was characterized by business methods strongly reminiscent of Frank Munsey and E. W. Scripps. His interests were not primarily editorial but financial. The basic technique he employed was to buy an ailing paper and resuscitate it by modern management methods, chiefly cost-cutting and the assiduous promotion of circulation and advertising. Newhouse also kept his chain out of the hands of bankers by paying cash for new papers, using profits made from properties already established. Sixty-five years old in 1960, Newhouse was at the peak of his career and worth, reputedly, nearly $200 million. He announced that he meant to plow back a good part of this fortune into good journalistic works, and made an impressive start in that direction in 1962 by giving Syracuse University $15,000,000 to found a great communications center.

Newhouse and all the other chain operators were dwarfed, however, by the vast empire being built in the 1960's by a hitherto obscure Canadian, Roy Thomson, who was already the first international press lord, with more properties to his name than even Hearst had dreamed of.

Thomson's spectacular rise, encompassing less than two decades, began in the environs of Toronto, Canada, where he forsook the auto accessory business to buy small Canadian papers and radio stations. From these humble beginnings, he went on to large newspaper and book-publishing enterprises and radio and television properties in Canada, Scotland, England, Africa and America. By 1962 he controlled more than a hundred newspapers, and it was said that he was about to supplement his few small American enterprises with larger ones.

What this might mean to the American newspaper was what it had already meant in the chain ownership of men like Newhouse—that is, a distinct advantage in the saving of unhealthy newspapers from extinction by the application of sound business methods and the resources of chain ownership.

The troubling aspect of the new order lay in the difference between the two kinds of chain management, new and old. Roy Howard had kept a close editorial watch on his newspapers for decades, and when he retired from the active direction of them, his able son Jack, equipped with the same passionate interest in the news, took over the reins and directed the editorial as well as the other operations of the chain. Similarly, Hearst had personally directed the editorial operation of his papers, which was continued after his death by his sons and editorial executives who had been close to him.

But the new chain entrepreneurs had no such intention. "Nobody knows better what to print than the editors on the spot," Newhouse had said. Much the same idea was expressed by Thomson, whose bedside reading was said to be balance sheets. Both these men had extraordinary ability in assessing the financial condition of a newspaper and knowing what to do about it. They were highly skillful in making solid properties out of failing newspapers. The editorial direction of the papers was left in the hands of the men who were put in charge. Presumably these were able men, but relatively faceless individuals, acting for owners who were nearly as unknown to the public.

Thus chain ownership had moved into a position where it was already a dominant factor in journalism, and likely to become more so, but in the process it had made a complete turnaround from the personal approach of Hearst and Scripps to the anonymity of New-house and Thomson. Whether the excesses of personal journalism were to be preferred to the gray sameness of the Thomson organiza-tion was a question difficult to answer. If the answer was a variety of newspapers operating with widely varying editorial viewpoints, there was little hope for a widespread fulfillment of that ideal as the decade of the Sixties began. The economics of publishing appeared to be slowly driving the personal, individual element completely out of journalism.

three

The Rise and Fall of Country Newspapers

THE CLASH OF GIANTS IN THE CITY and the shifting tides of metropolitan journalism have obscured the role of small town papers in the history of American newspapers, but their influence has not been inconsiderable. In a few instances country editors have attracted a national audience, but their chief preoccupation has been to provide the local voice for which no imported paper from a larger nearby town is ever a satisfactory substitute. It is this function which has enabled the small-town paper to survive, and even to prosper, well into the era of mass communications.

Country newspapers began as soon as printing presses moved outside Boston, Philadelphia and New York to the surrounding territory, as the early settlements pushed beyond their first boundaries. But the pattern of rural journalism was not set in a form likely to endure until Joseph Dennie came upon the scene in the closing years of the eighteenth century. Dennie was a Boston boy whose childhood was spent both there and in Lexington, where his parents fled when the British were at the gates of the city. In the manner of so many future editors, he read everything he could lay hands on in his father's library. The father had marked him for a business career, but it was obvious he had no talent for it, and even less for formal study. At Harvard he fought the discipline of work and despised the lectures, and hated the university until the day he died.

Dennie decided to be a lawyer, and was admitted to the bar, but his practice languished and he had a good deal of time to work at something he enjoyed much more—writing. His essays, derived from

Addison and Goldsmith in the fashion of the day, were printed in various New Hampshire weeklies, and their reception encouraged Dennie to start a paper in Boston in 1795, called the *Tablet,* in which he reprinted his own work, as well as new essays, some forty in all.

The *Tablet* expired after thirteen numbers and Dennie returned to New Hampshire, where he had served his apprenticeship as a law clerk. He came to rest in the village of Walpole. There he attracted men like himself—"wags, wits and literati," all Federalists—who drank and talked with him. These conversations inspired Dennie to new essay writing, pieces he signed "The Lay Preacher." They appeared in the local paper, the *Farmer's Weekly Museum,* begun years before by Isaiah Thomas, and they were, as Frank Luther Mott says, "probably the best periodical essays ever produced in America."

By this time weekly newspapers were sprouting like grass after rain, as journeymen printers traveled from one town to another, setting up papers where none had existed before. These papers were, quite naturally, highly imitative of those in the cities, and most made the fundamental mistake of filling their columns with items clipped from the larger, established papers instead of concentrating on the only commodity they had to sell, local news.

In these unimaginative organs Dennie's essays appeared as pearls in a bed of oysters, and they were quickly picked up by other papers, both daily and weekly. Their author soon found himself famous. Knowing a good thing when they saw it, the publishers of the *Farmer's Museum* made him editor in 1796. Dennie immediately got his friends to contribute, turned the paper into a strong Federalist organ, and in less than two years he had produced a newspaper that was read nearly everywhere in the settled parts of America.

He was already a personality in the new Republic, as much for his appearance as his essays. Joseph T. Buckingham, the *Museum's* printer's devil, later became a historian of journalism and in his "Specimens of Newspaper Literature," a standard source book, he describes Dennie as the editor looked in a Walpole tavern, where he often sat and talked with his friends and wrote pieces for the paper which Buckingham carried from tavern table directly to the composing room.

"In person he was below rather than above the middling height," Buckingham wrote, "and was of slender frame. He was particularly attentive to his dress, which, when he appeared on the street, on a pleasant day, approached the highest notch of the fashion. I remember him . . . dressed in a pea-green coat, white vest, nankin small-clothes, white silk stockings, and shoes or pumps fastened with silver buckles which covered at least half the foot from the instep to the toe. His small-clothes were tied at the knees, with ribband of the same color, in double bows, the ends reaching down to the ankles . . ."

Dennie's superlative talents did not save the *Museum* from teetering perpetually on the brink of ruin. Convinced that Walpole was too small an arena for him, Dennie moved to Philadelphia, where he worked for a time on John Fenno's *Gazette of the United States* until he founded in 1801 a weekly magazine called the *Port Folio,* which was the country's leading literary periodical until the *North American Review* was begun in 1815. In the *Port Folio,* Dennie continued his Lay Preacher essays, and the forty he had printed at Walpole were published as a book in 1803, becoming "the most popular work on the American continent," according to an English traveler. A second selection appeared in 1817.

When he died in 1812, Dennie passed into an undeserved obscurity. Not only were his essays of lasting worth, but in Walpole he had written the first noteworthy page in the history of American country journalism, brief as his time there had been.

Weekly journalism grew rapidly in America, and it was already flourishing by the time Dennie left the scene. From a beginning of fourteen weeklies in 1750, the number leaped to 422 in 1820, out of a total 512 papers in the nation. Sixty-six others were semi-weeklies or tri-weeklies, and only 24 were dailies.

Many of these weeklies before the Civil War were turned into dailies as the pressure of population created a demand, and as the mechanical means to satisfy it were invented. Those that remained in the small towns did not change as radically as those in the big cities, but they were able to improve their coverage as telegraph lines were extended, as far as Chicago and Milwaukee by 1848. Where the lines stopped, the pony express went on and served to carry the news until 1861, when the telegraph reached the Pacific. As settlements moved farther out from urban centers, secondhand printing presses and equipment moved with them.

Weeklies had a high mortality because so many of them were used for special purposes and were dropped when the purpose was satisfied. They advanced the shifting fortunes of political groups, promoted the settlement and sale of lands, served as organs for missionaries, and enlivened Army posts. The editors seldom showed enough enterprise to fill the whole paper with local news; two-thirds or more of the space was likely to be filled with "literary" material—essays, poems, sketches. They were usually four to six pages, laid out in six or nine columns. Their circulations seldom passed 1,000, and their advertising columns, aside from what retail lineage could be obtained, consisted of legal and patent-medicine ads. Almost every village as large as a thousand inhabitants had at least two papers, usually representing opposite political faiths.

The Civil War produced a device known as "patent insides," which came to be standard equipment in weeklies for generations afterward. It was invented by A. N. Kellogg, publisher of the Baraboo (Wisconsin) *Republic,* whose staff had been so reduced by enlistments that he was unable to fill his usual four pages. He used type set for the *Wisconsin State Journal* to fill pages two and three, leaving the outside for his own composition. Other publishers were enchanted by this labor-saving idea, and the *Journal* was soon kept busy supplying syndicated inside (or sometimes outside) pages to country weeklies. The advantage to an advertiser desiring to reach this broad market was obvious, and the accumulation of advertising reduced the price of the "patent insides."

After the war, business boomed in this kind of syndication until several syndicates were competing with each other and more than a thousand papers were being supplied by 1872. Kellogg himself owned the leading syndicate, centered in Chicago. This "readyprint" service, as it was often called, passed largely in 1901 into the hands of Kellogg's chief rival, the Western Newspaper Union, which was also distributing plates.

The importance of patent insides was plain in the decades following the Civil War, when the number of weekly papers, known commonly as "country papers" by that time, made a tremendous leap forward, from 4,000 in 1870 to more than 12,000 by 1900. They flourished largely in towns of under 10,000; larger ones were likely to have a daily. It was not impossible for towns of 300 or smaller to have a paper, and many of them did.

This ease of publication was due to the fact that country journalism was more or less still in the colonial stage. If a man had an old hand-press, a few cases of type and a foot-power press, he was in business. He could get credit for supplies, and his paper stock, already half-printed, came from the readyprint houses. All he needed was enough cash to pay for it, C.O.D., when it arrived in the express office. The publisher was often his own editor and printer, and needed no more help than a local boy to serve as printer's devil.

These all-around publishers were often as migratory as the journeymen printers. If they were not successful in one little town, they moved on and tried another. Wherever they went, the readyprints were there to help them, and two-fifths of the weeklies in the country, more than 3,000, were being supplied by twenty-one of these companies in 1880.

In spite of the transitory character of much of the country press, thousands of papers were well-established and prosperous. They were likely to be more independent than the big city papers, since the proprietors were personal journalists in the truest sense of the word. They were also important people in their small towns—more important even than the noted entrepreneurs of New York and Chicago, who were always competing with each other for attention. A circulation of 1,500 or so was enough to sustain the average country weekly, and a modicum of legal and retail advertising was enough to put the venture well into the black.

Country journalism had reached a peak in America by 1914. There were 14,500 weeklies, and their service was something the communities involved could not do without. The country paper recorded births, deaths and marriages, social events and the happenings of everyday life. The crime and scandal which were the stock in trade of big city newspapers at the turn of the century were unknown to these country weeklies. They faithfully reflected the life of the countryside, at least in its exterior aspects, and not even the coming of rural free delivery in 1897, bringing city dailies into farm mailboxes, shook their position. They were more prosperous than they had ever been, as national advertising began to add to income and both advertising and subscription rates increased.

The preoccupation with local news meant that the editors were prominent in local affairs, particularly in politics, and so the country press tended to be more partisan at a time when the city press was becoming less personal with the decline of the one-man show. National politicians tried to exploit the country press by distributing propaganda in plate and readyprint form, and succeeded for a time, but country editors were inclined to be independent as well as partisan.

No doubt the most independent of them all for some time was Edgar Watson Howe, known to the nation as Ed Howe, "The Sage of Potato Hill," publisher of the Atchison (Kansas) *Globe* for thirty-six years. The *Globe* was a daily, but Atchison was a typical small town, and its paper was the authentic independent voice of the small town editor, raised to a much higher level in this case by Howe's writing ability and iconoclastic mind.

Born in 1854, Howe was brought up in the rigid Methodism of his circuit-riding preacher father, in the hills of northern Missouri. As a boy he was compelled to listen to six-hour sermons, and was whipped if he fell asleep. The extreme discipline was bad enough for a growing boy, but it was compounded by the traumatic shock he suffered at fourteen when his father abruptly ran away with a lady member of his flock, leaving his wife and several children to look after themselves. It was understandable that he grew up with a permanent hatred of both religion and women.

Ed's father had relaxed his discipline enough to permit him to learn typesetting in the print shop he ran on the side in Bethany, Missouri, and so it was that after his father's sudden departure, the young man became a tramp printer, a part of his career in which the high point was a summer in Salt Lake City working for Brigham Young.

At twenty-one, Ed Howe came to rest in Atchison, then a bustling little community of 12,000, and there, with a backlog of $200 and the help of his brother Jim, he began publishing the *Globe*. Between them Ed and Jim did everything that had to be done, in the style of small papers everywhere, and the product they turned out looked no different from thousands of other small weeklies and dailies. What separated it from the others was Howe's particular genius for writing and editing. His work was so individual and outstanding that within a month the paper was operating in the black, and in a few years the town's two competing papers had to quit.

Howe's impact on the town of Atchison is unmatched in the history of American newspapers, and even now it is hard to believe. In this small town in the heart of Godfearing Kansas, he began an extraordinary personal campaign against religion and the churches. At first the citizens were incredulous. Then came the inevitable counterattack. There were advertising boycotts, cancelled subscriptions, and rival newspapers founded, all of which failed. Through it all Howe roamed the village streets and the surrounding countryside serenely, gathering news, and he prevailed. The reason was simply stated with a pardonable pride by his newspaper publisher son, Gene, who wrote later: "He was the greatest reporter in America; he was so regarded by many leading newspapermen. The *Globe* vibrated with his sparkle and humor, and it became the most quoted daily in the United States. Opposition could not stand against it; Atchison people simply could not resist reading his paper."

By the nature of things, however, it was inevitable Ed Howe should end as his son pictured him, "the most wretchedly unhappy man I ever knew." That was because he was a born crusader who happened to be crusading against institutions so firmly fixed in human life they could not be moved, or even substantially altered. Alternating between exuberant zeal and deep depression, Howe could not grasp this simple fact. "It's me and not my ideas," he would say. "I haven't been able to make people understand; I must make everything so plain, so simple that they will see the truth."

In retrospect, his views about religion and women seem incredible in so highly intelligent a man. Of the former he wrote: "To me, the most wonderful thing in civilization is religion. That people should have advanced so marvelously in everything else, as they have done, and carried along with them a doctrine they know to be untrue, is a fact I have marveled at all my life. Never have I known a sincere religious man or woman."

Howe told his readers that men and women were natural enemies, that civilization itself was threatened because women had become spoiled and extravagant, and he urged an actual revolt of the nation's men against women. He believed that a girl ought to have only one engagement and one marriage; he was shocked if a friend married a widow. In his opinion a woman ought to be her husband's chattel, without rights or privileges. If a husband ever sank to the point of helping his wife on with her coat, he said, then he should leave her at once because he was henpecked. Naturally, his own marriage was wretched and it ended in divorce by 1901, but not before his wife gave him three children—James, who became an AP man; Eugene, who was a noted publisher in his own right; and Mateel, a daughter who won a $10,000 prize with her first novel.

In time, Howe became a Kansas institution. Those who were offended by his views learned to overlook them; others were amused by what he wrote. Much of this tolerance may have derived from the fact that Howe put Atchison on the map. The *Globe* was quoted by newspapers everywhere, particularly Howe's "paragraphs," as he called them—sharp, witty aphorisms. One issue of the Boston *Globe* carried fifty-eight of these paragraphs. Atchison became known as "Ed Howe's town," and Howe himself was the most famous country editor in America. He added to his reputation by publishing in 1882 an excellent novel, *The Story of A Country Town*, and his autobiography, *Plain People*, published in 1929, remains one of the best written by an American.

Howe retired at fifty-seven, turning the *Globe* over to his son Gene, and amused himself by editing a magazine called *Ed Howe's Monthly*, in which he continued to make frontal attacks on everything in American life that displeased him, a list which included politicians, have-nots and liberals. As an extreme conservative, Howe's only god was business, but somehow the indignation and venom of these later years, printed in the magazine, did not attract a large audience, and he gave up the publication. He died in 1937, at eighty-four, consistent to the last in his viewpoints.

Ironically, Howe is better remembered for his pungent "paragraphs" than he is for his brilliance as an editor, his excellent novel or his fine autobiography. These snippets still glow with his sardonic wit:

> Families with babies, and families without babies, are so sorry for each other.
> Don't be ashamed if you can't play the piano! be proud of it.
> If you want to get a woman very angry, get someone to pray for him.
> Women like to attend weddings to hear the big, sweet, juicy promises the bridegrooms make.
> I once wondered how the banks made their money, but when I procured a loan, I found out.
> Nearly every unsuccessful man we ever met was a good billiard player.
> Some people never have anything except ideals.
> A man has his clothes made to fit him, a woman makes herself fit her clothes.
> A woman is as old as she looks before breakfast.
> What people say behind your back is your standing in the community in which you live.
> The difference between a good woman and a bad one is that a bad woman raises hell with a good many men, while a good woman raises hell with only one.

William Allen White, a fellow-Kansan who succeeded Howe as the best-known country editor in America, thought Ed was a "lovable, kindly old grouch." White himself was the antithesis, and much more typical of his breed in viewpoint. He was as uncompromisingly blunt in his beliefs as Howe, but he was blunt on the side of humanity and ideals, consequently he was more admired by his fellow-Americans.

White was born in February 1868, in Emporia, Kansas, the town in which he was to do his life's work. His training was on the Kansas City *Star* under Nelson, during which he absorbed the publisher's community service idea and carried it back to Emporia in 1895, where he bought the town's five-year-old *Gazette* for $5,000 and published it until his death.

His special talent was editorial writing, and he was the best since Godkin, although he spoke in a different language—the language of the people in small cities and towns everywhere in America. Intellectuals on city papers sometimes sneered at his folksy approach, but they underestimated him, because he could be biting and even cruel when he chose. He came to national prominence a year after he took over the *Gazette* with a single editorial: "What's The Matter With Kansas?"—a question he answered, in part:

> We all know; yet here we are at it again. We have an old mossback Jacksonian who snorts and howls because there is no bathtub in the statehouse; we are running that old jay for governor. We have another shabby, wild-eye, rattle-brained fanatic who has said openly in a dozen speeches that "the rights of the user are paramount to the rights of the owner"; we are running him for chief justice, so that capital will come tumbling over itself to get into the State. We have raked the old ash-heap of failure in the State and found an old human hoopskirt who has failed as a business man, who has failed as an editor, who has failed as a preacher, and we are going to run him for Congressman-at-large. He will help the looks of the Kansas delegation in Washington. Then we have discovered a kid without a law practice and decided to run him for attorney-general. Then for fear some hint that the State had become respectable might percolate through the civilized portions of the nation, we have decided to send three or four harpies out lecturing, telling the people that Kansas is raising hell and letting the corn go to weeds.

Read in the context of Kansas politics, this was an all-out assault on the Populist ticket. Picked up gleefully by the Republican newspapers, it elevated White in one stroke to be one of that Party's chief spokesmen. In later, less partisan years, he called the famous editorial "conservatism in its full and perfect flower."

But the editorial was a fair sample of the kind that flowed from White's pen for years in an unending, accomplished stream. Such talent made him so valuable to the politicians that in 1912 he was a Progressive Party national committeeman, in a brief flight from Republicanism, and later he was one of the chief movers behind the scenes to get Herbert Hoover into the White House, a careful undercover campaign which went on for years, and when it ended in success, succeeded only in disillusioning White, who found himself, as a liberal Republican, unable to go along with the President's conservatism.

White was a fearless editor who spoke out boldly no matter who might be offended. In the early Twenties he declared in a noteworthy editorial:

> The Ku Klux Klan is said to be reorganizing in Emporia. It is an organization of cowards. Not a man in it has the courage of his convictions. It is an organization of traitors to American institutions Not a man in it has faith enough in American courts, laws, and officials, to trust them to maintain law and order . . . It is a menace to peace and decent neighborly living and if we find out who is the Imperial Wizard in Emporia, we shall guy the life out of him. He is a joke, you may be sure. But a poor joke at that.

Later, in the spring of 1926, when the national Imperial Wizard, Hiram Evans, announced a speaking tour of Kansas, White predicted:

> He will find what was once a thriving and profitable hate factory and bigotorium now laughed into a busted community; where the cock-eyed hedragon wails for its first-born, and the nightshirts of a once salubrious pageantry sag into the spring breezes and bag at the wabbly knees. The Kluxers in Kansas are as dejected and sad as a last year's bird's nest, afflicted with general debility, dizziness on going upstairs, and general aversion to female society.

His prose was not always so exotic. He could slice cleanly and sharply, with an admirable clarity of language, through the texture of contemporary life, as in this comment on the Great Bull Market, written in 1926:

> What a sordid decade is passing! It will be known in American history fifty years hence as the time of terrible reaction . . . It will not be the story of a weak man like Harding nor a silent and unemotional man like Coolidge. They are mere outer manifestations of the inner spiritual traits of the people. The spirit of our democracy has turned away from the things of the spirit, got its share of the patrimony ruthlessly and gone out and lived riotously and ended feeding among the swine.

Until the end of his life, on January 29, 1944, White battled for what he believed was honest and right. He even criticized his fellow-publishers in terms which would have been resented far more than they were if they had come from anyone else. He wrote in 1939:

> The most serious danger that menaces the freedom of the American press is the obvious anxiety of rich publishers about the freedom of the press . . . The publisher is not bought like a chattel. Indeed he often is able to buy those who are suspected of buying him. But he takes the color of his social environment . . . The average publisher is pretty generally against organized labor. He is too often found opposing the government control of public utilities. He instinctively fears any regulation of the stock exchange. The right to strike seems to the rich publisher and his Chamber of Commerce friends to be sheer anarchy. It is inevitable that the managing editor and editorial writers who want to hold their jobs take their professional views and get their professional slant from their boss, the man who signs the payroll check . . . It often happens, alas too often, that a newspaper publisher, reflecting this unconscious class arrogance of the consciously rich, thinks he is printing news when he is doctoring it innocently enough. He thinks he is purveying the truth when much that he offers seems poison to hundreds of thousands of his readers who don't move in his social and economic stratosphere.

By the time White died, the influences in big city publishing he was talking about in his speech had permeated the fabric of the country press as well. Where once it had been lively, independent and politically diversified, the trend was to a gray conformity of conservative Republicanism everywhere in the nation except the South, where it was an even more conservative viewpoint representing the Southern Democrats. Metropolitan dailies had become big business; small-town papers had become small business. In both cases, the viewpoint was the same.

The small-town field itself continued to diminish after White's death. This decline had begun in the Twenties, with mergers and suspensions, and had been accelerated during the depression years. Mostly it was a reduction of competition; in 1930 the percentage of country weekly towns with only one paper was 86.5 per cent, and there were only 9,522 weeklies published in towns of 15,000 population or less. By 1951, the non-competitive figure had crept up to 89 per cent, while the number of weeklies had dropped to about 9,000.

Yet the country paper was not on the way out, by any means. Country editors of the old stripe have virtually disappeared today, with only two or three individualists like Henry Beetle Hough, of the incomparable *Vineyard Gazette,* in Edgartown, Martha's Vineyard Island, Massachusetts, still publishing newspapers easily distinguishable from any other. The old-style publisher has been replaced by the small daily and weekly operator who runs his paper on good business principles, often as part of a chain, but who shuns anything which might irritate his readers and advertisers.

Now and then a striking exception occurs, as when a newspaper in a conservative town strikes out against local bigotry, but for the most part the small-town paper has the same political coloration as its big neighbors. It functions as it always has, primarily as a community bulletin board, and it does the job much better than it did even twenty-five years ago. Better mechanical equipment, more use of pictures, application of modern management principles, and a more professional approach to the news has made the modern country newspaper a greatly improved product. Beset by expanding big-city circulation zones, and the advent of radio and television, it has concentrated on the one thing it does which cannot be duplicated, the coverage of purely local news. Western Newspaper Union discontinued its readyprint service in 1952, and country newspapers today develop their own features or buy more sophisticated material from the large services.

Recently the long-continuing trend toward contraction of the field has been reversed by two developments which are revolutionizing country journalism. One is the decentralization of great urban centers into smaller, suburban towns everywhere in the country. These new, expanding communities, often built on old ones and grouped around their own subdivisions and shopping centers, have inspired the growth of new suburban weeklies, which sometimes publish more often. Just as new machinery enabled the growing dailies to meet the expanding population of the nineteenth century, the rise of offset printing in the past fifteen or twenty years has enabled publishers in small towns, suburban or otherwise, to produce a new and better product.

The countryside is dotted today with these products, more than 500 of them, and their number is growing. Most of these newspapers are remarkably successful, smart-looking with the clean, sharp appearance in pictures and type which offset printing provides, and fat with advertising from the proliferating retail outlets in suburban towns. Color and individuality may have disappeared from country journalism, but they have been replaced by a bright new kind of well-organized, well-printed paper which satisfies the different needs of another time.

four

The Crisis of the Newspaper Business

IT IS SYMPTOMATIC OF THE DEEP, underlying illness in the press today that the fact of its crisis is so rarely discussed. The newspaper business has been highly resistant to criticism since the days of the first Bennett, and even more so since the era of its status as a business institution began. The only state of crisis admitted by publishers is the perennial controversy with the federal government, dating to Washington's time, in which the actors change while the argument remains the same. To this must be added the increasingly sharp conflict with organized labor, in itself part of a larger problem.

Publishers and their professional apologists insist that the American newspaper has never been in better condition, and in some respects that is true. Its technical production is superior to that of any other press in the world, and its general level of competence is higher than those of other countries. It is often said to be more free, but that is a comfortable self-delusion. The word "freedom" in its application to the press is subject to so many qualifications that it loses meaning at once, except in the sense that American papers, like those in all the countries of the so-called free world, are not subject to the kind of direct governmental control exerted by totalitarian or authoritarian governments.

Publishers waste a great deal of time today in fighting the federal government, but as we have seen, they have always done so. The practice, however, has steadily increased since 1933, during an era in which the trend has been steadily toward more liberal concepts of government while the press, like other conservative institutions,

261

has clung to a past which cannot be recaptured, and to principles which have been drastically altered by the vast change in human affairs taking place everywhere.

A large part of the press continues to live in an unreal world, fighting battles which were decided long ago by the inexorable course of events, while its real responsibilities go unfulfilled. In becoming a business institution, newspapers, with a dozen or so honorable exceptions, have utterly lost the sense of history which so possessed the nineteenth-century giants.

If the false and hollow battles over such shibboleths as "managed news" and "the people's right to know" were abandoned, it would be seen that the American newspaper confronts three real and formidable problems which it must solve before it can achieve its proper place in our democracy.

These problems can be stated simply. They are: the control of monopoly; the automation of the industry; and a redefinition of purpose. There is no order of importance because the problems are interrelated, and they must be solved within the common framework. Any history of the American press would be incomplete without a brief consideration of the elements involved, and an estimate made of the situation at mid-twentieth century.

To begin with monopoly, a serious problem both in Britain and America, it ought to be recognized at once that here we are dealing with an economic fact of life which is not going to be reversed through any kind of moral persuasion, nor by law.

Few people outside the business understand the extent to which the American press is monopolistic. Where there was once a healthy, competitive variety, only 10 per cent of dailies in the United States now have competition. As of 1962 there were 1,769 English-language dailies, but only 155 were in competition and many of these were losing money. Experienced observers believe that by 1970 there may be no more than twenty competing newspapers, and these will be confined to our ten largest cities.

Monopoly extends to the other means of mass communications as well. Newspapers presently own more than 750 radio and television stations, and in 76 American cities the only daily also owns the only radio station.

Some publishers of monopoly newspapers argue that monopoly is not necessarily a bad thing, if a community's sole newspaper is conscientious and fair in its news and editorial presentation. There are a few outstanding examples of this contention—the *Courier-Journal* in Louisville, and the *Journal-Bulletin* in Providence, to cite two. But a monopoly newspaper can present, in the end, only one viewpoint, and it is the diversity of viewpoint which is the strength (and, it must be admitted, sometimes the weakness) of democracy. A monopoly newspaper has an impregnibility which effectively ends opposition. In the present economic circumstances, it is virtually impossible for a competing newspaper to start operation in a one-newspaper town, and if it makes the attempt, the monopolist will do everything in his power to prevent it.

No matter what comforting things can be said about the practical operations of monopoly newspapers, monopoly is alien to our system and as unhealthy among newspapers as it is in any other segment of the economy; but whereas it is restrained by law in these other segments, economic law reinforces it where newspapers are concerned.

There is only one answer to this problem, and it does not lie in legislation, nor in any kind of control. Competition can only be restored by making it economically possible to start new newspapers, and this can only be done by materially reducing the cost of producing a newspaper.

Here we come to the second major problem: the automation of the industry. This is, to many publishers, the most important aspect of making a newspaper today, because automation is potentially capable of providing an answer to what had seemed an impossible dilemma.

The reason monopoly has been able to obtain a stranglehold on the newspaper business is the steadily increased cost of doing business in the last quarter-century. In towns where newspapers were competing, there was simply not enough income to go around, measured against costs, and the paper with the least business was eventually forced to the wall, unless it was a chain newspaper and the absentee owner could afford to siphon off profits from elsewhere to keep the paper alive until such time as the competition was weak enough to succumb.

Faced with these constantly rising costs in materials and labor, a newspaper could hope to increase its income only through more advertising, higher circulation and a higher price for the product. Unfortunately, there are ceilings on all these possibilities, and today they have been very nearly reached in all three.

The advertising dollar must now be stretched by national advertisers over television, radio, magazines and newspapers, and although the newspapers get their share, the high cost of television has been a drain which has weakened newspaper advertising potentials and nearly sounded the death-knell of mass magazines. The local retail advertising dollar, too, can be stretched only to a point, and the stretching process has been going on for some time. Circulation, moreover, is not keeping pace with population growth. The population increases at the rate of 1.85 percent every year, but newspaper circulation increases at the rate of less than one percent and shows every sign of decreasing that percentage. American net paid daily circulation amounts to 333 per thousand population; in Great Britain it is 573 per thousand. As for pricing the product, newspapers have gone from two and three cents to five cents and ten cents, but studies indicate that the public will not pay much more.

Having reached, or nearly reached, these ceilings, what is the newspaper publisher to do? The answer is to cut costs, and they can be cut substantially only in the composing room. A sudden upsurge of advances in printing technology during the last decade, the first major breakthrough since the nineteenth century, has pointed the way toward substantial reductions through automation. Already automatic processes can set type; computers can operate more than eight linotype machines at a time. The completely automated composing room is clearly visible on the horizon. Offset printing is already revolutionizing the small newspaper, and with further improvements, it will do as much for the big-city daily.

But the possibilities raised by these new labor-saving devices have run head-on into the human problems posed by technological unemployment. Strong unions are presently blocking the advances which will cut costs. The result has been incredibly costly strikes in New York, Cleveland, Minneapolis and a dozen other cities. Since the progress represented by automation is going to occur anyway, it would appear only sensible that the newspaper industry and the unions should jointly plan for the inevitable, instead of further weakening each other's positions. Little disposition to do so has appeared on either side. The alternative, however, is a steadily developing cost squeeze in the newspaper industry which, if not relieved by automation, will result in the further suspension of newspapers, the further loss of jobs, the further spread of monopoly.

If the problems of monopoly and automation are solved, or at least attempts are made toward their solution, there remains the question of purpose. It is a melancholy fact that there is virtually no serious consideration of this problem among publishers, although it may well be the key to everything else.

One of the elder statesmen in the business, J. David Stern, wrote recently in his reminiscences, *Memoirs of A Maverick Publisher*: "Granted our old-fashioned partisan press smelled to high heaven, it was the stimulating stench of human emotion. It roused the nation to brave deeds and great accomplishment. A newspaper was established to express a point of view. Publishers of the nineteenth century were concerned with public problems and they made their readers share this concern. Political zeal frequently exceeded the bounds of reason and decency, but it was an antidote to complacency, which is the Achilles heel of a nation grown rich and prosperous.

"Today most newspapers—especially monopoly and chain newspapers—avoid treading on toes. But there never was a worthwhile reform which did not bruise someone's pedal extremities . . . When the monopoly newspaper cannot avoid such a controversy it tries to be impartial."

The rôle of the newspaper in American life, as Stern suggests, has changed dramatically in the last half-century. It has, for example, lost its national political influence. That was obvious as early as 1936, when President Roosevelt was re-elected against the opposition of 90 percent of the press, and with the support of no more than a half-dozen metropolitan papers. It has become more evident with every national election since then, in spite of the most absurd manipulation of statistics in attempts to prove that newspapers are "independent."

The truth is that except when they are aroused by a candidate or a President who represents a challenge to the conservative business interests of which the press is a part, and which it defends, the publishers do not support even their own people with any passionate conviction. President Dwight D. Eisenhower, for example, commanded the virtually unanimous support of the press in 1956, but there has seldom been a quieter newspaper campaign. Crusading these days is left mostly to the columnists, except for local issues here and there. The tone of the nation's editorial pages is conservative, but few people are moved by them one way or the other.

Newspapers themselves have grown duller for a paradoxical reason. No one questions that the growth in advertising volume has saved the business from a much more serious reduction in numbers than has been the case. Advertising today is the lifeblood of the press. But it has also strangled the news, nearly to the point of extinction in many newspapers.

The change in this respect has been recent and dramatic. In 1940 the average number of pages in American dailies was 24.15 per day, and in these pages the balance was 10.4 advertising, 13.75 news and features. In just two decades the size of the papers has grown appreciably, to 37.5 pages a day, but the proportions are reversed—23.11 advertising, and 14.39 news and features. Advertising, in sum, has jumped 122 per cent, while news and features have increased only 5 per cent.

It is commonplace in many American cities today to find newspapers running seventy-four pages or more on a weekday. The solid news is to be found on pages one, two and three. For the remainder of the paper it forms an inconsequential border around the advertising on those pages which are not entirely occupied by ads.

Moreover, the proportion of hard news to entertainment and features in newspapers has steadily declined during the past twenty years. Most American dailies today are filled with syndicated features, comic strips, innocuous and routine local news, and a bare minimum of national and international news, unless that news is of crisis or disaster. The newspapers are impersonal and bland, for the most part. They are valuable and profitable as advertising media, they are useful as community bulletin boards, but they do not accomplish the primary function which newspapers must perform if they are to have any substantial place in the Space Age.

What is that function? It is, quite simply, to explain the world to the people who live in it. That is the news. It may be, as the distinguished Washington correspondent of the *New York Times* has remarked, that we need a new definition of news. News is not necessarily something that happens. It may be, and often is in our time, something that is *going* to happen. The changes taking place in the world may well be the most profound and far-reaching in human history. To cope with them, people must understand them. The charge against the communications media is that they are making few attempts to provide people with that understanding. Newspapers, for the most part, devote less and less space to news, as we have seen. Using techniques which have scarcely changed in the past half-century, they present a hopelessly inadequate picture of the world to their readers, often colored by attitudes which belong to other centuries.

It is often said in defense of newspapers that they give the people what they want, and that what people want is to be entertained and titillated, not to think or to learn. Without further reducing this threadbare argument beyond its present absurdity, it can be said that those who take it seriously are removing the only reason for the existence of the press, which is to communicate the facts and ideas that make the world move—to lead, not to be led. Newspapers cannot be operated by the business office and fulfill their purpose, but that is exactly what is happening to the American newspaper today, in spite of the fact that the new techniques of interpretive reporting are available and access to world news is greater than it has ever been.

The newspaper business is the only business in America which is given special protection in the Constitution by virtue of the First Amendment. This amendment was not written to give the newspaper a privileged sanctuary from which it could cry "freedom of the press" whenever it was criticized. It was written in recognition of the unique purpose the press serves in a free society, as the keeper of moral values. The American newspaper has not yet achieved that purpose in its nearly three centuries of history in this country, but it must if it is to have meaning and value in the society which history is now shaping.

Suggested Reading

THE LITERATURE OF JOURNALISM is far larger than is generally realized. Anyone motivated by this volume to explore it further might well begin with the bibliography in the field which has no peer: *The Literature of Journalism,* by Warren C. Price, professor of journalism at the University of Oregon. This book, published by the University of Minnesota Press, lists more than 3,100 entries in thirteen major categories. Since Professor Price was guided in the compilation by the availability of the works, his book is more than ordinarily valuable because the entries cited can be found in any moderately large library.

From this volume I have chosen a short list of titles in the fields of history and biography which may supplement the present work.

HISTORIES OF JOURNALISM

The definitive history is Frank Luther Mott's *American Journalism* (Macmillan), recently issued in a handsome new revised edition. It is not likely to be surpassed.

The Press and America, by Edwin Emory and Henry Ladd Smith (Prentice-Hall), is the most recent general history, thorough and excellent, especially valuable because it places the history of journalism in its proper perspective, as a part of the political, economic and social scene. This broadening of scope extends to the chapter bibliographies. It has recently been reissued under Professor Emory's name, and remains indispensable.

Highlights In The History of the American Press: A Book of Reading, by Edwin Emory and Edwin H. Ford (University of Minnesota Press) is a collection of twenty-seven articles which tell the story of the press in terms of men and trends. Introductory essays by the editors link the articles and make the book, in effect, a briefer history than the longer volumes.

The Presidents and The Press, by James E. Pollard (Macmillan), is a scholarly yet readable analysis of the relationship between newspapers and the Chief Executive. It is the only detailed work in this special field. Source notes are excellent.

BIOGRAPHY

Post Biographies of Famous Journalists (University of Georgia Press), edited by John E. Drewry, contains twenty-two sketches of twentieth-century editors and writers, taken from issues of the *Saturday Evening Post* between 1928 and 1942. A companion volume, *More Post Biographies*, adds twenty-two further pieces culled from *Post* issues between 1937 and 1946.

Ladies of the Press (Harper), by Ishbel Ross, is subtitled "The Story of Women in Journalism by an Insider," and it is exactly that, beginning with Anne Royall and continuing to this century.

A Treasury of Great Reporting (Simon & Schuster), edited by Louis L. Snyder and Richard B. Morris, has valuable biographical material in the editorial forewords preceding the selections, which begin with the sixteenth century. Most of the book is devoted to American journalism.

The Two Franklins: Fathers of American Democracy (Little, Brown), by Bernard Fäy, considers Benjamin Franklin and his grandson, Benjamin Franklin Bache. It is based on original sources, and quotes freely from the *Aurora,* the *Gazette of the United States* and *Porcupine's Gazette.*

The Man Who Made News: James Gordon Bennett (Duell, Sloan and Pearce), by Oliver Carlson, remains the best biography of James Gordon Bennett Sr. The definitive book about the two Bennetts and their times still waits to be done.

Timber Line (Covici-Friede, reprinted by Garden City Publishing Co.), by Gene Fowler, is not only the best book about Bonfils and

Tammen and the Denver *Post,* but it is one of the best journalistic biographies ever written.

Specimens of Newspaper Literature, with Personal Memoirs, Anecdotes, and Reminiscences (Redding and Co.), by Joseph T. Buckingham, based on Isaiah Thomas' *History of Printing,* describes forty-five early American newspapers.

Where Main Street Meets The River (Rinehart), by Hodding Carter, Pulitzer Prize-winning editor of the Delta *Democrat-Times,* in Greenville, Mississippi, is an excellent account of life on a small paper by a liberal southern editor.

Peter Porcupine In America: The Career of William Cobbett, 1792-1800 (University of Pennsylvania Press), by Mary Elizabeth Clark, is the only biography of Cobbett which deals exclusively with his life in America.

The Amazing Nellie Bly (Dutton), by Mignon Rittenhouse, is described by Professor Price as "perhaps the best biography of a stunt reporter."

Dana and The Sun (Dodd, Mead), by Candace Stone, is an analytical study of Dana's editorial policies, but is more useful than the other books about Dana, which are either authorized or otherwise inadequate. Dana is another figure in American journalism who waits for his biographer.

Richard Harding Davis: His Day (Scribner's), by Fairfax Downey, re-creates the romantic life and times of the romantic reporter.

Joseph Dennie and His Circle: A Study in American Literature from 1792-1812 (Bulletin of the University of Texas, No. 40), by Harold M. Ellis, is scholarly and is the only full-length study extant of this important figure in American journalism.

The Marshall Fields: A Study In Wealth (Dutton), by John Tebbel, covers the whole Field dynasty, but it has sections on Marshall Field III's newspaper activities, describing the history of the newspaper *PM* and the beginnings of the Chicago *Sun.*

That Rascal Freneau: A Study in Literary Failure (Rutgers University Press), by Lewis Leary, is the definitive study of Freneau, and includes much material on his journalistic career.

My Last Million Readers (Dutton), by Emile Gauvreau, is one of the best accounts extant of New York tabloid journalism of the 1920s, particularly the *Graphic* of which Gauvreau was editor, and Hearst's *Mirror,* of which he was an executive.

Life and Letters of Edwin Lawrence Godkin (Macmillan), by Ogden, who was once Godkin's colleague and later became editor of *The New York Times.* This two-volume work is the best available on Godkin and is well worth reading.

Henry W. Grady: Spokesman of the New South (Knopf), by Raymond B. Nixon, is an excellent and detailed study of Grady and how he built the Atlanta *Constitution.*

Horace Greeley: Nineteenth Century Crusader (University of Pennsylvania Press), by Glyndon G. Van Deusen. Scholarly, well documented, and much the best of numerous books about Greeley.

Citizen Hearst (Knopf), by W. A. Swanberg, is the most recent and the most comprehensive of Hearst biographies. *The Life and Good Times of William Randolph Hearst* (Dutton), by John Tebbel, published a year after Hearst's death, is cited by Professor Price (before Swanberg's book) as "perhaps the best balanced treatment."

Country Editor (Doubleday), by Henry Beetle Hough, may well be the best book of this century on country journalism. Hough describes the first twenty years of his career on the *Vineyard Gazette,* in Edgartown, Martha's Vineyard, Massachusetts, which he and his wife bought in 1920. A second volume, *Once More The Thunderer* (Ives Washburn), carries the story a decade farther.

King News: An Autobiography (Stokes), by Moses Koenigsberg, is an inside look at Hearst chain journalism by a man who was one of its organizers and executives.

Victor Lawson: His Time and His Work (University of Chicago Press), by Charles H. Dennis. Semiofficial and respectful, but based on exhaustive research and therefore valuable.

An American Dynasty (Doubleday), by John Tebbel, covers the careers of the McCormicks, Medills and Pattersons in their operation of the Chicago *Tribune,* the New York *Daily News,* and the Washington *Times-Herald.*

Mr. Miller of the Times: The Story of An Editor (Scribner's), by F. Fraser Bond. Miller was with the *Times* first in the George Jones era, then on through the first quarter-century of Ochs. An excellent account of the *Times* during that period.

An Honorable Titan: A Biographical Study of Adolph S. Ochs (Harper), by Gerald W. Johnson, is described by Professor Price as "the only effective full-length treatment of Ochs's career."

Fremont Older (Appleton-Century), by Evelyn Wells. Uncritical, but the only full-length biography of Older.

Joseph Pulitzer: His Life and Letters (Simon & Schuster), by Don C. Seitz. Pulitzer, like Dana, does not yet have a definitive biographer, but this biography by an editor who worked for Pulitzer on the *World* through two decades and was the paper's business manager is the best presently available.

Raymond of the Times (Norton), by Francis Brown, is an excellent and probably definitive biography of Raymond, based on exhaustive research. The author is the present editor of *The New York Times Sunday Book Review*.

Lusty Scripps: The Life of E. W. Scripps, 1854-1926 (Vanguard), by Gilson Gardner. Scripps designated his old associate, Gardner, to write his biography but characteristically ordered it to be as candid as possible. Should be read with Scripps's own *Damned Old Crank: A Self-Portrait of E. W. Scripps* (Harper), edited by Charles R. McCabe, which is more revealing than anything written about him.

Fifty Years A Journalist (Doubleday), by Melville E. Stone, is "among the better autobiographies in journalism," according to Professor Price.

From 'Prentice to Patron: The Life Story of Isaiah Thomas (Appleton-Century), by Annie Russell Marble. The standard biography of Thomas, well documented.

A Giant of The Press (Editor & Publisher), by Barnett Fine. The only biography of Van Anda, great managing editor of the *Times*. Also tells much of *Times* history.

'Marse Henry': An Autobiography (Doran), by Henry Watterson. This two-volume work is as long as "Marse Henry's" editorial columns, but it is a fascinating, if discursive, story.

The Autobiography of William Allen White (Macmillan), is, as Professor Price remarks, "one of the most valuable autobiographies of American newspapermen."

The Trial of Peter Zenger (New York University Press), edited by Vincent Buranelli. Contains a reprint of the trial text with spelling and punctuation modernized, plus biographies of principal figures in the case, a discussion of the "Meaning of The Trial," and a good bibliography.

INDEX

The Author and His Book

JOHN TEBBEL *was born in Boyne City, Michigan, in 1912. He received his A.B. from Central Michigan University in 1935 and an M.S. from Columbia in 1937. In 1939 he married Kathryn Carl. He was city editor of the Isabella Co.* Times-News *(Mt. Pleasant, Michigan) 1935-36; a writer for* Newsweek *magazine in 1937; a reporter for the* Detroit Free Press, *1937-39; feature writer and roto news editor of the* Providence Journal, *1939-41; managing editor,* The American Mercury, *1941-43; Sunday staff writer,* The New York Times, *1943; associate editor, E. P. Dutton & Co., 1943-47; assistant in journalism, School of Journalism, Columbia, 1942-46, now Chairman of the Department of Journalism, New York University, formerly Director of the Graduate Institute of Book Publishing.*

He is the author of such notable books as An American Dynasty *(Doubleday, 1947);* The Marshall Fields *(Dutton, 1947);* George Horace Lorimer and the Saturday Evening Post *(Doubleday, 1948);* Makers of Modern Journalism *(Prentice-Hall, 1950);* Life and Good Times of William Randolph Hearst *(Dutton, 1952);* The American Indian Wars *(with Keith Jennison; Harper, 1960);* The Inheritors *(Putnam, 1961);* Epicure's Companion *(with Ann Seranne McKay, 1962).*

This book was set in type by Spartan Composition Company, Hackensack, New Jersey, and printed and bound by the Book Press, New York City. The text is set in Times Roman, originally designed for the use of the London Times.

A HAWTHORN BOOK